THE BUSINESS VALUE OF

IT

Managing Risks,
Optimizing Performance,
and Measuring Results

THE BUSINESS VALUE OF

IT

Managing Risks,
Optimizing Performance,
and Measuring Results

Michael D. S. Harris
David Herron
Stasia Iwanicki

CRC Press
Taylor & Francis Group
Boca Raton London New York

CRC Press is an imprint of the
Taylor & Francis Group, an **informa** business

AN AUERBACH BOOK

Auerbach Publications
Taylor & Francis Group
6000 Broken Sound Parkway NW, Suite 300
Boca Raton, FL 33487-2742

© 2008 by Taylor & Francis Group, LLC
Auerbach is an imprint of Taylor & Francis Group, an Informa business

No claim to original U.S. Government works
Printed in the United States of America on acid-free paper
10 9 8 7 6 5 4 3 2 1

International Standard Book Number-13: 978-1-4200-6474-2 (Hardcover)

This book contains information obtained from authentic and highly regarded sources. Reprinted material is quoted with permission, and sources are indicated. A wide variety of references are listed. Reasonable efforts have been made to publish reliable data and information, but the author and the publisher cannot assume responsibility for the validity of all materials or for the consequences of their use.

Except as permitted under U.S. Copyright Law, no part of this book may be reprinted, reproduced, transmitted, or utilized in any form by any electronic, mechanical, or other means, now known or hereafter invented, including photocopying, microfilming, and recording, or in any information storage or retrieval system, without written permission from the publishers.

For permission to photocopy or use material electronically from this work, please access www. copyright.com (http://www.copyright.com/) or contact the Copyright Clearance Center, Inc. (CCC) 222 Rosewood Drive, Danvers, MA 01923, 978-750-8400. CCC is a not-for-profit organization that provides licenses and registration for a variety of users. For organizations that have been granted a photocopy license by the CCC, a separate system of payment has been arranged.

Trademark Notice: Product or corporate names may be trademarks or registered trademarks, and are used only for identification and explanation without intent to infringe.

Library of Congress Cataloging-in-Publication Data

Harris, Michael D.S.
    The business value of IT : managing risks, optimizing performance, and measuring results / authors, Michael D.S. Harris, David Herron, and Stasia Iwanicki.
        p. cm.
    ISBN 978-1-4200-6474-2 (alk. paper)
    1. Information technology--Economic aspects. I. Herron, David (David E.) II. Iwanicki, Stasia. III. Title.

HC79.I55H39 2008
004.068--dc22   2007044640

Visit the Taylor & Francis Web site at
http://www.taylorandfrancis.com

and the Auerbach Web site at
http://www.auerbach-publications.com

Contents

v

PART IV: HOW SHOULD WE CHANGE?

Foreword

Establishing the cost/value relationship of IT for a business increasingly vexes the CIO. With the growth of IT from a peripheral part of organizations' internal systems infrastructure to its present central and dominant role in operations, the CIO now needs to demonstrate the value of the expenditure in IT to a business audience of increasing diversity. CIOs are no longer only found in Fortune 500 firms — they are members of the CxO community in businesses of all sizes and industry sectors and are full business partners in such. How then can the significant and ever-growing cost of IT be expressed in terms that the business leaders relate to and come to understand as investment and efficient operations rather than growing overhead? How can that equation be expressed in language that the business leaders can understand?

In another class of businesses, IT <u>is</u> the product. This is the world that I personally live in. SW is central to the business; the value of IT is more directly expressed (impact on margin) and also more visibly part of the cost of goods. This hardly simplifies the value conversation — in fact, it forces IT managers to evince even more directly. Are our costs of operations in line with best industry practices? Does our software shop produce products efficiently and more effectively than our competition? What is the value of new technology? When do we outsource/insource? How should we manage our suppliers?

We all live in multi-vendor environments not dreamed of twenty years ago. I have project teams existing simultaneously in India (many locations therein), Poland, Russia, the Netherlands, New York, Chicago, and Los Angeles (I'm not recommending this). This virtual team operates 24/7/365 and it all hinges on standards, measures, and processes for success. There's little time to learn on the job. Bringing the right package of practices and standards to such a diverse team is exigent.

The industry providentially comes to our rescue with a plethora of methodologies, measures, benchmarks, best practices, and shared experiences. There's no shortage of highly refined alternatives to shop from for the CIO. This richness, however, takes us forward stepwise, but without completeness.

The *Business Value of IT* knits this landscape together. It provides a reference for the full range of value, demonstrating and managing practices that have emerged from our industry. An encyclopedic knowledge of the full range of the standards and substantial practical experience in the application of such gives the polymath authors (Michael D. S. Harris, David Herron, and Stasia Iwanicki) a unique ability to present what is available in relation to each other and in the context in which the CIO should consider them. Having personally worked bottom up discovering, learning, introducing, and living with much of the best practices this text exposes, the context of these solutions in framing business value was found by hard discovery. This text lucidly establishes the relationships, provides an invaluable context among solutions, and ascribes the intrinsic value to each. It's an excellent reference for the CIO and for the line manager seeking to engage the business with the transparency into the investment and cost equation they demand to justify the cost of IT.

Mike Antico, CTO
Wolters Kluwer
New York

Preface

As consultants for the David Consulting Group and in our earlier careers, we have been involved with IT for at least 25 years. During that time, we have been involved in many successful projects and have been confronted by many challenges. Our collective experiences have culminated in a certain amount of "professional wisdom" and learned knowledge that we have drawn upon in creating this book.

The role of IT within organizations has undergone many changes over the years. The responsibilities of the CIO and Senior IT Management Team and the ways that their IT teams interact with and support the business have changed just as much. We believe that IT Providers must be viewed as strategic business partners requiring the CIO to be a pivotal part of a supply chain, well versed in both technology and the business.

There have been numerous publications with regard to the latest methodologies, techniques, and management practices all positioned to make the IT environment more productive and responsive to the business. Amid this sea of change and among all of the unique situations that IT managers face, there are a number of common questions that arise. There is the constant challenge of making the business case for IT in a global marketplace.

We felt that the time had come to write this book and to gather together answers to some of the questions that we have been hearing from business leaders. We attempt to share our collective experiences and wisdom touching on topical areas. Each author brings to this publication a unique and valued perspective. We have tried to keep the original thoughts intact while presenting a very readable and useful book for all to enjoy.

Acknowledgments

It is almost impossible to recognize all those individuals who have ultimately made this book a reality. Our collective knowledge is comprised of both tangible and intangible experiences, both personal and professional. We each have individuals and companies woven into our hearts and minds and we are deeply appreciative of their support over the years. We hope and trust that they know who they are even if we have not mentioned them here.

The obvious beginning point is to acknowledge the love and support that we have received from our families. They have endured the many trials and tribulations that come with professionals who are constantly on the road and all too often experienced the delays to travel or demands of clients that made us late or away for dinner or other important events. Thanks and love to our significant others: Mary Herron, Jane Harris, and Jamie Bird; to our children: Josh, Jay, Alex, and Elizabeth Herron; Catherine, Vicki, and Deri Harris; and Jack Iwanicki, and Corbin and Griffin Bird; and to our parents, Mildred Herron, Dave and Lyn Harris, and John and Judy Iwanicki whose lives have enriched our lives beyond measure.

Of course, there are our clients who have contributed to our learning experience and have provided us with the experiences and knowledge that have led to the writing of this book. We have been blessed with a majority of successful engagements and our customers are, on the whole, a well-satisfied bunch. We are ever so grateful to the following for the opportunities and ongoing support: David Garmus, Frank Sanchez, Mike Sanchez, Joe Waterman, Richard Phillimore, Rob Hoerr, Meghan McGuire, Matt Lessig, Matthew Bohnert, Teresa Sande, Will Tumulty, James Bailey, James Haworth, Marlene Boyanner, Tom Cagley, Barry Young, Allyson Van Steenbergen, Patricia Siegle-Eberle, Erik McClure, and, of course, Mike Antico.

Along with our natural families we have the pleasure of working with the DCG family of consultants. These individuals are the collective "face" of DCG. Their loyalty and professionalism have made DCG one of the industry leaders in the area of software performance measurement and process improvement. Thanks are due to them all but particular thanks are due to Fiona Thompson for all of her efforts in pulling this book together.

Finally, we must thank our reviewers who helped us with the all-important fine tuning of the book: Andrea Canfield, Diane Bloodworth, Phil Chenard, and Timothy Ryan Smith. Any remaining errors are, of course, ours alone.

Introduction

Business value is just one output of the collection of processes through which businesses today try to maximize the age-old equation of profit equals revenue minus expenses.

Business value is not identical to profit or revenue or expense. Rather "business value" is a multi-dimensional output and different observers apply different weights to different dimensions at different times. For example, business value can be the financial return on the investment made in the development of a new product or service. There is business value in building an infrastructure, such as a shopping mall, that facilitates other business. There is business value in ensuring that a current business service continues to be available to customers and does not fail when it is needed. There is business value in beating competitors to market. There is business value in being able to respond very quickly when your competitor beats you to market.

Which of these examples is the most valuable or the least valuable? Again, different observers apply different weights to different dimensions at different times. The intent of this book is to provide answers that will most often satisfy these observers in this order: CEOs, CFOs, CIOs, software development heads, and project managers. To be able to answer the question more satisfactorily, it is necessary to be able to gather as many measurements as possible of outputs and inputs so that different options can be compared against each other using common yardsticks. These examples also begin to show that business risk, or the management of business risk, is a dimension of business value.

Most businesses today rely on information technology (IT) to realize some of their business value. It has been argued in recent years that IT may not provide as much value as it once did.* This book will provide leaders of businesses and IT Providers with a set of yardsticks for measuring IT inputs and outputs to business processes and discuss processes for transforming these measured IT inputs and outputs into business value metrics appropriate for your environment.

---

* Carr, Nicholas G. 2004. *Does IT Matter? Information Technology and the Corrosion of Competitive Advantage.* Harvard Business School Press.

How do we measure the value of information technology? It's a question that is on everyone's mind, from business managers to board rooms. Interestingly enough, the question itself contains the key phrase that unlocks the mystery — how do we measure?

This book aims to show that the right metrics are available, can be implemented, and have been shown to work. There is a widely held view that "IT has traditionally measured itself in very technical terms that don't mean much to people outside of IT." In this book, we tackle this problem in two ways: by identifying IT metrics that do have meaning for people outside of IT; and by explaining some important IT metrics in a way that people outside IT can readily appreciate. We also discuss why many organizations do not use some or all of these metrics and how to change this dynamic.

If business value can be an output of an IT-driven or IT-supported business process, then it is necessary to consider both the IT inputs to those business processes and the IT outputs which may or may not be identical to the business outputs. Two issues dominate this consideration today: software development and outsourcing.

Measurement of software development has been notoriously elusive for a long time. It has been relatively easy to do for some time but the business value of measuring software development has not been as widely recognized as it should have been.

In recent years, the IT landscape has changed dramatically through outsourcing. Accordingly, throughout this book we refer to the plural, "IT Providers," rather than the IT Department.

By focusing this book on the needs of business executives whose business outputs depend on IT and the senior-level IT managers who serve them, we are seeking to deliver business visibility into IT performance by providing practical advice based on industry best practice. Whether the individual is new to his or her senior-level position or a seasoned veteran, he or she will find the answers to some of the more challenging questions.

The book includes techniques, methods, and processes to identify and assess risks, to measure performance, to put a dollar value to IT, and to measure and justify the value of the measurement program. The content of this book is based on the authors' combined experience of over 75 years of implementation and consulting experiences. These are the tools, techniques, methods, and practices we have successfully brought to our internal and external clients over those years. In return, we have gained insight as to what works well and what doesn't.

The ultimate value of measuring IT may come from the dynamic caused by the measurement activity itself which focuses our attention on where we can improve to deliver value to the business more effectively. In brief — measure results, improve IT processes, deliver value — then do it again!

The book tackles four challenges — business value, governance, performance, and implementation as four parts, in that order. Extracting value from IT has to start with the business. In each of these four sections, the chapter headings are titled in the form of a series of questions. These are questions that a business executive or senior IT manager should ask. Businesses care most about the "coal face" of the business—IT interface, the operational IT issues of running their applications in production. While this book has that ultimate priority firmly in mind, by the time an application is in production, the biggest opportunity to maximize business value has been missed. Consequently, this book puts more emphasis on maximizing value through the "soft" application development and service management aspects of IT rather than on the "hard" value issues such as minimizing the production costs of servers, networks, and application hosting.

In the first part of the book, we pose the question, "What does IT contribute to the business?" This section seeks to identify the potential outputs of an IT organization that can be of value to a business. It introduces techniques for measuring this value and for balancing the dreams of huge delivered value with the reality of constrained inputs. The IT industry has an interestingly mixed reputation for delivery in the public consciousness based on well-established facts reported in the media. It has a great reputation for delivering continuous innovation and a terrible reputation for delivery on time and on budget on some major projects. This part seeks to provide some insight into how businesses can extract the value they need, avoid unintended consequences, and maybe even get some extra value they didn't know they needed through the application of risk management.

The second part addresses the question, "Why should we care about IT governance?" This part introduces processes to ensure that the activities of the IT organization are prioritized to maximize the value delivered to the business or businesses being served in the short, medium, and long terms. It examines the alternative frameworks available to business today and identifies what might be appropriate in different circumstances. This part considers how outsourcing should be structured, managed, and measured to maximize value and minimize risk. Finally, this part looks at the tools that should be considered for IT.

In the third part, this book tackles the question, "How should we measure IT performance?" It should be noted from the start that the question, "Why should we measure IT performance?" is assumed to have been answered if you have picked up this book. If you can't measure it, you can't manage it.

In the final section, the book focuses on the challenges of implementing change through people. Many businesses have successfully implemented the techniques described in this book and have realized business value as a result. Why haven't all businesses done so? What is stopping them? How can obstacles be removed?

About the Authors

Michael D. S. Harris brings to this book a wide range of perspectives on IT. His international career has taken him from production management through R&D, project management, and academia to consulting before planting him firmly in charge of a large software engineering group for a public company. Most recently, he decided that he liked one of his former vendors so much that he would buy the company. Mr. Harris is now the owner and president of the David Consulting Group and a partner in the joint venture, IT Decisions Coaching. He is a Chartered Engineer (CEng.), a member of the Institution of Engineering and Technology (MIET) in the United Kingdom, and a member of the Institute of Electrical and Electronic Engineers (MIEEE) in the United States.

This is **David Herron**'s third book. His first two books were co-authored with his business partner David Garmus on the subject of functional measurement. Mr. Herron's professional experience includes 20 years of working within IT in various management positions and another 15 years consulting with Fortune 1000 companies in a variety of IT-related areas. He is most known for his work in the performance measurement arena. As one of the co-founders of the David Consulting Group he helped to create a unique consulting environment providing clients with solutions that resulted in quantitative improvements in productivity and quality. Besides his two books he has authored numerous industry-recognized articles and white paper studies on various measurement-related topics. Most recently Mr. Herron is engaged with IT Decisions Coaching, where he is applying his years of experience to coaching and mentoring senior leaders and project teams within IT.

Stasia Iwanicki is an accomplished IT executive with 18 years of experience leading large-scale global programs. She is a passionate process advocate, a Six Sigma Black Belt, and a certified Project Management Professional® who has led the development of SDLCs at JPMorgan Chase, Bank of America (formerly Fleet Bank), and the transformation of IT while at Capital One. Foremost, she is a business advocate who bridges the business to IT gap. She brings her experience to this work, mindful of approaches to simplify complex concepts focusing on how to utilize them to achieve world-class results.

List of Commonly Used Acronyms

AD/M:	Application Development and Maintenance
CEO:	Chief Executive Officer
CFO:	Chief Financial Officer
CIO:	Chief Information Officer
CI:	Configuration Item
CMDB:	Configuration Management Database
CMM:	Capability Maturity Model
CMMI®:	Capability Maturity Model Integration
COBIT®:	The Control Objectives for Information and related Technology
COTS:	Commercial Off-The-Shelf (software)
DoD:	U.S. Department of Defense
EVA:	Earned Value Analysis
FMEA:	Failure Mode and Effects Analysis
FP:	Function Point
FPA:	Function Point Analysis
FTE:	Full-Time Equivalent (staff)
GQM:	Goal-Question-Metric (methodology)
GUI:	Graphical User Interface
HR:	Human Resources (department)
IEEE:	Institution of Electrical and Electronic Engineers
IFPUG:	International Function Point Users Group
IRR:	Internal Rate of Return
ISACA:	Information Systems Audit and Control Association
ISBSG:	International Software Benchmarking Standards Group
IT:	Information Technology
ITIL:	Information Technology Infrastructure Library
ITSM:	Information Technology Service Management
M&A:	Mergers and Acquisitions
MIS:	Management Information Systems

MIT:	Massachusetts Institute of Technology
Opex:	Operating Expenses
P-CMM:	People-Capability Maturity Model
PMBOK®:	Project Management Book of Knowledge
PMI®:	Project Management Institute
QA:	Quality Assurance
RFC:	Request For Change
RFP:	Request For Proposals
ROA:	Return On Assets
ROI:	Return On Investment
SCAMPI:	Standard CMMI Appraisal Method for Process Improvement
SEI:	Software Engineering Institute
SLA:	Service Level Agreement
SOX:	Sarbanes–Oxley (Act)
TCO:	Total Cost of Ownership
YTD:	Year To Date

WHAT DOES IT CONTRIBUTE TO THE BUSINESS?

Chapter 1

What Should the Business Expect from IT?

This chapter sets the scene for the rest of the book. Our goal is to introduce a view of IT from the perspective of the businesses that use it. Further, this chapter seeks to make current IT best practices accessible and understandable to business managers. Too often, IT projects and operations fail because business expectations for them are unrealistically high based on ignorance of what can be achieved in a given time at a given quality and budget. Also, too often, IT Providers' deliverables in a given time at a given quality and budget are unrealistically low. This is based on IT Providers' ignorance of (or disregard for) what can be achieved by combining a clearly prioritized set of business needs with well-established, but woefully underutilized, IT industry best practices. This chapter seeks to provide an overview of those industry best practices that businesses should expect in the hope that their expectations will become more realistic and, at the same time, the accountability of IT Providers will improve.

The business should expect great service at a low cost. Too simplistic? There is an old joke about a group of buddies who are sitting around a campfire when they are interrupted by an angry grizzly bear. While the humans scatter in all directions as fast as they can, one guy sits to take the time to put on and tie up his sneakers. He figures he only needs to run faster than the slowest one of his buddies to avoid being eaten by the bear.

So perhaps the business should expect better service than the competition gets from its IT Providers at a lower cost than the competition pays for its IT. This may be setting the sights a little low. What if there were two bears? Nonetheless,

3

this old joke introduces six key concepts in establishing realistic but aggressive business expectations:

1. Information for Decisions (How fast can I run? How fast can they run?)
2. Value for Money (No need to pay for a Ferrari if a pair of sneakers will do the job.)
3. Risk Management (Is there one bear or two bears? Have those sneakers ready!)
4. Process (Don't trip over my untied laces.)
5. Responsiveness (Does the situation demand that I run? Do I have time to put on my sneakers before the bears reach me?)
6. Innovation (What if I am the slowest runner next time even with my sneakers on?)

These concepts are discussed in more detail later in this chapter.

Before continuing, it is necessary to explain a few terms that will be used in this book. In these days of outsourced IT functions and geographically distributed IT departments, it is appropriate to refer to an enterprise having "IT Providers." Generally, all IT Providers are managed through the single, internally staffed IT department, but this is not always the case. We believe that the term "IT Providers" better captures the opportunities and challenges inherent in enterprise IT delivery today than the more usual "IT Department." When we refer to "IT Department," we refer explicitly to the internal staff. When we refer to "IT," we refer to the general function.

Throughout this book, we refer to the chief information officer or CIO. This is a title that we use as a form of shorthand to infer the member of the executive team who has responsibility for all IT functions. Very often in an organization, there is no one person who would properly or adequately fit into this singular position but rather a broader gamut of executive management who have varied roles around IT. We do not imply that there is a right or better model from an organizational perspective, we simply use CIO to mean all of those folks.

It is important to understand the impact of IT on the business. Too often, both the business and the IT Providers have in mind the traditional relationship model shown in Figure 1.1. The presumption is that the business is the interface to the "real world" of customers, stakeholders, employees, other businesses, and the government. The IT Providers do not have, and do not need, a huge understanding of the dynamics of the businesses' interaction with the "real world" because the business will buffer, translate, and interpret for IT. Studies of the personal characteristic traits of individuals who are successful in business or IT environments tend to show that this model suits the players just fine.

However, we are moving quickly toward a modified model of the world, some would argue we have already arrived, where IT is involved in every interaction between the business and the "real world." This new model looks something like Figure 1.2. The new IT buffer represents the increasing use of IT for interaction

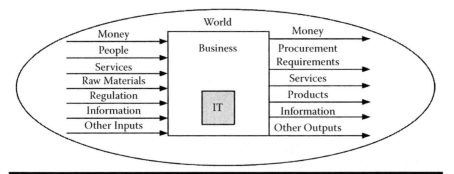

Figure 1.1 Traditional view of world-business–IT relationship.

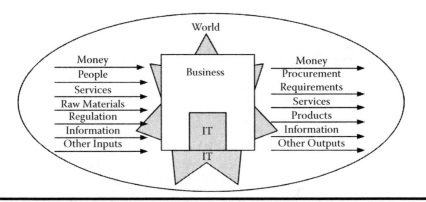

Figure 1.2 The new view: Businesses touch the world through IT.

between the business and the outside world. At the most obvious level, it is the sale of products over the Internet and email communication with employees and contractors. At another level, it is the capture of incoming information, such as invoices, into digital form as soon as they arrive in the office. Today, even many very small transactions become records in a point-of-sale system or stock control system.

The important point here is that IT and IT Providers are inseparable parts of the operations of most businesses. A small failure or improvement of IT can have a dramatic effect on the business' ability to operate and perhaps to influence its profitability.

Information for Decisions

The much quoted adage, "If you cannot measure, you cannot manage," is critical to understanding what the business should expect from its IT Providers. The business needs clear, concise, relevant, and timely information from the IT Providers to understand whether all of its other expectations are being met. Unfortunately, IT Providers tend to be much better at generating data than generating information.

Any discussion about the information needed by the business must start with identifying the information needed to inform the business whether its strategic and tactical goals are being met. This should then lead to a discussion about what operational performance measurements for the IT Providers need to be monitored to ensure continued success. Finally, a set of measurements are required to give the business information about whether the current supplier of IT services is providing value for money (i.e., compared to their own previous performance and, relative to other providers).

Expectations for those measurements that are related to the performance of the IT Providers should be captured in a written agreement between the business and the IT Providers, typically called a Service Level Agreement (SLA).

If the metrics defined are to be used effectively, they need to be built into an automated collection, storage, processing, and delivery information system that can deliver dashboards and reports designed to show the right level of information for decisions at any given level of management. These systems also need to allow managers to drill down to deeper levels of detail if required.

In designing an information or measurement system, it is appropriate to use a formal technique such as the Goal-Question-Metric (GQM) technique[1] to establish the metrics that need to be gathered. This technique was developed by Victor Basili and his colleagues at the University of Maryland while working with NASA. Basili and his co-workers defined GQM as a set of six steps where the first three steps identify the right metrics from the business goals and the last three steps gather and use the data from the metrics to enable effective decision making:

1. Develop a set of corporate, division, and project business goals with associated measurement goals for productivity and quality
2. Generate questions (based on models) that define those goals as completely as possible in a quantifiable way
3. Specify the measures needed to be collected to answer those questions and track process and product conformance to the goals
4. Develop mechanisms for data collection
5. Collect, validate, and analyze the data in real-time to provide feedback to projects for corrective action
6. Analyze the data in a postmortem fashion to assess conformance to the goals and to make recommendations for future improvements

Value for Money

The business must hold its IT Providers accountable for "Value for Money." However, before it applies a blanket strategy across all its functions and all IT Providers, the business must establish its own current priorities for IT. In a discussion of the roles and responsibilities of the CIO, Karl Schubert[2] lists ten questions that a CEO should ask his CIO. One of these is particularly relevant to a business' expectations of its IT Providers, "Do you view IT as an expense or an investment?"

This is not a trivial question. It must be noted here how important it is for the business to answer this question seriously, honestly, and with a view to the medium term (on the assumption that very few businesses actually look to the long term even if they claim they do). The answer may or may not be industry based. For example, for banks IT is clearly an investment. For a construction company, it may not be.

Is IT part of what makes your business competitive? Is it a strategic differentiator? If it is, then you should answer that you view IT as an investment. This has implications for what your business can fairly consider "Value for Money." Your tolerance for failure of mission-critical systems will be lower and, hence, your IT costs higher. The positive impact of IT innovation on your business will be higher, so your willingness to tolerate IT experimentation should be higher and your acceptance of the failure of some of those experiments should be higher.

On the other hand, if IT is a "necessary evil" in your business, then "Value for Money" for you can focus on delivering satisfactory services for the lowest possible cost with some acceptance of risk.

Of course, in most enterprises, there will be some environments at some times in which IT is viewed as an investment and others where it is viewed as an expense. These will change over time and businesses need a clear understanding of their current portfolio. There will be times when a binary answer is too simplistic.

Measuring IT value is covered in more detail in Chapter 2.

Risk Management

The one thing that CEOs and all senior managers hate is surprises. The business has a right to expect no surprises from its IT Providers. The only way to avoid surprises is to engage in a dialogue about risk management.

In IT, there is a certain mystique about the risk management process area and it is generally ignored. The IT industry is bedeviled by an incomprehensible optimism, indefensible in the light of the industry's track record for on-time and on-budget delivery (this parallels the saying in theater, "It'll be alright on the night!"). This optimism and unwillingness even to think about risk management is interesting in that it runs counter to most engineers' (or even a local car mechanics') reaction to even the most simple request — a sucking sound made by a sharp intake of breath. There is a real gap between the difficulties that we as IT practitioners can enumerate for others and those that we admit to ourselves.

It is necessary for businesses to drive their IT Providers to enumerate and quantify all possible risks. Businesses should expect each risk to be accompanied by one or more mitigation strategy with associated costs. A business should then choose the risk management strategies it can tolerate in terms of consequences and expense.

Essentially, businesses have the right to expect IT Providers to be prepared for different failure scenarios by appropriate forward thinking and planning.

A relatively new phenomenon for businesses and IT Providers is the interest being taken in IT by external auditors of the organization. This may or may not be driven by specific regulations, such as the Sarbanes–Oxley Act in the United States. External auditors have become increasingly aware of two broad and related risks:

1. An IT operations failure can seriously disrupt or destroy an organization's ability to operate and its reputation with its customers.
2. One of the most likely causes of an IT operations failure is the introduction of new software.

Interestingly, in seeking to assess the scale of the second risk in organizations, external auditors are now working their way back along the software development life cycle processes seeking reassurance from evidence of auditability and best practices.

Monitoring of key metrics is an essential part of risk management. Businesses should not expect to understand or even receive the data from the IT monitoring systems but they should expect their IT Providers to set performance thresholds that will give early indication of a possible failure situation in the future. The appropriate time span for "future" is the time required to have the option of taking corrective action.

Finally, an often neglected aspect of risk management is the management of people risk. Significant IT capital is tied up in the business' intellectual property that is in people's heads. It is all too easy to view staff as fungible "resources." In most organizations, there are key individuals whose knowledge and expertise is the difference between success and failure in the short and medium term. IT Providers must be required to perform the same risk management planning for their people as they do for their hardware! This is a particular risk during merger and acquisition events. The business should expect a succession plan for, and from, the CIO.

The special nature of people issues in IT Providers is covered in more detail in Chapter 15.

Innovation

Innovation tends to be thought of as the introduction of something new. We prefer a much tighter definition which is the introduction of something new that improves measured performance in desirable ways. In IT, an improvement in the measured performance of one parameter may be at the expense of a reduction in the measured performance of other parameters. Businesses need to be mindful that IT Providers may be offering innovation on a narrow front. The bigger picture is always needed.

With the proviso that businesses must understand their view of IT, as discussed in the "Value for Money" section, businesses have a right to expect innovation from

IT. Innovation in and through IT has become such a norm in our society that businesses sometimes forget to think about it in that way. New software or new operating systems or new hardware can become a "pain" that we would rather not deal with — "innovation for innovation's sake." Businesses must remember that the improvement-enabling power of IT endures. That any manual process is a candidate for automation is so obvious that it should not need stating but when did you last look around your business for manual processes?

Our technology is not yet so perfect that it cannot be improved. If it were, the emergence of new approaches such as search engines and Web services would find few takers.

The business should expect creative energy from its IT Providers whether it's that top consulting company coming in with a new idea to make millions; the offshore software maintenance company inventing a better, cheaper way to service customer bug fixes; or the CIO proposing to save a fortune by combining two different business units' similar needs. These all boil down to finding new ways to deliver value for money. IT Providers are uniquely qualified to identify potential applications of new technologies to old problems and potential applications of all technologies to new problems.

Businesses need to create an environment in which their IT Providers can contribute thought leadership, business creativity, and process innovation coupled with sound business cases. The definition of "sound" will vary from business to business but it should not exclude big ideas. Return on investment is crucial but the definition of "return" should include consideration of broader value. It is notoriously difficult to predict the unintended consequences of implementing IT changes but it should be remembered that sometimes the unintended consequences can be hugely rewarding.

One way to enable but manage innovation in IT, and to make unintended consequences a positive force, is to use some form of Agile Methodology using the principles of the Agile Manifesto.[3] We are firm believers in this approach to incremental value delivery in an innovative project.

Process

Defined processes ensure repeatability and provide a springboard for continuous improvement. Most businesses do not have the time or the knowledge to create best practices for the management of IT. Fortunately, much of the work of best practices capture and codification has been done already. Businesses should view the implementation of process by their IT Providers as a huge step forward in risk management. Through the implementation of industry-recognized processes, businesses are benefiting by avoiding the mistakes that others have made to find out what constitutes best practice. Your auditors will be much easier people to satisfy if your IT Providers implement these processes. Of course, in the spirit of "no surprises"

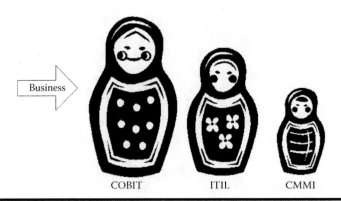

Figure 1.3 Process dolls.

in front of the auditors, implementing these processes also requires that you implement your own internal audit capability.

Numerous processes have been defined for IT. Many are very useful, some are internationally recognized and standardized, and a relative few have become operationally important at the interface between the business and the IT Providers. For the purposes of this particular section, we believe that all businesses should expect to have a discussion with their IT Providers about why they have or have not adopted the following models (or frameworks): COBIT®, ITIL®, and CMMI®.

We provide introductions to COBIT, ITIL, and CMMI in Chapter 6. To understand the differences and overlaps between them, it is important first to understand that these three models were developed and defined independently. Initially, they did not acknowledge each other and did not attempt to interface with each other explicitly. This limitation has been best addressed by version 3 of the ITIL. From the business perspective, think of the three models as three Russian nesting dolls (see Figure 1.3). The outer doll is COBIT, which is designed to provide a framework for governance and control of IT Providers. The middle doll is ITIL, which focuses on best practices for the IT operations or, more succinctly, keeping what's running, running. The inner doll is CMMI, which is focused on best practices for systems and software development. It is appropriate for any business to expect its IT Providers to have implemented all three of these models or to articulate very good reasons for not doing so. The day-to-day involvement that the business needs to have in each of the three is symbolized by the three Russian dolls, most involvement with COBIT, much with ITIL, least with CMMI.

In addition to these three models, businesses and their IT Providers may wish to consider using Six Sigma as a quantitative approach for identifying and rectifying areas in need of improvement (particularly relevant for CMMI Level 4 and the CMMI continuous representation).

Six Sigma is not an IT-specific model and has both pros and cons for the business–IT interface. On the plus side, Six Sigma may be in use in the business for business process improvement purposes and using the same approach in IT could be powerful in reinforcing corporate culture. On the minus side, if IT Providers do not have a reasonable level of IT maturity, the focusing effect of Six Sigma may leave too many IT capability gaps.

Customer requirements or the needs of other parts of the business (e.g., manufacturing) may lead the organization to consider (or require) compliance with ISO quality standards in its IT Providers.

Finally, project management is a key capability for all IT Providers, and the Project Management Institute (PMI®) provides a number of models of best practice.

Six Sigma, the ISO standards, and the best practices of the PMI are described in Chapter 6.

Responsiveness

The business must expect responsiveness from IT to three key stakeholders who may not seem so visible (or important) to the IT Providers as they do to the business:

1. Business customers
2. Business users
3. Business managers

It may seem odd to prefix all of these stakeholders with the term "business" but it is important to recognize that IT customers, users, and managers are often different from those of a specific business unit. Indeed, two business units usually have different customers, users, and managers by definition. Even good IT Providers who are on top of their game in serving their businesses can face conflicts of priorities between different business units.

Unless the business sells IT services or products, the best form of responsiveness that IT Providers can deliver to business customers is invisibility. The technology should never be the problem and, if it is, the IT Providers should get IT out of the customers' eyes as quickly as possible.

For business users, the IT Providers should be expected to share the urgency of the business need. Further, the IT Providers should establish processes for engaging with the business users. These engagement approaches include participation in requirements gathering, training, support, and easy accessibility.

For business managers, IT Providers must be expected to provide information, not data. The distinction being that IT Providers must be able to report to business managers in context-relevant ways to enable business decision making. IT Providers should be required and able to participate in business planning and provide responsive leadership to offer the business IT-based opportunities for business growth and cost savings.

Summary

This chapter describes six things that a business should expect from its IT Providers. The chapter introduces the important process best practices that IT Providers should implement. Like any successful partnership, the business–IT partnership will succeed through mutual support and mutual understanding of the expectations in both directions. Running IT is a tough job and good CIOs are hard to come by. To do the job properly, a good CIO will expect to contribute to all of the same critical success factors that drive the business executives. So, in its dealings with IT and the CIO, the business leadership must be openhanded with information, evenhanded in risk management, fair-minded in resolving conflicting priorities, and tough-minded in evaluating value for money and return on investment.

References

1. Van Solingen, Rini and Berghout, Egon. 1999. *Goal/Question/Metric Method*. McGraw-Hill Education.
2. Schubert, Karl D. 2004. *CIO Survival Guide — The Roles and Responsibilities of the Chief Information Officer*. John Wiley & Sons.
3. Beck, Kent, Beedle, Mike, van Bennekum, Arie et al. 2001. Manifesto for Agile Software Development. http://agilemanifesto.org/ (accessed May 10, 2007).

Chapter 2

How Do I Measure the Value of IT?

The phrase "beauty is in the eye of the beholder" could equally apply to value as to beauty. This chapter seeks to suggest some objective and subjective ways to measure or compare value. Whichever approach or combination of approaches is chosen, it is important to remember this fundamental perspective.

This chapter reviews the most frequently used financial and non-financial measures of IT value and suggests how these can be combined to facilitate comparison of options and trends.

What Is Value?

The Merriam-Webster Online Dictionary[1] offers the following seven definitions for the term "value":

1 : a fair return or equivalent in goods, services, or money for something exchanged

2 : the monetary worth of something : MARKET PRICE

3 : relative worth, utility, or importance <a good *value* at the price> <the *value* of base stealing in baseball> <had nothing of *value* to say>

4 : a numerical quantity that is assigned or is determined by calculation or measurement <let *x* take on positive *values*> <a *value* for the age of the earth>

5 : the relative duration of a musical note

6a : relative lightness or darkness of a color : LUMINOSITY **b** : the relation of one part in a picture to another with respect to lightness and darkness

7 : something (as a principle or quality) intrinsically valuable or desirable <sought material *values* instead of human *values* — W. H. Jones>

Table 2.1 Grady's Definition of Value

Value	=	Benefits	−	Costs
		■ Product capability ■ Time to market ■ Timeliness ■ Product evolution		■ Development ■ Rework ■ Knowledge recovery

Source: Grady, Robert B. 1997. *Successful Software Process Improvement.* Prentice Hall.

For our purposes, definitions 5 and 6 can be discarded. Crudely summarizing the other definitions, value is something that must be measured objectively (definition 4) and yet may require subjective judgments such as fairness or desirability. This is a perfect introduction to the problem businesses face in measuring value from IT Providers.

In Table 2.1, Robert Grady[2] provides the following simple definition of value for software development that applies equally well to general IT Providers:

Product capability assumes that the functional or utility value to the customer will be increased. For example, they will increase revenue or reduce costs or realize some other benefit (increased security, less risk, etc.).

Time to market assumes that there is value in having the enhanced product earlier rather than later. For example, having a system to sell tickets for the Olympics three weeks early could mean three more weeks to sell tickets.

Timeliness assumes there is value associated with meeting delivery commitments. For example, a maintenance contract on an old system has not been renewed because the new system should be delivered and operational before the old maintenance contract ends.

Product evolution assumes there is value in being able to evolve the product to give it a longer useful life. For example, converting an application from COBOL to Java to make it easier and cheaper to maintain and enhance.

The definition of benefits reinforces the notion that value can be very much "in the eye of the beholder." For this reason, it is absolutely essential that the business retains control of the decision-making process with respect to value measurement. Further, different entities in the business might have different priorities and assign different values to the same benefits. For example, sales may assign high value to capabilities that generate high prices; the customer service department might assign high value to capabilities that improve customer ease of use or satisfaction. The business has to establish a broadly inclusive process for establishing the value of different capabilities.

Why Is It Important to Measure IT Value?

All eyes are on IT investments. IT consumes significant resources relative to other functions because of the cost to operate and manage the IT infrastructure and the ubiquity of IT throughout most modern organizations. Even if businesses minimize their IT-supported innovation (a risky strategy), there are ongoing costs for networks, systems, applications, and a highly skilled work force.

How do you know if you are getting value for money from your IT investments? How can you maximize the likelihood of success in your IT investment choices? How can you tell if you need to make as much investment in IT as you are making now?

The challenge is to characterize how an IT investment, for new capabilities or for "keeping the lights on," helps the business that bears the cost to achieve its financial performance targets and business objectives. IT must consistently deliver value in economic terms that make sense to its business customers. Smarter IT executives have realized that IT alone does not create value unless, perhaps, you are in the business of selling IT products and services. In truth, value emerges from the impact of IT on business processes (an ultimate truth even for IT vendors). However, IT also contributes value to the businesses and the organization in ways that are not adequately reflected by purely financial measures. That said, the IT budgets of some organizations are a complete mystery to the businesses that pay for them and may not be delivering commensurate value. For example, Ben-Menachem and Marliss[3] reported in 2005 that:

> Many analysts are inclined to measure corporate maturity by the percentage of revenue spent on IT. This percentage has grown steadily over the past two decades. In fact, IT's size tends to grow commensurate with the maximum that the organization's resources can support.

It is interesting to note that this common metric of IT expenditure as a percentage of revenue varies widely by industry with a range in 2004 of 1.7 percent (oil and gas production) to 7 percent (financial services and banks). Clearly, this measure alone is insufficient to tell us whether those industries are getting value from their IT Providers.

In his excellent book for those interested in these challenges, Mark Lutchen[4] reminds us that successful measures must be

- Relevant
- Practical
- Actionable
- Reported or communicated
- Owned

As Lutchen states, "The reality is that the right IT metrics are neither the same nor relevant for every organization."

In late 2006/early 2007, Michael McShea published two excellent articles on this topic for the IEEE's *IT Professional* journal.[5,6] His articles provide the structure for the two following sections. For deeper insight into this topic, see Steve Tockey's book, *Return on Software: Maximizing the Return on Your Software Investment.*[7]

Financial Value Measures

Total Cost of Ownership (TCO)

TCO, which came to prominence in the 1990s, seeks to capture the full cost of an IT asset from initial purchase through implementation and operation to maintenance and "end of life" costs. Although this is a cost-based approach which does not equate to value, it can be useful for measuring IT value because it allows comparison of alternative implementations that will meet the same business need and, presumably, have very similar values to the business. If the TCO of one alternative is significantly less than the others, then it represents better value for money. It is also true that by including such considerations as training costs, security costs, scalability costs, and the costs of reliability deficiencies, TCO incorporates perspectives that are not purely financial.

Of course, a limitation of TCO is that it involves predicting future costs. This limitation can be minimized over time by tracking actual costs but, by then, the investment decision has been made.

Return on Investment (ROI)

ROI means calculating the revenue that the business generates or the costs that it saves in return for the investment that it is making. Clearly, for an IT investment to be approved by the business, the IT Providers and the business must work together to demonstrate that the business will get its money back with a nice profit in an acceptable period of time (the payback period). In practice, ROI is typically expressed as a percentage of the investment, either annually or over the duration of the project with the cash flows rendered as net present values. Typically, the assumed discounting rate is called the internal rate of return (IRR) and is linked to the cost of capital of the business or the amount of interest the business will pay to borrow the money to make the investment. Acceptable IRRs and payback periods vary immensely from business to business but an IRR of at least 20 percent and a payback period of one to three years are a reasonable starting point for a discussion.

ROI is very widely used to justify IT investments, particularly for new projects. Although there is still the problem of predicting the future, ROI provides a good way to compare the financial value of very different projects and also provides hurdles, through the payback period and IRR, that quickly cut off further, costly consideration of some projects.

One practical problem with the use of ROI is that organizations often have good systems established for making their investment decisions using ROI but may have weak systems for monitoring the actual ROI achieved and using historic data on project ROI results to inform their current and future investment decisions. In short, are the ROI numbers that we are basing our decisions on realistic? For a single project, if the ROI is less than expected, at what point should the business cut its losses and cancel the project? Over a period of time, if the ROI for many projects is consistently more or less than the current target, then the IRR could be adjusted accordingly.

Another practical problem with ROI is that cost savings must be in real money rather than theoretical "efficiencies." For example, a projection that an IT investment will save the business 10 percent of staff time is only a real cash flow if it results in the employment of 10 percent less staff. It is fair to note that the staff may not necessarily be terminated but may deploy their efforts to other productive work; however, this is rarely monitored or measured carefully.

Economic Value Added (EVA)

The Economic Value Added approach starts with the assumption that the organization exists to provide economic value to its shareholders. This may not be entirely true for not-for-profit organizations but the approach still has value. The calculation and comparison of Economic Value Added is very similar to ROI except that the benchmark used for making investment decisions is not the IRR but the opportunity cost of using the money to make other business investments, (e.g., leaving the money in the bank rather than funding projects).

Real Options Valuation (ROV)

ROV is a more complex technique than the methods described so far. It is based upon the financial estimation techniques used in stock option theory. Without going into the detail of the mathematics, ROV is used to modify the ROI calculation by taking into account the value that the current project could contribute to future projects. This approach typically enhances the ROI of projects such as IT infrastructure where the cost of implementing a whole new infrastructure for just one project for one business unit's needs is so burdensome that no one business unit could ever justify starting the new infrastructure. However, the overall value of the new infrastructure to all the business units in the organization could be huge. ROV provides a technique for justifying that first project based on the future derived value.

Return on Assets (ROA)

Widely used to measure the performance of companies, ROA can also be applied specifically to the IT assets. For the organization, ROA is calculated by dividing the net income by the value of the assets being used to generate the net income. Similarly, ROA for IT assets can be calculated by isolating the IT-specific assets from the organizational assets and the net income due to IT assets from the overall net income. This can be hard to do and the accounting systems need to be set up appropriately to provide any chance of achieving this on a repeatable basis.

In his book, *Software as Capital*,[8] Baetjer argues that economic capital goods embody, or are, knowledge. He goes on to argue that, as an embodiment of knowledge, software can be considered as capital. Baetjer extends this argument in a number of interesting ways that are beyond the scope of this chapter but the key point is that an ROA approach has deeper implications than might be immediately obvious.

Ben-Menachem and Marliss describe in some detail the importance of IT asset valuing and offer a three-step process for calculation. Of key importance in this process is the need for a working IT-asset inventory system that contains all of the IT assets (hardware and software) used in the organization. The Information Technology Infrastructure Library (ITIL®) provides details of how such an IT assets inventory (Configuration Management Database or CMDB) should be established and used as part of its Configuration Management process. The Capability Maturity Model Integration (CMMI®) also contains a configuration management process area. ITIL and CMMI are discussed further in Chapter 6. To add a valuation context to the CMDB, Ben-Menachem and Marliss' three steps are

1. Categorize all items, creating groups.
2. Assign values to each item.
3. Classify each item into one of three categories, say A, B, and C, where A-level items represent the top 20 percent of items in terms of value and C-level items represent the bottom 20 percent of items in terms of value.

Clearly, both Class A and Class C items demand significant attention with respect to continuing investment decisions but for very different reasons.

Return on Infrastructure Employed (ROIE)

ROIE is similar to ROA but it focuses on IT services rather than IT assets. With ROIE, IT service cost (including depreciation) is the basis for computing a return. While ROIE can be used for a single project, it works best when calculated for aggregations of projects. For example, it might be used to compare the performance of different in-house or outsourced IT Providers. ROIE might be improved by providing the same IT service at a lower cost or by containing the cost growth of providing a particular IT service to less than the rate at which the organization's net income is growing.

Interestingly, if the organization's net income is shrinking in a particular period, the ROIE will worsen if nothing changes on the IT services. To maintain or improve ROIE under this scenario, the IT services costs must be flexible enough to reduce, perhaps, the quantity of the service being provided.

Non-Financial Value Measures

The most frequent criticism of purely financial valuation methods is that they provide no measure of the value of the activities in the context of the business strategic goals. For example, the ROI for an IT investment is the same in a business pursuing a customer intimacy strategy whether the investment will improve customer intimacy or destroy it.

Multi-Dimensional Value

The need for a broader measurement of the strategic and tactical value that IT can bring to the business has lead to the consideration of multi-dimensional IT valuation approaches that include other aspects of value in addition to the financial valuation. McShea separates these approaches into three types:

1. Multi-criteria approaches have their roots in multi-attribute utility theory with various approaches to combining the scores from different dimensions. The end result usually takes a normalized score (between 0 and 1) and applies it as a multiplier to the ROI. Table 2.2 shows a summary of representative techniques.
2. Strategy framework approaches explicitly define strategic objectives for the organization or business and establish key parameters for measuring success. Candidate IT investments are assessed against these success parameters. Table 2.3 shows a summary of representative techniques.
3. Portfolio management approaches take strategy framework approaches a stage further by grouping IT investments into sets that share the same objectives. Under this approach, different portfolios can have different objectives. Table 2.4 shows a summary of representative techniques.

Lutchen offers another perspective on tying different metrics to different categories of IT investments as summarized in Table 2.5.[4]

What might these non-financial value considerations include for a business trying to assess the value of its IT Providers? Jones[9] offers the following value

Table 2.2 Multi-Criteria Approaches

Method	Description
Information economics (IE)	IE provides a scoring mechanism taking into consideration ten variables: six business domains and four technical domains. Business domain includes enhanced ROI and risk and business alignment issues. Technical domain includes architecture alignment and technical risk factors.
Applied information economics (AIE)	Built around principles of measurement theory, decision theory, and actuarial sciences, AIE reduces each variable to a range of ROI outcomes with assigned probability. The impact of all risks is quantified in this way, along with intangible benefits. The result is a probability distribution for ROI, e.g., 75 percent chance of an ROI of 30 percent.
Total economic impact (TEI)	TEI calculates traditional costs and business benefits using financial methods, adds a quantitative measure of benefits related to future flexibility based on ROV or other techniques and then adjusts the probability distribution based on risk factors. The result is an ROI that has taken into account real options and risk.
Total value of opportunity (TVO)	TVO combines quantitative and qualitative measures. Costs are derived using a TCO approach. Metrics convert IT benefits into bottom-line business results in three main categories: demand management, supply management, and support services. The TVO methodology considers four other qualitative measures including risk, architecture alignment, business process impact, and strategic business alignment.

Source: McShea, Michael. November/December 2006. IT value management: Creating a balanced program. *IT Professional,* IEEE. With permission.

points that could be combined in a set of metrics according to their relevance to a particular business:

- Safety improvements
- National security improvements
- Risk reductions
- Synergy (compound values)
- Cost reductions
- Revenue increases
- Market share increases
- Schedule improvements
- Competitive advantages
- Customer satisfaction increases
- Staff morale increases
- Mandates or statutes

Table 2.3   Strategy Framework Approaches

Method	Description
Balanced scorecard (BSC)	The BSC has four layers: financial, customer, business process and learning, and growth (sometimes referred to as the "people" layer). Each layer has specific, company-unique strategic objectives with defined metrics that are linked to other objectives in other dimensions to reflect strategy. A strategy map is constructed by linking objectives to show cause and effect, i.e., "linkage."
IT scorecard	The IT scorecard has four categories: user orientation (user satisfaction), operational excellence (efficiency in development and operations), business contribution (financial), and future orientation (approach to skill set development and innovation). Critical success factors identified in each are based on business strategy.

Source: McShea, Michael. November/December 2006. IT value management: Creating a balanced program. *IT Professional,* IEEE. With permission.

So much thinking about IT is focused on "things" like hardware and software that it is all too easy to forget how much IT is dependent on people, especially when change is required (i.e., all the time). In considering these metrics, businesses should remember to constantly challenge their IT Providers to include the fact that the need to gather, report, and control these metrics extends outside the organization to all IT Providers. Often, in outsourcing arrangements, businesses and IT groups lose sight of some of these key metrics. Lutchen identifies important non-financial metrics that businesses should require their IT Providers to report:

- The rate of movement and mix of IT skills, compared to the business objectives
- The ability of the IT Providers to continue to grow and evolve their skills base to accommodate new and changing technologies and business needs
- The total compensation (base, individual and team bonuses, and market premiums) needed to change behaviors in the IT Providers
- The leverage effect of teaming as an IT organizational imperative
- The overall morale and the ability of the IT Providers to continue to effectively absorb and cope with continuous change

Strategic Value

Denne and Cleland-Huang[10] introduce the concept of a "Minimum Marketable Feature" (MMF) defined as "components of intrinsic marketable value" or units of software value creation. Candidate MMFs are identified through the cooperative efforts of the business and IT groups by considering the application domain,

Table 2.4 Portfolio Management Techniques

Method	Description
Giga Information Group portfolio framework	This method categorizes projects on two axes: IT impact on operations (low to high) and IT impact on the business (low to high). Quadrants: In terms of IT's role (operational impact and business impact), projects are support, factory, strategic, or turnaround. Allocating IT projects to quadrants reflects IT's role in the organization and strategy.
Ross and Beath investment quadrants	This method categorizes projects on two axes: technology scope (infrastructure or business applications) and strategic focus (short-term profitability or long-term growth). Quadrants: Infrastructure projects are renewal (short-term profitability focused) or transformational (long-term growth focused). Business applications are process improvements (short-term profitability) or experiments (long-term growth).
MIT Center for Information Systems Research portfolio pyramid	In this technique, four defined asset classes focus on risk versus reward and IT projects' varying profiles along these lines. Investment profiles are geared toward agility versus cost-driven strategies. Rather than a quadrant-based approach, a pyramid is constructed with infrastructure investments at the base and supporting transactional projects (internal business process focused) at the next layer. Informational (management decision support) and strategic projects (external market-driven) form the pinnacle.

Source: McShea, Michael. November/December 2006. IT value management: Creating a balanced program. *IT Professional*, IEEE. With permission.

shareholders' needs and constraints, and the current business context. Note that MMFs are probably not synonymous with tasks on the IT team's project plan, although they should be close to the high-level requirements in the product backlog of an agile development team. To derive the value of MMFs, Denne and Cleland-Huang ask some key questions:

1. What type of value will this MMF return?
   a. Savings in resource costs?
   b. Increased sales revenue?
   c. Improved customer retention?
2. Can the value of the MMF be expressed in monetary units (e.g., dollars)?
3. If not, how can intangible benefits be justified or compared?

Table 2.5 Business Value Measures for IT

Technology Investment	Categories of IT Investment	Business Value Characteristics	Typical Business Value Outcomes	Key Business Value Measures
... to gain competitive advantage or to position the company in the marketplace to increase market share or sales	Strategic	Competitive advantage Competitive necessity Market positioning Innovative services Increased sales	50 percent fail Some spectacular successes Two- to three-year lead time Higher revenue per employee	*Business unit financial* Revenue growth Return on investment Return on assets Revenue per employee
... for managing and controlling the organization at the business unit level (e.g., financial control, decision support, planning)	Informational	Better information Better integration Improved quality Increased control	Shorter time to market Superior quality Premium pricing Improved control	*Business unit operational:* Time — new product to market Sales — new products Product/service quality
... to process basic repetitive transactions of the company; focus is on high-volume transactions and cost reduction	Transactional	Increased throughput Cost reduction	25 to 40 percent return Higher ROI/ROA Lower risk Improved control	*Business unit IT application:* Time — application implementation Cost — application implementation
... to construct foundation IT capability (e.g., PCs, servers, networks, maintenance, help desks)	Infrastructure	Standardization Flexibility Cost reduction	Utility-type reliability Supports and facilitates change Creates compatibility	*Enterprisewide IT infrastructure:* Infrastructure availability Cost per transaction Cost per user

Source: Adapted from Lutchen, Mark D. 2004. *Managing IT as a business: A survival guide for CEOs.* John Wiley & Sons, Inc. (Pricewaterhouse Coopers LLP). With permission.

4. What are the risk factors associated with this MMF?
5. What cost and effort is required to develop this MMF?
6. What is the anticipated timeline to generate the MMF and realize the associated benefits?

Note that the value of individual MMFs may be dependent on the delivery sequence. For example, online customer access to their bank statement is valuable only after up-to-date bank statements have been delivered online.

This theme of the business and IT working together to link value measurement to strategic focus is extended by Broadbent and Kitzis[11] who assert the importance of business and IT executives working together to agree on practical courses of conduct to deliver value. Their idea is to ask what IT capabilities are required for the implementation of particular strategic initiatives. Importantly, they link these initiatives to the three high-level value disciplines first proposed by Treacy and Wiersema[12] in six ways:

1. Cost focus: Drawing on the value discipline of operational excellence
   a. Price products and services at lowest cost
   b. Drive economies of scale through shared best practices
2. Value differentiation as perceived by customers: Drawing on the value discipline of customer intimacy
   a. Meet client expectations for quality at reasonable cost
   b. Make the customers' product selection as easy as possible
   c. Provide all information needed to service any client from any service point
3. Flexibility and agility: Drawing on the value discipline of product and service innovation
   a. Grow in cross-selling capabilities
   b. Develop new products and services rapidly
   c. Create capacity to manufacture in any location for a particular order
4. Growth: How the base of the business will expand
   a. Expand aggressively into underdeveloped and emerging markets
   b. Carefully grow internationally to meet the needs of customers that are expanding their business
   c. Target growth through specific product and customer niches
5. Human resources: Where people policies fit in
   a. Create an environment that maximizes intellectual productivity
   b. Maintain a high level of professional and technical expertise
   c. Identify and facilitate the movement of talented people
6. Management orientation: Different aspects of business governance and decision making
   a. Maximize independence in local operations with a minimum of mandates
   b. Make management decisions close to the line
   c. Create a management culture of information sharing (to maintain or generate new business)

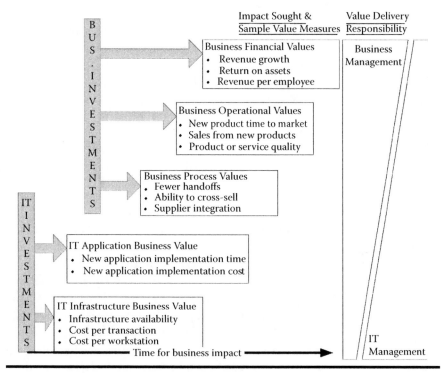

Figure 2.1 Hierarchy of business value measures.

Practically, Broadbent and Kitzis suggest a four-step approach for CIOs seeking to link the value of their IT group to the value goals of the business:

1. Start with some measure of business value at as high a level of the enterprise as possible
2. Look for strategic initiatives in place to improve that value
3. Identify how IT can support and add value to those initiatives and programs
4. Attach metrics to the specific IT investments and initiatives contributing to achievement of the business value

In Figure 2.1, Broadbent and Kitzis take these high-level ideas a stage further by proposing appropriate sample measures.

Using IT Value Measurements for Decisions

All measurements, including IT value measurements, are only useful and worth making if they are used to guide decisions. This means that all measurements have to be available to or, better, be regularly presented to decision makers. In the context of businesses making decisions based on the value of IT, this means that IT must regularly present its measurements to the business decision makers. Different decision makers require different information and different levels of detail of the same information. For example, a project manager needs to know the detailed status of a project such as progress against milestones, resource consumption, etc., although the CEO may only be interested in a summary level that shows whether a project is one of 20 that are "on schedule."

Dashboards

A useful tool for presenting measurement information to managers at different levels is the "dashboard." This tends to be an on-screen presentation of trend charts, typically showing the four to ten most important measurements for the viewing decision maker. Often, the charts represent an aggregation of other measurements so that the decision maker can "drill down" to greater levels of detail if needed. For example, the CEO may start by looking at a dashboard reflecting measurements across the entire organization. If the CEO notices a significant trend change in one of the measurements, say sales revenue has dropped this month, additional detail is available on that chart. By drilling down, an additional, more detailed screen would show sales revenue for each of the business units, indicating whether sales were slightly lower across the board or one particular business unit had a bad month.

When businesses look at dashboards at the highest level, it is important to understand that IT value will be only one of a number of measurements that will be displayed. Broadbent and Kitzis suggest the hierarchy of dashboards shown in Figure 2.2. In Figure 2.2, the IT measurements are reporting basic operational performance. It is noteworthy that although IT value is not identified explicitly, it is implicit in each of the six metrics identified:

	Demand Management	Market Responsiveness	Sales Effectiveness	Product Development Effectiveness
What the Business Watches	Supply Management	Customer Responsiveness	Supplier Effectiveness	Operational Efficiency
	Support Services	Human Resources Responsiveness	IT Responsiveness	Finance and Regulatory Responsiveness

IT Responsiveness

	System Performance	IT Support Performance	Partnership Ratio
What IT Reports to the Business	Service-level Effectiveness	New Projects Index	IT Total Cost Ratio

Figure 2.2 Hierarchy of dashboards.

1. System Performance is the percentage of time that systems, applications, and infrastructure services are available when needed and are performing at levels required by the users. Clearly, service level agreements (SLAs), where they exist, would form a large part of the reporting under this heading. In the interests of decision making, only the most important applications and infrastructure systems should be included. Availability and performance should be reported on a trend basis with indications of agreed significant thresholds.
2. IT Support Performance is the percentage of time that IT support staff and organizations are available to help with problems and new requests, and perform at the level necessary to address these requests properly. Again, note that availability and performance are measured and reported separately. The IT support performance measurements are based on a combination of service desk and customer care metrics.
3. The Partnership Ratio is an index of the percentage of business projects and initiatives in which IT Providers have a partnership or leadership role with the business early in the strategic planning process. Interestingly, although IT Providers can report the number of projects that they are involved in, only the business can provide the total number of projects — presumably, there will be projects that IT Providers do not know about because they are not involved.
4. Service-level Effectiveness is a measure of IT customer satisfaction based on surveying the customer. This metric reflects the possibility that system performance may be satisfactory but the business may not be happy because the SLAs are inadequate in breadth or depth. This may be due to changes in the needs of the business or simply because the SLAs were not adequately defined in the first place.
5. The New Projects Index is a measure of IT's ability to deliver new projects that meet the agreed requirements on time and on budget. Clearly, the business also has a role to play in this.
6. The IT Total Cost Ratio is a measure of the total cost of IT, directly and indirectly, as a percentage of revenue and expenses.

It should be apparent that IT Providers deliver value in all of the other metrics being reported at the business level in Figure 2.2. For example, if we consider "Human Resources (HR) Responsiveness," undoubtedly some of the investment in HR funds the IT systems that support HR. Are these investments delivering value for money? Could HR be more effective if its IT was enhanced? Is there a business case for that? If there is not extensive IT in use in HR today, should there be?

The Business Case

So how do we report IT value? We need to include IT value indicators in each of the measurements being reported at the business level. As we have noted, the value of IT to the business is very dependent on the business value priorities (e.g., operational excellence, customer intimacy, product/service innovation). Different business units may have different priorities.

What common management tool applies internally valid measures of value to new investments? The business case. The business case for any new project (including non-IT projects) should include quantification of the value of the project to the business in terms of tangible and intangible benefits. It should be possible to track the value of these benefits in monetary units against the project costs throughout the life of the project.

This approach to measuring IT value is so simple that it is bound to raise a number of questions:

- What if the benefits are all intangible and cannot be easily measured? The advisability of starting the project should be seriously questioned.
- This might be good for all new projects but what about our legacy systems? First, there may be a number of old business cases available. The sum of all the legacy systems in a particular area provide some percentage of the business value being generated today (ignoring all new projects). Hence, a one-off legacy business value calculation based on some percentage of revenue minus costs should result in a historic IT value measure. The components of this calculation can be tracked going forward. For example, using the HR example again, the cost of the IT resources needed to provide the HR systems last year should be relatively easy to calculate (ultimately, the costs associated with each of the business units must sum to the total cost of IT). The challenge is to decide what value the system provides to HR. If we assume that the HR department prioritizes customer intimacy, one simple way to do this is to calculate the number of full-time equivalent staff (FTEs) that would need to be employed in HR to provide the same level of service as the computer system. The value then is the difference between the projected annual cost of the FTEs and the annual cost of the computer system. But this is too simplistic. Another approach is to consider the sum of the costs associated with the minimal acceptable IT solution plus the extra FTEs in HR and IT that would still allow HR to meet its SLAs.
- If this process is so simple, why don't we track the "actual versus planned" figures for business case returns today? Why indeed — it is amazing how rarely this is done when we consider just how much energy and angst goes into creating a typical business case.
- Do we really need a business case for every project when many of them are very small. The answer is "yes." There are lots of trade-offs in efficiency and effectiveness between small and large IT projects but no organization can survive with exclusively all small or all large projects. Getting the right mix and controlling the relative level of investment is an important IT governance issue.

- Isn't this just earned value analysis (EVA)? No. EVA is a very useful tool in development projects because it gives an indication of the progress of the project based on the completion status of the various sub-components of the project. However, EVA typically stops when the development project is completed with 100 percent of its earned value delivered. A business case is much more about the real cash flows after the project is developed and implemented in operations — the cost of development is just one part of the investment in the project.

This use of the business case for new projects is compelling but what about the recurring IT expenditure to "keep the lights on"? How can we construct business cases for the existing IT spend as opposed to the new IT spend? How can we compare the two?

The answer to this takes us into the area of risk management, which will be covered in more detail in Chapter 14. In considering the value to the business of continuing to spend on existing IT, the business needs to capture the cost avoidance benefits of the expenditure. In considering the value of another year's expenditure on legacy systems, the business case needs to consider the cost implications of a system outage. These costs include the immediate repair costs plus the impact on revenue. For example, a one-day outage of the Amazon.com or e-Bay Websites could be caused by a simple software defect that would take a short time to detect, fix, and redeploy but the lost revenue (and damage to reputation) would be huge.

Value Visualization

Over many years, the process and measurement experts at the David Consulting Group (DCG; www.davidconsultinggroup.com) have studied, taught, implemented, and audited almost all of the process improvement methodologies and best practices that have come, gone, and stayed around. Current examples of these, described elsewhere in this book, include Six Sigma, GQM, CMMI, ITIL, and COBIT. From our experience we have seen that all of these have value in certain circumstances and a few have value in all circumstances. We choose, and use, all of these approaches as knowledge steps to move our clients along paths toward their desired goals based upon our intimate understanding of their current capabilities and potential.

With such a variety of tools available, how can you ensure continuous improvement, test for effectiveness or, indeed, test for "mission accomplished"?

DCG has evolved the Value Visualization Framework^{SM} (VVF) shown in Figure 2.3. The framework is based on the simple philosophy that any project (in our case, process improvement and measurement projects) must deliver value and that value must be visible. The VVF is unique in that it takes a holistic view of the organization and facilitates the selection of the best practices (one or many)

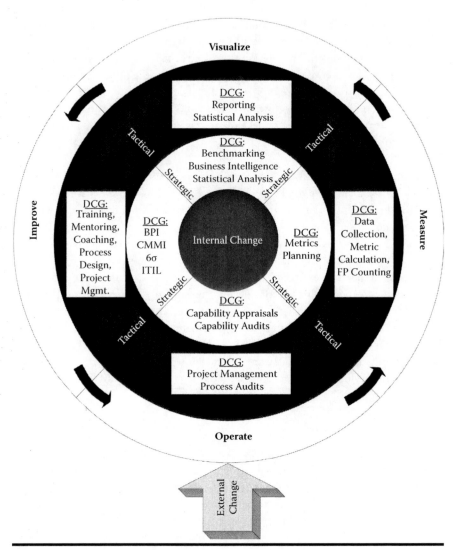

Figure 2.3 The Value Visualization Framework^{SM}.

to meet the different needs of the current situation based on clear definition of the value that can be delivered by this iteration of the framework. This avoids the need to "bet the business" on one particular methodology when maximum improvement and, more specifically, value can only or best be achieved by cherry picking combinations of parts of methodologies (that minimize risk) for this situation.

At DCG, evidence-based value modeling is used to test the potential ROI of individual best practices or combinations of best practices with reasonable probability and risk levels. More generally, any of the value measurement techniques described in this chapter can be used to facilitate regular value visualization for the business.

Summary

Clearly, there are many techniques that can be used for measuring the value of IT. The "right" ones are right for a particular business–IT Provider relationship. Business cases, or something similar, should be the vehicle for capturing the agreements between business and IT regarding how the value will manifest itself to the business, and how this value will be measured, monitored, and reported. The cost of measuring, monitoring, and reporting should be included in the business case at least through to the projected date when the expected and agreed return is achieved.

References

1. http://www.m-w.com (accessed Sept. 20, 2007)
2. Grady, Robert B. 1997. *Successful Software Process Improvement*. Prentice Hall.
3. Ben-Menachem, Mordechai and Marliss, Garry S. July/August 2005. IT assets — Control by importance and exception: Supporting the paradigm of change. *IEEE Software*.
4. Lutchen, Mark D. 2004. *Managing IT as a Business: A Survival Guide for CEOs*. John Wiley & Sons, Inc. (Pricewaterhouse Coopers LLP).
5. McShea, Michael. January/February 2007. Communicating IT's value in a modern business climate. *IT Professional*, IEEE.
6. McShea, Michael. November/December 2006. IT value management: Creating a balanced program. *IT Professional*, IEEE.
7. Tockey, Steve. 2005. *Return on Software: Maximizing the Return on Your Software Investment*. Pearson Education, Inc.
8. Baetjer, Howard. 1998. *Software as Capital: An Economic Perspective on Software Engineering*. IEEE Computer Society Press.
9. Jones, Capers (International Function Point Users Group). 2002. *IT Measurement: Practical Advice from the Experts*. Pearson Education, Inc.
10. Denne, Mark and Cleland-Huang, Jane. 2004. *Software by Numbers — Low-Risk, High-Return Development*. Sun Microsystems Press (Prentice Hall).
11. Broadbent, Marianne and Kitzis, Ellen S. 2005. *The New CIO Leader — Setting the Agenda and Delivering Results*. Harvard Business School Press.
12. Treacy, Michael and Wiersema, Fred. 1995. *The Discipline of Market Leaders: Choose Your Customers, Narrow Your Focus, Dominate Your Market*. Perseus Books.

Chapter 3

How Much IT Is Enough?

IT is a strategic differentiator. Often, it is a single force that determines the speed and agility of an organization. Think of it as the vehicle for the journey toward world-class results. It can provide different combinations of safety (quality), speed (high performance), and capacity at different fuel efficiencies. Do you need a Lamborghini? Do you want one? How about the cost? The question is, what specific attributes do you want or need from this vehicle? Why buy luxury add-ons when base model options will do? What passenger capacity or towing capacity is required? How long does this vehicle need to last? One year? Three years? Seven-plus years?

Decisions about IT spending are a series of trade-offs. The key to making the right decisions lies in first knowing the compelling needs to achieve the business strategy. Establishing the strategic enablers (most critical elements necessary to deliver on the strategy) generates the focus for planning activities to achieve this desired future state: efficient IT, nimble IT, high-quality IT, world-class IT, etc.

Performance is defined differently depending on the strategic enablers critical to the business. In Chapter 11, we provide performance data for the dimensions of:

- Productivity
- Cost
- Duration
- Quality

These apply for both new development and enhancement activity. Comparison of these dimensions supports decisions about where to prioritize spending against the known strategic enablers.

To determine how much IT is enough, the scope of the IT budget must be defined. Typically, the IT budget is comprised of some mix of the people, processes, and technology (hardware and software) spending for an organization. The IT budget can be managed as a cost or profit center, functioning through a department, a business unit, an entire division, a company, or a set of such entities that we call IT Providers.

We have defined a number of ways to measure IT value in Chapter 2. Here we present four value metrics to explore how to examine when the level of IT spending may be enough. Each dimension on its own can stand alone; however, together they provide a multi-dimensional picture of technology spending in relation to macro indicators or high-level characteristics:

- Return on investment (ROI)
- IT spending as a percentage of gross company revenue
- IT distribution analysis
- Organizational evaluation

Finally, we consider the trade-off between cost containment and innovation.

ROI or Return on Investment for IT Spending

The ROI is as easy as thinking of the return rate for your savings account. You deposit $10,000 at an annual percentage rate of 5 percent. One year later your account is valued at $10,500. Your ROI is $500, 5 percent of the $10,000 investment.

Technology is an investment. The spending provides a return. This is also true for required changes like Sarbanes–Oxley compliance or other regulatory requirements. It represents the cost of remaining a going concern (cost of staying in business) or keeping your CEO on (or off!) the front page of the *Wall Street Journal*.

Consider the following example: a business unit requests a business application that will create a competitive advantage in the marketplace. That "advantage" needs to be understood and communicated by the business to the IT Providers:

- How is this application expected to improve revenues?
- How is it expected to reduce expenses?
- Are there secondary benefits to be realized by streamlining a process or improving the customer experience?
- How should this initiative be prioritized versus all other opportunities in the queue?
- What competitive advantage does this application provide? For how long?

The business states that the CEO designated this as a top priority. It is expected to bring $10MM in increased sales over the next five years.

Now the IT Providers have to estimate the expense to develop the new application. Technology costs will be $2.5MM and take six months to be in full production. (Note that we are assuming an efficient and effective estimation process based on historic data — unfortunately this is not as common as we might expect and hope.)

$$ROI = (total\ benefits - total\ expenses)$$

$$ROI = (\$10MM - \$2.5MM)$$

$$ROI = \$7.5MM\ over\ five\ years$$

The results can also be expressed as a ratio: in this case 1:4 representing $4 of return for every dollar invested over the same five-year period. Often, the ROI is expressed in annual terms for easier comparison to commonly used interest rates. Over the five years the ROI is 300 percent. Making some simple assumptions, the annual ROI would be roughly 25 percent. An excellent investment!

There are many other factors that should be included in the expense base such as the total cost of ownership to support and maintain the new application. Factors like these vary for each organization. The most important consideration is to use one method consistently to allow for a true comparison from one internal investment to another.

How much ROI provides enough return or a return soon enough? As we noted in a previous chapter, "beauty is in the eye of the beholder." What return do you expect on a car purchase? The only vehicles that appreciate are the Lamborghini and various antique cars — hardly a good model for an IT system! ROI is a single dimension in a decision of whether to move forward; it affords a direct financial look at the potential for return.

To understand some of the limitations of using only the ROI dimension, consider "Growth Bank" and "Old Bank." Growth Bank sought tremendous organic growth at almost any price. A persistent belief was that spending $1 to make $2 was a good investment. Growth was explosive and organic. It took years for the analysis of total cost of ownership to catch up but eventually it did. IT was very expensive in comparison to peer groups, their applications were built independently, and there was tremendous redundancy in the services they provided.

Old Bank moved at a slow pace, carefully considering every investment. It targeted projects with a two-year payback. ROI had to be at least 5:1. Innovation was rare. Expenses were always toward the lower end of peers. Time to market for new products was always behind industry peers. Growth was through acquisition.

Both examples are approaches of very different, real-industry peers. Both banks are in the top ten, even today. ROI is not a single-threaded answer.

IT Spending as a Percentage of Gross Company Revenue

Defined as the total IT expense divided by the total gross revenue of the organization or company, this includes the entire IT budget, the staff, hardware, software, licenses, contracts, application development, and support. For example:

Company X gross revenues from sales	$200 million
Company X IT expenses	$18 million
Percentage IT spending	= (IT expense / gross revenue)
Company X	= 9 percent of gross revenue is spent on IT

In our experience, we have seen these numbers as low as 3.4 percent and as high as almost 12 percent. The spread tends to be smaller in specific industries. In an industry like financial services (in a growth year) we would see targets of 6 to 9 percent[1] depending on factors such as:

- The need for new development in technology
- The organization's reliance on technology
- Opportunities for consolidation

IT spending as a percentage of gross company revenue is a measure that has been collected and reported for years, so there is a substantive amount of data available by industry and other factors (U.S., non-U.S., CMMI® level, company size). Unfortunately, the missing parameter in using this data is whether the industry is in a growth year or a year of restructuring (e.g., lower marketing spending resulting in lower revenues means higher IT spending as a percent of revenue without changing the IT demand). It is still a telling number to calibrate for year-over-year spending. For example, this measure can help paint the picture of a truly neglected IT department which has flat IT spending in a steadily growing company. The percentage of technology spending in relation to revenue will show a steady decline year over year, as illustrated in Figure 3.1.

IT Distribution Analysis

IT distribution analysis is a technique used to understand the relative amounts of people, spending, applications, customers, etc. in relation to the amount of technology maintained and developed in an organization.

This data reveals the current level of resource utilization which achieves the current output or level of support. You can think of this as the miles per gallon

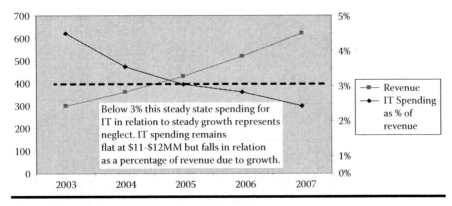

Figure 3.1   Neglected IT. Flat IT spending in a growing company.

(or kilometers per liter) rating for your technology investment. The results are points for understanding and discussion within the current organization. There is also industry data available if a comparison to peer groups is desired (see Figure 4.1 through Figure 4.3 in Chapter 4).

It can be very productive to analyze the cost of maintenance as a percentage of the overall IT budget. Jim Fister of Intel notes that "as much as 90 percent of today's IT budgets go to maintenance." If maintenance expenses are 80 percent or more of the IT budget, then there should be room to make savings to devote more funds to new capabilities. Follow-up questions address which of the applications require the most support and what solutions are more effective.

The same approach can be applied to each technology category. The analysis should be performed according to categories that already represent the way your IT Providers support the client base, usually by departments of sales, marketing, operations, human resources, finance, manufacturing, etc. (see Figure 3.2). Another approach is analysis by core process area. This can be more difficult but it provides more insight (see Figure 3.3).

Figure 3.2   IT spending by supported client base (example).

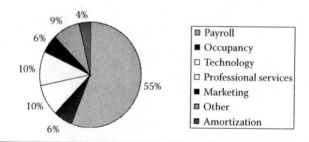

Figure 3.3   IT spending by function.

The next question to ask is whether the IT budget is proportionally targeted to the right areas to achieve the business strategy.

Looking at the percentage distribution for each department as a pie chart (see Figure 3.2), can the portions be reallocated to solve business problems or client dissatisfaction or better align with business strategy? For example, if 30 percent of the company's non-IT budget is spent on marketing this year, then should 30 percent of the IT budget (or the "discretionary" IT budget) also be allocated to marketing?

As an aside, the "discretionary" IT budget is one name for that part of the IT budget that is available to be spent each year "at the company's discretion"; that is, IT budget that is not already committed to maintenance. As noted previously, this is often a minority of the budget.

The results of this internal analysis can be illuminating. The discussions often generate champions within the client base for increased funding for IT. Other observations of organizational need and pain points surface which can form grounds for conversations about change.

An important point for discussion, though not obvious, is "How did we get here?" What elements are present in the culture or structure of the organization that led to the current state?

What organizational factors, cultural norms, or customer demands contributed to the current state of spending or distribution of IT resources? This determines the influencing factors such as operations receiving the greatest share of IT resources (see Figure 3.3).

What is the prioritization process for approving new IT applications or enhancements? Failing to prioritize often leads to spending on the wrong things or the squeaky wheel project (or people).

Does a target architecture exist? Are design standards adhered to? Conversely, persisting with antiquated disparate systems significantly increases maintenance costs and allows for many costly independent acquisition or development paths to emerge. Having a vision of the target solution allows measurement of progress toward the target and a sense of what "done" looks like.

Watts Humphrey once said, "Watch what people do when something goes wrong, that's the process." What is the process in the IT organization? What do people do under stress? Avoiding key steps in a standard process erodes quality and contributes to a chaotic culture where deviations become the way of doing business.

Answering the questions presented here is critical to understanding the current state of performance for the organization. The answers are also key to understanding how the current state of spending came to be. To make lasting changes, the norms of behavior must also change. An excellent source for more on this topic is *Leading Change* by John Kotter.[2]

Organizational Evaluation

Organizational evaluation is an evaluation of the skills needed to run the IT organization. The human assets of the organization are always a delicate topic; it is important to take every step in this process or none at all:

1. Establish guiding principles. These principles become the guardrails for the evaluation. The guiding principles should answer the question: "Why are we doing this?" Some examples are
   - Align IT outlets to deliver business strategy
   - Enable our target architecture
   - Evaluate IT spending
   - Support the need to consolidate
   - Support the need for rapid growth
   - To fund a new function
   - We're taking a disciplined approach to realigning the organization

   The principles you establish are used to confirm the resulting actions, ensuring alignment with the original intent of the organizational evaluation.
2. Engage the clients. Often called "users," the clients of the IT Providers have plenty of valuable input to determine the skills lacking in IT. This engagement can be captured through survey data, designed workshops, and focus groups. Prioritize the results. Remove outliers, observations that might be compelling but very rare. Seek to solve for the top three to five items.

   Client engagement is necessary to understand what issues really need to be solved. A lack of role clarity or no clear support might influence moving to a client-focused allocation of IT resources. This structure would align whole teams to focus on a specific business area. This structure is excellent for team focus, aligned goals, and client satisfaction. The trade-off is a poor structure for functional support (all developers are not in the same group). It often costs more and can be difficult for central roles like architecture to support so many groups. As such, it is an important decision point in IT budget allocations.
3. Engage IT Providers. Many people within the IT organization from bottom to top possess knowledge about what needs to be corrected. They will also have valuable information about the existence of barriers to change and the

associated risks. Again, prioritize the results. You should see overlap with the theme of the input from the clients.

4. Establish goals for the outcome of this exercise. These goals will be reviewed with the leadership in the organization, at a minimum. Include the time frame in which the results will be announced, the sooner the better.

   These goals could include onshore to offshore ratios of staff, like a 60/40 or 70/30 split, improving the client perception of IT, or faster throughput. Regardless of the goals of the exercise, formal documentation is required.

5. Skills evaluation. Start with the future state of the organization. Use documents like the three-year business strategy, technology target architecture, or other forward-looking information to define high-level position types. Use a table similar to Table 3.1 to analyze the results.

6. Select the organization design. In technology there are two clear choices or a hybrid approach:

   – A functional alignment of groups and reports of like functions, (e.g., analysts, project managers, developers, testers, etc.). This design may be the most efficient because like functions are in a single team. Its limitations can be the lack of alignment with client goals, and IT roles and teams that are siloed.

   – A client-focused design aligns entire delivery units according to client groups. This often entails diverse roles reporting to one manager (e.g., project mangers, analysts, developers, and testers). Benefits include high client satisfaction and faster delivery through greater focus. Limitations of this design include less efficiency through teams developing their own processes, duplicating functions, and not providing clear priorities for shared resources like design or architecture.

7. Assess the organizational design according to the goals from step 4. Ensure the new design will fill the gaps identified. Communicate the results to leadership, plan for the communication and rollout of the changes.

Containing Cost Versus Innovation

Striking the right balance between innovation and controlling IT cost is a continual challenge. Being innovative means some initiatives will fail. To breed a culture where risks are taken, failure must be an acceptable, even celebrated, result. It took Thomas Edison thousands of experiments to find the right amount of the right material to make a long-lasting light bulb. Edison viewed each failure as one more option eliminated, thereby getting closer to his goal. Building for innovation and developing a culture for taking risk does not need to clash with cost consciousness. However, an appropriate structure or system of support to foster innovation is necessary.

Table 3.1

Future Role	Future Competencies	Future Technical Skills	Number Required	Can This Position be Outsourced (why or why not?)
Business analyst	Facilitation skills Requirements elicitation	Use case development Risk analysis	18	
Project manager	Communication Collaboration Organization Discipline Leadership	Earned value management Business case development	10	
Development manager			4	
Process engineer		CMMI ITIL	3	
Architect		Business and technology knowledge	2	
Developer	Documentation	List technologies needed	30	
Tester		List testing tools	15	

The following steps establish innovation as an important element of the IT culture and budget:

- Establish a budget for innovation.
- Assign responsibility for innovation to a senior member of the IT organization.
- Set annual goals for innovation.
- Provide the time necessary for staff to work on innovative ideas.
- Celebrate failure.

Summary

This chapter describes a general philosophy and detailed measures for starting a discussion about whether "enough" is being spent by the business on its IT.

References

1. Gartner Consulting Worldwide IT Benchmark Service Trends and Findings for 2007.
2. Kotter, John. 1996. *Leading Change.* Harvard Business School Press.

Chapter 4

Am I Paying
Too Much for IT?

IT budgets have been on the rise every year for the past decade. Research indicates that global spending for IT, that is the complete operating budget for IT goods and services purchased as well as internal budgeting for IT, has increased at rates of 5 percent or above annually in recent years.[1] Jed Ruben of Gartner reported spending on IT for 2006 increased by 6 percent on average for the year. Knowing whether IT spending is at a steady state, growing, or shrinking helps one to IT expectations and where your organization's IT spending is in relation to the world at large.

According to Dr. Howard Rubin, founder of the Worldwide IT Benchmarking Database (now owned by Gartner), technology spending has been steadily gaining momentum; the velocity of IT spending continues at a rapid pace. Consider the following statistics on the past 20+ years of IT spending:

- From 1980 to 1990, IT spending totaled US$600 billion
- From 1990 to 2000, IT spending totaled US$3 trillion
- From 2000 to 2005, in just five years, IT spending reached US$4.3 trillion

This represents a steep increase in significant IT investment. Rubin suggests that we are going to start seeing technology being used to fight more competitive battles. Technology spending is going to be king in terms of strategic advantage and leverage.

In a 2006 interview with Michael Militus of CAI, Dr. Ruben stated, "More and more people are going to be asking themselves questions like, 'How can I guarantee that I achieve my deadline and lower my risks and manage my financial loss?'. And then they'll either get into the engineering and process discipline or they'll fall off the planet."

In this chapter, we explore

- What is a budget?
- Defining a budget for IT
- IT as a percentage of revenue and as a percentage of total operating expenses
- IT budgeting (IT as a strategic business partner or strategic weapon)
- Capitalizing IT expenses
- Monthly budget reviews
- Monthly project reviews

What Is a Budget?

First we have to understand what is meant by the term "budget." A budget is a financial plan. The budget for IT is usually comprised of all IT expenses for hardware, software, licensing, maintenance, staff, and professional services. It is viewed (and reviewed) differently depending on the climate and focus of the organization. It is most important to know how the budget is regarded by the executive team. For example, is the budget a guide, viewed as a guardrail for decision making? Is the budget sacred, no changes allowed? How closely are the numbers reviewed and revised?

In most cases, a budget is established annually and reviewed (that is, compared to actual expenses) monthly. Some organizations allow changes on a quarterly basis, allowing a reforecast for the rest of the year. In others, the budget is regarded as immobile, all deviations must be accounted for and brought within a 3 to 5 percent expectation. In these cases all under-runs (spending less than budgeted) are given back to the corporate books monthly, not to be carried into future months.

Regardless of the philosophy of the organization, it is important for IT to be as close to the budget as possible. Great deviations of more than 20 percent in either direction indicate poor planning, a division that is slow to deliver, a department whose spending is out of control, or all of these.

Defining a Budget for IT

In this section we will break down the major components and some sub-components of a typical annual budget for IT. It is critical for the person responsible for the budget to work closely with the organization's financial controller or designee from the CFO's office to ensure continuity in the process and to build support for the various decisions that lead to the final budget.

■ Personnel. This portion of the budget includes the salaries and bonuses for all full- and part-time employees of the IT department. Benefits such as health insurance, vacation, life insurance, etc. often fall in this category. By way of example, in the United States, benefits are usually estimated at 30 percent of the base salary. Each organization has a method for estimating the amount, and information is available from the organization's financial controller. Payroll taxes, training, and staff welfare (motivation and support) or team building comprise the rest of this budget line item. Payroll taxes vary (even state to state), and again the financial controller should have the detail. Training is a matter of organizational culture, priority, and success (based on our experience, in 2007 a guideline is to estimate $500/day, five to ten days per IT employee per year), Team building and staff morale are important to improve the cohesiveness of the unit. A good rule of thumb for this more general staff investment (in 2007) is US$300 to $500 per IT employee per year although, again, organizational culture and financial position will be very influential here.

When money is tight, training is often the first item cut from many budgets. Our advice is to look elsewhere. This is roughly a 2 percent annual investment in the employees to keep skills current and improve morale. Correctly targeted, this investment rarely fails to pay dividends, even in tough times.

■ Professional services. These are the line items for ongoing temporary help, staff augmentation, and consulting services. The leadership team must think about achieving the business strategy for the coming year. What does IT need to deliver to help the business achieve those goals? Improve delivery? Improve production support? Increase the quality of delivery? New systems or services? Any new introduction of technology, process or quality improvement, sizing, or estimating will require some level of professional services support. Programs can run without this additional support but will often take longer and cost more in the long run, especially if core staff are diverted from what they are good at to areas where their competence and experience are limited.

■ Software. The costs here are basically licensing and depreciation. Licensing costs consist of COTS (commercial off-the-shelf) software, purchases of licenses, renewal of licenses, and maintenance agreements or upgrades. Depreciation is the expense of any previously capitalized asset. The useful life for typical IT acquisitions accounting purposes is usually three years. Software either developed internally or purchased for any expense in excess of a number agreed upon by the organization and its tax advisors (e.g., $500K) is booked as an asset and depreciated over its useful life. The budget will incur a monthly expense (e.g., 1/36th of the value of the asset if the depreciation period is three years).

■ Hardware. This represents the purchase or lease of equipment including servers, switches, routers, hubs, fail-over equipment, desktops, printers, laptops, and monitors. Included here as well are the annual maintenance agreements for hardware. Most hardware, other than very low cost or disposable items, is usually depreciated.

■ Travel and expenses. Travel expenses are a part of most environments today. Travel varies by company, geography, culture, and industry. The simplest way to develop a forecast for this line item is to use the previous year's run rate and add or subtract for any large changes. For example, a good approach is to think in terms of "likely number of trips per person." Domestically in the United States, a trip for one week with airfare, rental car, hotel, and food may cost about $2500. Trips abroad, flying business class, can be $10,000 or more.

■ Communication, supplies, and other. This includes voice and data line fees, communications like voice mail, paper, pens, ink, subscriptions, memberships, and even occupancy including cubical builds or office moves.

Together these line items comprise the basic IT budget. To perform a true comparison to others in the same industry, a benchmarking study should be performed. In Chapter 11 we review such studies.

IT as a Percent of Revenue

This metric for IT spending is often used as a stick, not a carrot. It is a very flat statistic in that it does not provide any dimension regarding what is at stake for the organization (i.e., the delivery required to make this year's revenue). All that said, it is still a keen data point for use as just that, one point on a spectrum of delivery measures.

Table 4.1 shows spending as a percent of revenues as characterized by Silicon Valley expert Dean Lane from his book *CIO Wisdom: Best Practices from Silicon Valley's Leading IT Experts.*[2] A balance to this characterization is the benchmark forecast in Figure 4.1 from Gartner, the IT spending as a percentage of revenue as planned for various industry types.

Normally, revenues are recorded by the business units, not by IT, and so, in situations where IT expenses are distributed, it is important to capture and understand all IT spending holistically for the organization. See Figure 4.2.

IT as a Percent of Total Operating Expenses (OPEX)

Operating expenses are the total expenses for the whole organization, known as the operating budget or plan. When IT spending as a percentage of OPEX is used as a benchmark, it provides for a more grounded analysis than IT spending as a percentage of revenue. The percentage of OPEX is especially useful when compared to an industry peer group. It is also more effective for non-profit organizations or government agency comparisons.

Table 4.1   IT Spending as a Function of Revenues

Percent of Revenue	Consequences for the IT Organization
<1	IT is under-funded. This level cannot be sustained.
1–2	Difficult corporate environment in which to make IT a successful partner, few sustaining projects, little to no strategic investment.
2–3	Healthy zone for manufacturing companies or large companies achieving economies of scale.
3–6	Indicates solid funding from within the organization. IT can be a successful partner. This can sustain a few growth projects each year.
6–15	Very aggressive investments in IT, high depreciation and external service fees.
>15	Alert! IT is over-funded. Bring spending under control.

Source: Lane, Dean. 2003. *CIO Wisdom: Best Practices from Silicon Valley's Leading IT Experts.* Prentice Hall. With permission.

Using completed versions of Figures 4.1 through 4.3 is an effective way to determine the rate of IT spending in relation to industry groups more subjectively. The following questions are a guide to analyze IT spending; answers to these questions without satisfactory responses indicate an organization is paying too much for IT:

- What is your IT spending in relation to revenue?
- Where is it on Table 4.1?
- Where is it on Figure 4.1?
- Where is it on Figure 4.3?
- If it is more than 3 percent higher on Figure 4.1 or Figure 4.3, are there substantial influencing factors the organization understands and accepts?
- Is your spending in IT increasing annually at a rate of more than 6 percent? Why?

If answers to these questions resulted in sub-par spending, IT may be under-funded. Refer to Chapter 3, Figure 3.1. To address the issue of an under-funded IT department, one must first gain agreement with "C"-level leaders that there actually is an issue and that it needs to be addressed. This analysis may be used to engage in a broader conversation of delivery and execution in relation to spending.

IT as a Strategic Business Partner

Budgets are produced to control IT expenses. This is an important role but what if IT were viewed as a strategic weapon for the organization? What if IT were a key differentiator among the competition? How then would an organization approach the budget process?

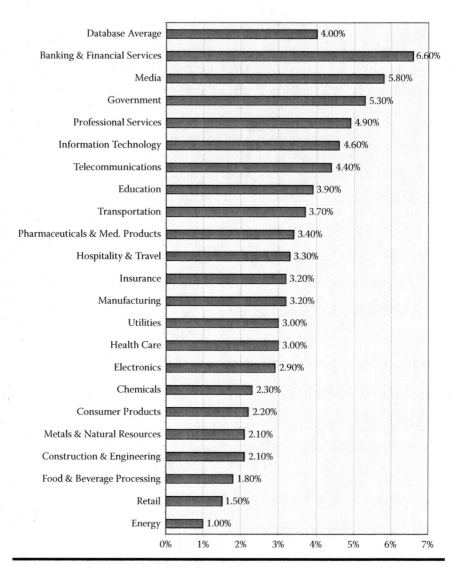

Figure 4.1 IT spending as a percent of revenues by industry. *Source:* **Gartner Worldwide IT Benchmark Service Trends for 2007. With permission.**

First and foremost IT would have advocates in the senior team and within the ranks of the organization. Business client (business customers)-facing IT staff would be acknowledged for their depth of business knowledge and true understanding about the challenges and goals for the departments they serve and the organization as a whole.

The client organizations seek guidance and partnership when designing solutions to achieve strategic intent. These business partners participate in the building

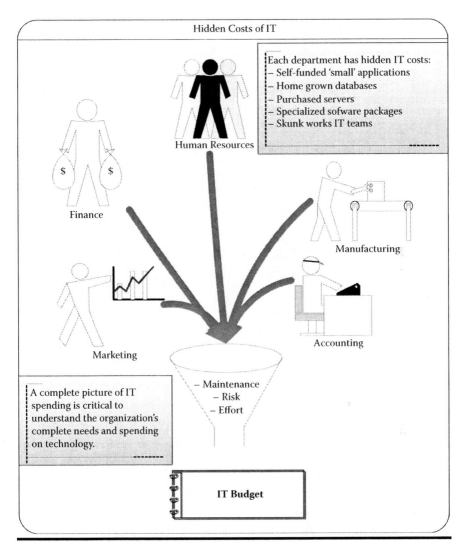

Hidden Costs of IT

Each department has hidden IT costs:
– Self-funded 'small' applications
– Home grown databases
– Purchased servers
– Specialized sofware packages
– Skunk works IT teams

Human Resources

Finance

Manufacturing

Marketing

Accounting

A complete picture of IT spending is critical to understand the organization's complete needs and spending on technology.

– Maintenance
– Risk
– Effort

IT Budget

Figure 4.2   Hidden costs of IT.

of the annual IT budget, and they contribute content and prioritization of key programs contained therein.

Client participation and support in IT projects is crucial to the success of the whole organization to ensure alignment, improve communication, and build an understanding of the work. It is well understood that non-IT managers often have to make process or organizational changes when large IT projects like a new financial system are installed. How about a small project? Let's take, for instance, a new change request system. Is it safe to assume the impacts are all internal to IT? No. There are often new demands that must be completed by IT personnel but must

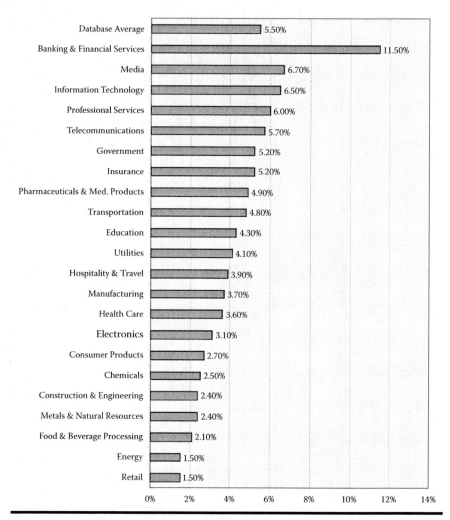

Figure 4.3 IT spending as a percent of OPEX spending.

be supported or determined by the client (see Figure 4.4). These are characteristics like the severity of the change to the business, the priority, the financial impact, etc. Lack of client participation often leads to very dissatisfying experiences with IT. Client involvement in all IT projects mitigates the risk of introduced change and improves alignment with the organization.

No IT projects exist without client participation or sponsorship. This sounds easy for projects that deliver immediate value for the client, like a new call center or a new marketing program. However, this also includes internal projects like upgrading to new hardware, process improvement projects, and building an enterprise data warehouse. If an IT system does not impact the IT client, it is fair to ask why it is even in the organization!

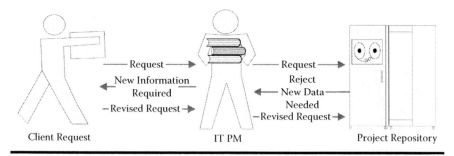

——Request——▶		——Request——▶
◀——New Information		Reject
Required		◀——New Data——
—Revised Request——▶		Needed
		—Revised Request——▶
Client Request	IT PM	Project Repository

Figure 4.4   Example of new change request system.

Figure 4.5 shows a typical Project Request form that builds client participation into the process. The key is in a field titled Client Participant in Section 2. This is the catalyst for identifying the named resource for the new IT project.

IT Poised to Enable the Business Strategy

The most senior representatives of the IT Providers should ensure that the prioritization of projects visibly delivers on elements of the business strategy while maintaining the integrity of the future state of IT. Key elements of the target architecture should deliver the foundation necessary for the growth and agility the business requires to dominate the market.

Unfortunately, discussion between the business and IT Providers too many times degrades into negotiations about trade-offs, of "keeping the lights on" (meaning performing the necessary maintenance and regulatory work), or delivering on the business strategy. It is the role of IT to provide full visibility and forecasting as well as offering creative alternatives for the realities of the current state of IT delivery. Therein lies the genius of any well-run IT organization: *full visibility and creative alternatives.*

The business may require elements of technology that are slated for the future. Fulfilling these requirements is dependent upon key infrastructure or architectural elements. It is the responsibility of the IT organization to present the trade-offs at hand. For example, the earlier installation of new software may require a substantial rewrite once a new database is in place. An often overlooked option is to show an earlier installation with some functionality limitations; a planned chunk of business-critical delivery with another chunk coming at a future date. This is a fundamental philosophy of agile delivery methods; however, this approach also applies to more traditional methods as well.

Discussions about funding for those IT elements that enable the business strategy are much less contentious. The discussion is "how will we fund," not "if we will fund." In some organizations the departments that will benefit most from the initiatives fund the IT programs to ensure prioritization and commitment. In

Project Request: Mission Critical IT Project		
Section 1: To be Completed by IT Project Manager upon Receipt from Client		
Date:		**Project ID #:**
Impact Analysis Assigned to:		**Estimated Completion Date:**
Section 2: Request Initiation/ to be Completed by Requestor		
Date Submitted:	**Client:**	**Client Participant:**
Department:	**Project Name:**	**Project Request Name/Title:**
Brief project description: (describe)		
Reason/Justification: (describe)		
Priority: (immediate = Show stopper; Urgent = Critical to the business, regulatory; Important = Good functional improvement, enhancement; Less Important = all other low priority changes; Strategic = achieves an element of the strategy)		
Section 3: Request Initiation / to be Completed by Client Sponsor		
Date Received:		**Accepted for Estimation:** (Yes / No)
Accepted by:		**Date:**
Section 4: Impact Analysis Summary / to be Completed by IT Project Manager		
Impact Analysis Recommendation/Potential Alternatives:		
		Date Accepted:

Figure 4.5   Project Request form.

other organizations where the IT budget is constrained, the discussion focuses on "what not to do." This is a more difficult planning discussion but much more powerful as well. It results in careful discussion and consideration of each program. Capturing the points considered and the outcomes forms an archive of the factors that influenced the decision making. Table 4.2 provides a template for capturing these points.

Capitalizing IT Expenses

A difficult item on the minds of many management personnel is the capitalization of IT expenses. The challenge is that capitalized investments in IT must be depreciated and become (seemingly endless) line items of monthly expense. The confusion

Table 4.2 IT Enabling the Strategy; Business Prioritization

Business Initiative	How it Enables the Strategy	Funding Source	Points Considered	Outcome

derives from interpreting national and international accounting rules and understanding what is required and how the industry at large handles the regulations from the perspectives of two groups with radically different world views, languages, and experiences: IT professionals and accountants.

By way of example, it is the responsibility of U.S. organizations today to recognize any investment in technology over $500,000 in development as an asset to the organization. That is to say that any purchase of hardware or software or internal development reaching $500K must be amortized over its useful life and depreciated monthly. Seems simple enough. However, implementation and interpretation of this rule vary for internally developed software. A challenge in performing this task is that it is left largely on the shoulders of the IT project manager who needs to work with a designee (usually with an accountant's background) from the CFO's office to forecast the expenses and timing of the implementation of these initiatives. It's easy when a server is purchased for $65K but internally developed software is different. What expenses should be considered development? When does development begin? When does it end? What if not all groups are in a phase of development at the same time; does it still count toward the asset value? This has a direct impact on budgeting. Consider the following (simple) example. If, say, 100 resources build a system worth US$100M in one year, then their budgeted cost in that year is only one third of their actual cost (assuming a three-year depreciation). Great news! Maybe. Next year, if the same 100 persons work on mainly small projects with no capitalization, their budget cost will be their actual cost, plus one third of last year's cost.

Take this discussion one level higher, up to the budget of IT, or up one more, to the level of the organization. Here there are additional points to consider. Too much capitalization can seem like a mortgaged future; a payment for the sins of the past, large expenses for which it feels as though there is no present value. Decisions governing how and when large IT programs will be capitalized and what will be included in the capitalization must be carefully considered going forward. Once established, these rules of governance must be followed consistently for all future programs.

For many of our past and present clients, the amount capitalized for people (or booked as an asset and depreciated over the useful life) are the expenditures

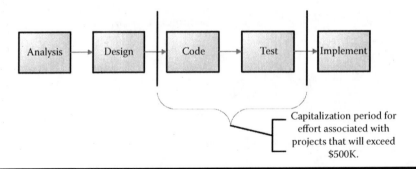

Figure 4.6 Capitalizing IT expenses for software development projects.

attributed to the coding phase through the start of the implementation phase of the project. This is illustrated in Figure 4.6. This assumes that:

- All development life cycles have phases corresponding to analysis, design, code, test, and implementation.
- Organizations track the resources and capital expenditures associated with all large projects expected to exceed $500K in development.
- Resources are people, full-time IT employees, part-time IT employees, consultants, and contractors who dedicate time to the project.
- Non-human resources tracked are any expenditure that is necessary for the project over $500K including servers, software, other hardware, licenses, etc.

Monthly Budget Review

Applying discipline and routine to a monthly review of the IT budget estimates against actual results is critical to understanding and steering the spending. There is no single activity that can be performed that produces a greater and more lasting effect on spending than the monthly review process. The best practice is to meet monthly with senior managers across the organization to review and understand the financial results of IT spending.

The business should create a charter for the monthly budget review meeting defining the purpose, frequency, attendees, recommended agenda, inputs, and outputs of the meeting. The business must publish the results of the meetings for more visibility, to drive responsibility and understanding, and to gain and prove commitment. Mid-level managers and even individual contributors should have access to this information. The charter should include the following:

- The purpose of the meeting is to perform a review of actual spending in relation to the forecast and to make changes as needed to the projected spending. It may also include a review of deviations greater than 5 percent on any line item or for a given amount like ±$25,000.

- Recommended frequency is monthly but may vary due to organizational need. No more than monthly, no less than quarterly are guardrails.
- The attendees should include the CIO, at least one major sponsor from the client organization, the senior team from IT, and the CFO or designee who can prepare the reports and review the results.
- Agendas should follow a standard format of outstanding items from the last meeting, review of the results, trend analysis, forecast changes for established trends, and discussion of future spending and cuts if necessary.
- Input to the meeting is the report of actual spending compared to the forecast and action items from the previous meetings. Additional reporting of the year-to-date (YTD) run rate and year-over-year trend analysis are recommended but they are not mandatory. Meeting attendance is also a required input to the meeting. Without critical mass, the effort will not achieve the brain trust and commitment needed to influence change.
- Outputs from the meeting include minutes for critical items discussed and any action items. In less mature organizations, it may seem risky to publish the results. Information sharing is a best practice. The best way to achieve the needed buy-in for change is to engage the organization. Sharing this critical and sensitive information with the organization accompanied by requests for involvement or change is an opportunity for a leader to leverage.

Monthly Project Review

Similar to the budget review is a review of all critical projects currently underway or "in-flight." We have found it is a best practice for IT departments to perform a monthly project review with the business. This forum provides executives visibility into the progress of projects and focuses the organization on those that are most important. It also instills a sense of commitment and healthy anxiety in the IT staff contributing to the projects. No one wants to walk in with a bad report. The review process can remove layers of management and bureaucracy that often separate the CIO from the teams actually performing the work.

It is common for executives to "drop in" on project team meetings for projects they sponsor or have a vested interest in. It's difficult for the same executives to readily identify which of those activities underway are draining critical time and talent. According to the much-referenced Chaos study from the Standish Group,[3] only 16 percent of all IT projects will come in on-time, on-budget, delivering desired functionality. The monthly project review is an opportunity to view all development currently in-flight, risks, barriers, and issues requiring escalation. Just as important, a large cross-section of IT Providers have the opportunity to see the executive team in action and hear the topics they care about. The executives also have the opportunity to celebrate success by rewarding successful teams.

Most organizations have multiple projects in-flight at once. Establish a hard stop on the time allotted for the meeting to ensure an effective use of everyone's time. Encourage all project managers to attend. Develop a rhythm to achieve the coverage necessary and keep the meeting on course. Use a "parking lot" to capture follow-up items.

Some large financial institutions afford five minutes for each project in these meetings. Other companies only review the top projects; those in the top half of their size, those key to the strategy, or those with high resource utilization. All the companies we have seen use a common format for project reporting to facilitate a discussion or review of only the most important points. The format of this project sheet is a single page which includes

■ Project Title	■ Business Sponsor	■ Project Number
■ Start Date	■ Targeted Finish Date	■ Brief Description
■ Budget	■ Spending To Date	■ Status
■ Milestones	■ Issues (top three)	■ Risks (top three)
■ Accomplishments	■ Project Manager	

The monthly project review provides a forum to gain an understanding of the resource utilization and progress on projects. It is during these sessions that the reality of the current state of spending, project progress, quality, and speed can be endorsed by leadership or required to change.

Summary

In summary, the budget for IT is comprised of multiple line items representing expenses incurred by IT. Budgets for IT have increased over the last 25 years almost algorithmically and are likely to continue as IT is viewed as a competitive weapon. IT spending as a percentage of revenues and percentage of OPEX spending are common reference points for comparison to understand IT spending. Two key tools to use to manage spending and organizational focus are a monthly budget review and monthly project review.

References

1. Gartner Consulting Worldwide IT Benchmark Service Trends and Findings for 2007.
2. Lane, Dean. 2003. *CIO Wisdom: Best Practices from Silicon Valley's Leading IT Experts.* Prentice Hall.
3. www.projectsmart.co.uk/docs/chaos-report.pdf (accessed Sept 20, 2007)

WHY SHOULD WE CARE ABOUT IT GOVERNANCE?

Chapter 5

Who Governs IT?

The thought of IT governance can make any executive shudder and the IT practitioners run for cover. The job of CIO is one where in a line of ten people, nine will step back, none forward. In this section, we will review the role of IT governance with regard to leadership, management, clients, and users of IT. We will also review effective organization structures to establish governance that seeks to achieve business goals and the contributions to those structures of the practitioners within IT Providers. We'll define the principles and help identify governance intentions according to critical questions for the organization.

The referenced best practices in this section are based on research from the MIT Sloan School of Management captured in the book *IT Governance: How Top Performers Manage IT Decision Rights for Superior Results*,[1] by Peter Weill and Jeanne W. Ross. Their work on IT governance was developed through their research on 250 enterprises worldwide and research performed by the MIT Sloan School Center for Information Systems Research (CISR). In most other chapters in this book, we have gathered and summarized data from many sources in an attempt to present a diversity of ideas and approaches. In this chapter, we make no apologies for mainly using what we consider to be the best single source for research and reference information on operational IT governance.

What Is IT Governance?

Effective governance addresses three questions:

1. What decisions must be made?
2. Who should make these decisions?
3. How will we make and monitor these decisions?

Weill and Ross define IT governance as "specifying the decision rights and accountability framework to encourage desirable behavior in using IT." This ensures compliance with the enterprise's overall vision and values. Through their governance research, Weill and Ross have been able to conclude that effective IT governance is the single most important predictor of the value an organization generates from IT.

For our purposes here, governance is not about creating bureaucracy but determining what decisions must be made, by whom, and how they will be monitored. Providing clarity to the organization about the results of governance decisions and, more importantly, the process of decision making streamlines communications and removes ambiguity. Uncertainty by managers or project teams about how to proceed when making critical decisions can cause delays and, worse, indecisiveness. This translates into lost time and a loss of passion for the work to be performed. The right governance for IT results in a clear process for decision making.

The top performing organizations implement IT governance most effectively to support their strategies. The CISR research shows that the top performing organizations generate up to 40 percent higher returns on their IT investments than their competitors with weak IT governance.

Key Elements of IT Governance

Table 5.1 is a starting point for the IT governance model because it identifies the key types of IT governance decisions. All of these are candidates for inclusion in an IT governance model.

IT Principles Decisions

Organizations need to decide which three or four principles (or strategies) will dictate the culture of their IT Providers. Even when IT Providers are external to the organization, these principles should play a part in deciding which outsourcing partners are most compatible. By way of example of the type of principles we are talking about, Table 5.2 shows examples of IT principles aggregated from a number of different organizations (note that no single organization had more than five!).

Some key questions to ask for IT principles governance are

- What is the enterprise's operating model?
- What is the role of IT in the business?
- What are IT-desirable behaviors?
- How will IT be funded?

Table 5.1 Key IT Governance Decisions

IT Principles Decisions: *High-Level Statements About How IT is Used in the Business*		
IT architecture decisions: Organizing logic for data, applications, and infrastructure captured in a set of policies, relationships, and technical choices to achieve desired business and technical standardization and integration.	IT infrastructure decisions: Centrally coordinated, shared IT services that provide the foundation for the enterprise's IT capability. Business applications needs: Specifying the business need for purchase or internally developed IT applications.	IT investment and prioritization decisions: Decisions about how much and where to invest in IT, including project approvals and justification techniques.

Source: © 2003 MIT Sloan Center for Information Systems Research (CISR). With permission.

IT Architecture Decisions

It is natural for businesses to treat IT architecture as unfathomable technical babble. However, it is important for business leaders to ask questions in non-technical language and require answers in equally non-technical language. Some key questions to ask for IT architecture governance are

- If we adopt this architecture, will the following things get better or worse (if you are told that all are going to get better, then seek independent advice!):
  - Capital investment levels?
  - Time to market?
  - Performance?
  - Quality?
  - Maintenance costs?
  - Vendor dependencies?
- What are the core business processes of the enterprise? How are they related?
- What information drives these core processes? How must the data be integrated?
- What technical capabilities should be standardized enterprisewide to support IT efficiencies and facilitate process standardization and integration?
- What activities must be standardized enterprisewide to support data integration?
- What technology choices will guide the enterprise's approach to IT initiatives?

Table 5.2   Examples of IT Principles

■ Benchmarked lowest total cost of ownership	■ Federal IT organization
■ Architectural integrity	■ Develop project, process, and technical competence within IT
■ Consistent, flexible infrastructure	■ Standardize project procedures
■ Rapid deployment of new applications	■ Standard technology platforms; single sign-on
■ Measured, improving, and communicated value and responsiveness	■ Seamless escalation across multiple support levels leveraging centralized competence centers
■ Enable the business	■ Adopt a process view of the firm
■ Ensure information integrity	■ Build a corporate infrastructure to support cross-functional processes
■ Create a common customer view	■ Build and leverage a standardized environment
■ Promote consistent architecture	■ Focus on the customer
■ Utilize industry standards	■ Provide business information
■ Reuse before buy; buy before build	■ Integrate processes, functions, and companies
■ Manage IT as an investment	■ Make it easy for customers to do business
■ Early adoption without penalty	■ Share and reuse technology enterprisewide
■ Commercial orientation of IT	■ Federal IT organization
■ Creation of business cases and measurement of IT impact	■ Develop project, process, and technical competence within IT

IT Infrastructure Decisions

As for IT architecture, it is natural for business to treat IT infrastructure as unfathomable technical babble. Some key questions to ask for IT infrastructure governance decisions are

- What infrastructure services are most critical to achieving the enterprise's strategic objectives?
- For each capability cluster, what infrastructure services should be implemented enterprisewide and what are the service level requirements of those services?
- How should infrastructure services be priced?
- What is the plan for keeping underlying technologies up to date?
- What infrastructure services should be outsourced?

Business Needs Decisions

Is it reasonable to question why "business needs" appear to be only a subset of the considerations for decisions when surely they should drive all IT decisions? To answer this question, it is important to remember that this chapter is about constructing an appropriate IT governance model. Hence, this is really about how decisions on business needs will be made alongside other IT decisions. The assumption is that the real, major business decisions are being made in the context of a corporate governance model (which is at a hierarchically higher level in the organization than the IT governance model). Some key questions to ask for business needs IT governance decisions are

- What are the market and business process opportunities for new business applications?
- How are experiments designed to assess whether they are successful?
- How can business needs be addressed within architectural standards? When does a business need to justify an exception to standards?
- Who will own the outcomes of each project and institute organizational changes to ensure the value?

IT Investment and Prioritization Decisions

In previous chapters, we have given a lot of information about measuring the value of IT. These should be reviewed before setting up an IT governance model.

One fundamental aspect of IT investment and prioritization is deciding how to manage the organization's IT applications portfolio (e.g., HR systems, finance systems, software development systems, etc.). One approach to IT portfolio analysis is the concept of IT investment portfolios. Much like a financial investor's portfolio of stocks, bonds, real estate, and cash, an IT investment portfolio should be reviewed according to the distribution by categories important to the organization. The classifications should be easy to understand and number five or less to facilitate high-level analysis. Recommended categories include

- Strategic
- MIS (Management Information Systems)
- Transactional
- Infrastructure

Utilizing these categories to evaluate the planned IT spending can facilitate the analysis of IT portfolio spending in relation to the strategic direction of the organization. If improving the customer experience is a strategic initiative, what percentage of the planned spending is marked for customer facing systems?

Evaluating the IT portfolio as an investment is intended to validate the budget distribution or drive discussion in the organization to support the distribution. If the distribution is easily explained, matching well to the needs of the organization and the overall priority, the exercise will underscore the strength of the decisions. If the distribution is very different than the stated goals of the organization for cost-saving initiatives or strategic goals, they must be reconciled as a divergence exists and the expectations of the organization will not be met.

Some further key questions to ask for business needs IT governance decisions are

■ What process changes or enhancements are strategically most important to the enterprise?
■ What are the distributions in the current and proposed IT portfolios? Are these portfolios consistent with the enterprise's strategic objectives?
■ What is the relative importance of enterprisewide versus business unit investments? Do actual investment practices reflect their relative importance?

Decision Input and Decision Making Models

To establish models for who will make decisions and who will have input to those decisions, it is useful to identify a set of archetypical scenarios. Table 5.3 defines a set of typical models for input to and making decisions.

Note that in an IT duopoly, input is gathered or decisions made as a result of a consensus discussion between the IT Provider and the business group or groups directly concerned with the decision. Two separate models are used for duopoly where one IT Provider must consult or make decisions with many business groups.

Table 5.3   IT Governance Archetypes

Model	Who Has Decisions or Input Rights?
Business monarchy	A group of business executives or individuals (CxOs), includes committees of senior business executives, excludes IT executives acting independently
IT monarchy	Individuals or groups of IT executives
Feudal	Business unit leaders, key process owners or their delegates
Federal	C-level executives and business groups (e.g., business units or processes); may also include IT executives as additional participants, equivalent of the central and state governments working together
IT duopoly	IT executives and one other group (e.g., CxO or business unit or process leaders)
Anarchy	Each individual user

Source: © 2003 MIT Sloan Center for Information Systems Research (CISR). With permission.

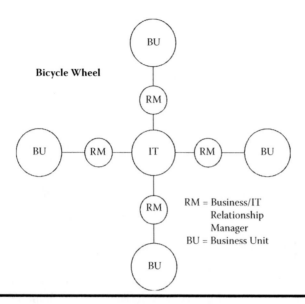

Figure 5.1 Bicycle wheel IT duopoly. *Source:* © 2003 MIT Sloan Center for Information Systems Research (CISR). With permission.

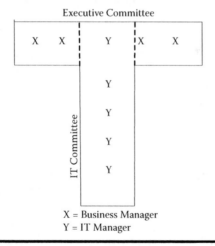

Figure 5.2 T-shaped IT duopoly. *Source:* © 2003 MIT Sloan Center for Information Systems Research (CISR). With permission.

In the first model, the "Bicycle wheel IT duopoly" (see Figure 5.1), the IT Provider interacts with each of the many interested business groups separately through business/IT relationship managers. In the second model, the "T-shaped IT duopoly" (see Figure 5.2), the IT Provider interacts with all of the many interested business groups together. It is worth noting here that the T-shaped duopoly is more scalable in the situation where there are multiple IT Providers. The seat on the Executive Committee would be taken by the most senior IT Provider (usually the in-house CIO) but all IT Providers can be represented.

It should be noted that, for IT governance, the players defined (e.g., CxOs) may be at a lower level in the organization but the models are still sound.

The research conducted by Weill and Ross shows that although there are a wide variety of approaches to the models used for input and decision making, there are some that are used more commonly than others as shown in Table 5.4. The shaded boxes in Table 5.4 represent the models most commonly used for input to decisions, and the shaded boxes highlight the models most often used for actually making the decisions. The numbers in each cell are percentages of the 256 enterprises studied in 23 countries. The columns sum to 100 percent.

Of course, simply because most organizations govern IT in a particular way, it does not necessarily follow that this is the most effective way to govern IT. To pursue this thought, Weill and Ross examined the core business strategies (maximization of profit, growth, or return on assets) used by enterprises in the survey and identified the governance strategies used most often by enterprises with most success against their core business strategies. The results are shown in Table 5.5. The shaded boxes in Table 5.5 show the decision-making model used most across all organizations surveyed (successful and unsuccessful). Table 5.5 has some profound implications for businesses seeking to build IT governance. It seems clear from this research that organizations seeking to maximize return of assets should leave IT decision making to the individual business units without imposing any standard structures. It is equally clear that, generally, for profit and growth maximization decision making, a business monarchy is the best structure.

A common problem in organizations today is too many "number one" projects. There are so many initiatives anointed as "critical" or "top priority" that the real business imperative can not be determined. Will the top project please step forward? This situation clouds decision making. Top projects often compete for system resources, funding, and skilled team members. Having multiple projects designated as "number one" is like having multiple bosses all with equal authority and competing requests.

Throughout this book there are many tools and models referenced to help resolve the issue of having too many top priority projects. Differentiation among the top priority projects is necessary to influence the right behavior and decision making when issues arise and trade-offs have to be made. In Chapter 2, value is shown to be an excellent attribute to be used as a differentiator among project peers to determine the overall benefits to the organization. Determining how to prioritize and how to communicate the results will be different depending on the organization. However, the outcome should be clear, priority 1, priority 2, priority 3, and so on.

All of these inputs contribute to the governance design framework proposed by Weill and Ross to define an IT governance framework (see Figure 5.3).

Table 5.4　How Enterprises Govern

Decisions Archetypes	IT Principles		IT Architecture		IT Infrastructure Strategies		Business Application Needs		IT Investment	
	Input to Decisions	Decision Making	Input to Decisions	Decision Making	Input to Decisions	Decision Making	Input to Decisions	Decision Making	Input to Decisions	Decision Making
Business monarchy	0	27	0	6	0	7	1	12	1	30
IT monarchy	1	18	20	73	10	59	0	8	0	0
Feudal	0	3	0	0	1	2	1	18	0	3
Federal	83	14	46	4	59	6	81	30	93	27
Duopoly	15	36	34	15	30	23	17	27	6	30
Anarchy	0	0	0	1	0	1	0	3	0	1
No data or don't know	1	2	0	1	0	2	0	2	0	0

Source: © 2003 MIT Sloan Center for Information Systems Research (CISR). With permission.

Table 5.5 IT Governance Models Used by Most Successful Companies

Decisions Archetype	IT Principles Decision Making	IT Architecture Decision Making	IT Infrastructure Strategies Decision Making	Business Application Needs Decision Making	IT Investment Decision Making
Business monarchy	Profit Growth	Profit	Profit	Growth	Profit Growth
IT monarchy			Profit		
Feudal					Growth
Federal					
Duopoly				Profit	
Anarchy	ROA	ROA	ROA	ROA	ROA

Source: © 2003 MIT Sloan Center for Information Systems Research (CISR). With permission.

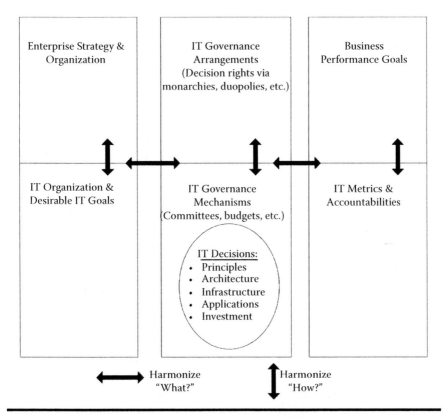

Figure 5.3 IT governance design framework. *Source:* © 2003 MIT Sloan Center for Information Systems Research (CISR). With permission.

We recommend utilizing these tools for discovery and analysis to define the right IT governance framework for the organization and to ensure alignment with strategic goals.

Summary

The role of IT governance is "specifying the decision rights and accountability framework to encourage desirable behavior in using IT." We reviewed models and research based on the work of Peter Weill and Jeanne W. Ross to examine the role of leadership, management, clients, and users of IT. We defined the principles and governance intentions according to three critical questions:

1. What decisions must be made?
2. Who should make these decisions?
3. How will we make and monitor these decisions?

Reference

1. Weill, Peter and Ross, Jeanne W. 2004. *IT Governance: How Top Performers Manage IT Decision Rights for Superior Results.* Harvard Business School Press.

Chapter 6

What Models Should IT Use?

All models are wrong, some are useful.

— George Box

No model has the capacity to be all things to all people. The value of a model lies in its ability to focus effort on a shared intent. Hence, there must be leadership commitment to using the model or methodology selected. Once a commitment is made, a model serves as a framework to measure and achieve progress toward a stated goal, much like a map. A map is a tool, it will not set your direction, but it is useful in planning the route you'll take and the distance you'll travel. It provides information to help determine the duration of travel and the supplies needed to get to the destination. There are limits. It will not provide resistance data like traffic congestion or construction.

It is a logical implication of our "model as map" metaphor to realize that, first, you have to determine where you are now. That is, the starting point for the models we'll review is determined by evaluating how your organization is operating in relation to the characteristics of the model. The next step, deciding where you want to go, requires an assessment of which attributes of the model are needed to achieve the goals of the organization. Knowing where you are is critical to determining your path forward. In IT circles, Watts Humphrey is credited with the saying, "If you don't know where you are, a map won't help." Many organizations have started improvement initiatives without baselining current performance effectively, only to learn that this is a costly misstep. Both time and money are wasted when the organization must go back and recalibrate performance. More than the tangible aspects of wasted time and money or steps forgotten, the energy of the staff and the momentum of the program suffer. Know where you are before you begin the journey of improvement!

So, can an organization improve or exhibit excellence without using a model to do so? Of course it's possible but the question is, why would you even consider it? Why expend all that energy reinventing the wheel when proven frameworks exist? Unless building improvement programs is a core competency within the organization, the do-it-yourself approach will prove more costly. To use an analogy, it is possible to design and build your own car but very few people have the time and energy to engage in such an arduous task.

There are many models available today. These include the Capability Maturity Model Integration (CMMI®), International Organization for Standardization (ISO), Control Objectives for Information and related Technology (COBIT®), Information Technology Infrastructure Library (ITIL®), Six Sigma (6σ), and Project Management. In this chapter, we'll provide the highest level of information about these models and methodologies as the most popular ones referenced elsewhere in this book. We'll start by providing a lens to aid in applying context for consideration and effective use. To do this, we'll review the origin of the framework, the purpose for which it was built, its most popular audiences, and an abridged description of the framework or methodology. This overview of these tools is intended to provide the context for comparison of theses frameworks to facilitate decision making. There are many sources available for more information on any model and the tools deployed in addition to the specialist consulting firms available for assistance. Readers should note that we use the terms "model" and "framework" interchangeably in the book.

Capability Maturity Model Integration (CMMI®)

CMMI is maintained by the Software Engineering Institute (SEI) of Carnegie Mellon University in Pittsburgh, Pennsylvania. The SEI was founded by the Department of Defense (DoD) in response to the "software crisis":

- Software was continually produced late, with overruns, and laden with defects.
- They needed a method to evaluate software contractors.
- Carnegie Mellon University won the contract.
- SEI is now funded by both the DoD and its own revenues.

The mission of the SEI is "to provide leadership in advancing the state of the practice of software engineering to improve the quality of systems that depend on software."

CMMI is the evolution of the Capability Maturity Model (CMM v1.0). According to the SEI, the CMM was established to (1) serve as a framework for organizations' software process improvement programs and (2) serve as a basis for software organizations to be evaluated by their prospective customers. The initial release of the CMM, v1.0, was reviewed and used by the software community during 1991 and 1992. A workshop was held in April 1992 on CMM v1.0, and was attended by about 200 software professionals. This led to the publication of the CMM v1.1 in 1993 as a result of the feedback from that workshop and the ongoing feedback from the software community.

The CMMI was sponsored by the DoD and the National Defense Industrial Association (NDIA) as an evolution of the CMM. The effort involved collaboration between commercial and private industry from around the world, government, and the SEI. CMMI seeks to improve the usability of capability maturity model technology across multiple disciplines. According to the SEI it can be used to guide process improvement across a project, a division, or an entire organization. It helps integrate traditionally separate organizational functions, set process improvement goals and priorities, provide guidance for quality processes, and provide a point of reference for appraising current processes.

To determine performance according to the CMMI model, an organization's capability or maturity is assessed according to the Standard CMMI Assessment Method for Process Improvement (SCAMPI[SM]). It is an appraisal performed by a trained team of software professionals to determine the state of an organization's current software process, to determine the high-priority software process-related issues facing an organization, and to obtain the organizational support for software process improvement.[1] SCAMPI provides a consistent method for both internal assessments and external evaluations. Appraisal results are valid for up to three years after the end date of the appraisal, when the results expire and the organization can no longer claim compliance.[2] During this three-year period, an organization can claim the level associated with the results of the assessment. For example, a large banner visible to the public hangs on a walkway at Grumman's Baltimore facility; the banner reads "CMMI Level 5." Other organizations have been known to hang entryway banners exclaiming "Alert: You are now entering a Level 3 facility." More than just bragging rights, once an organization has been assessed, their results are auditable by the SEI and assure some level of consistency and quality due to the formality and constraints of the process itself. In addition, some government agencies require a minimum assessed CMMI level as a precondition for awarding software- or systems-related contracts.

The premise for the development and continued use of the CMMI is summarized well in the following quote: "The quality of a system or product is highly influenced by the quality of the process used to develop and maintain it."[3] This foundational thought pervades the contents and approach used by the SEI in developing and evolving the CMMI.

The version in use today is the CMMI v1.2. This model has incorporated feedback from the software community and data from almost 20 years of use to evolve to its current state. The model does not prescribe how to run a software or systems development group. It indicates what goals should be achieved and practices should be performed. In essence, the CMMI will tell you what you should look like if you are a mature organization.

The target audience for CMMI is anyone who develops software for either internal or external use. The CMMI incorporates an engineering approach to address the need for process improvement. Though its roots are in the original need from the DoD, today over 68 percent of those implementing CMMI-based improvement processes are commercial businesses and in-house technology groups, 28 percent are military contractors, and 3 percent are government agencies.[4]

The CMMI has worldwide recognition and respect, software customers demand its use, and competitors are using it to improve performance, quality, and capability to create competitive advantage. Many organizations use a CMMI-level as a marketing tool to signify performance capability.

The CMMI model is often called non-prescriptive, meaning it does not provide a step-by-step improvement plan at the task level. It provides a framework for staged growth. An assessment will benchmark an organization's process and capability maturity, not the product or any other delivered outputs. It focuses on the management aspects of an organization's adherence to set standards which generate consistency, repeatability, quality, and ultimately the commitment to continuous process improvement.

A Capability Maturity Model (CMM) typically defines five levels of maturity that an organization can strive to achieve and, more importantly, sustain. Level 1 is the lowest level and the easiest to achieve although its value to an organization is low. Level 5 is the highest level. The CMM approach has been applied to a number of different problem spaces so you will hear of initiatives such as "people CMM" or "business development CMM" which may be credible initiatives (caveat emptor) but they are not directly related to CMMI.

Under a simple CMM, an organization has its processes and practices independently appraised against the requirements of a nominated level of the model, say Level 3. If the appraisal found that the organization met all of the requirements of Levels 1, 2, and 3, then the organization would be recognized as having achieved Level 3. Under CMMI, this approach is called the "staged representation" of the model and the levels are called Maturity Levels, e.g., Maturity Level 3 (see Table 6.1).

CMMI introduced a second way to ascend the capability maturity model, called "continuous representation." The rules are slightly more complex but, put simply, instead of having to achieve all of the requirements of a level to be successfully appraised against that level, the continuous representation allows organizations to seek appraisal against subsets of the requirements at different levels. Under the continuous representation, the five levels are still relevant but they are called "capability levels" (see Table 6.1).

Table 6.1 Comparison of Capability and Maturity Levels

Level	Continuous Representation Capability Levels	Staged Representation Maturity Levels
0	Incomplete	N/A
1	Performed	Initial
2	Managed	Managed
3	Defined	Defined
4	Quantitatively managed	Quantitatively managed
5	Optimizing	Optimizing

Why the complexity? Actually, it is driven by the needs of business. Broadly, there are three business drivers for seeking CMMI for a software development group:

1. It's the right thing to do to develop software effectively, efficiently, and economically to gain competitive advantage.
2. Clients are insisting on it as a contract condition.
3. The organization has specific problems in software development that need to be addressed.

The staged representation:

- Provides a defined road map for process improvement in the form of the five levels, then the process areas within each level contain generic and specific practices to achieve
- Each maturity level provides a mandatory foundation for the next level
- Process areas are fully contained within a single maturity level
- Results in a maturity level rating

The continuous representation:

- Allows flexibility in addressing process areas most critical to an organization's business objectives (i.e., process areas of higher levels can be addressed individually)
- Each process area has generic and specific practices at capability levels (0 to 5)
- Provides guidance for incremental improvement approach within each process area

Staged CMMI is best for organizations that:

- Are concerned about benchmarking their maturity level versus competition or using it for industry performance comparison

- Have achieved a maturity level and have a formal assessment as a goal
- Have little previous experience in process improvement and desire a proven path

Continuous CMMI is best for organizations that:

- Have no interest in having a formal appraisal or measuring their overall maturity level
- Have previous experience in process improvement and can map specific processes to their business objectives
- Have goals or a need to improve in specific processes
- Are migrating from using other continuous models
- Desire increased visibility into the capability within specific process areas
- Are already using ISO/IEC 15504 (see section on ISO in this chapter)

Each level of the CMMI contains a number of "process areas," which form the subsets of requirements that can be addressed in a continuous representation approach. Table 6.2 shows that, in addition to being organized by levels, the process areas are also grouped into the "categories" of engineering, project management, support, and process management. Typically, an immature software development group will be heavily focused on engineering with some project management. It can come as a shock to some organizations that they even need the support and process management process areas. Hence, these areas can represent the biggest opportunities for organizations to benefit and the biggest challenges to implementation and sustenance of the model.

It is worth noting here that CMMI is a very project-oriented model when it comes to appraisals, and organizations can be selective in the domain of the group that they are seeking to have appraised. For example, an organization might have a commercial development group and a government development group but only choose to implement CMMI and be appraised in the government development group. That said, a formal CMMI appraisal must be carried out by a lead appraiser certified by the Software Engineering Institute against very specific guidelines. These guidelines do not allow an organization to pick which projects will be appraised.

Although this may change over time, the current industry view of the CMMI levels is broadly that CMMI Level 5 is a highly desirable goal for large organizations that compete on their ability to perform software development, e.g., large defense contractors and major software development outsourcing vendors in India and elsewhere. Level 4 is a stepping stone to Level 5. Level 3 demonstrates an acceptable level of maturity for most contractual purposes and is a credible achievement for a development group. Level 2 is a minimally acceptable level for contract purposes; it demonstrates that a development group is getting its act together and shows that it could be on its way to Level 3.

Table 6.2 Process Areas and Associated Categories and Maturity Levels

Process Area	Category	Maturity Level
Requirements management	Engineering	2
Project monitoring and control	Project management	2
Project planning	Project management	2
Supplier agreement management	Project management	2
Configuration management	Support	2
Measurement and analysis	Support	2
Process and product quality assurance	Support	2
Product integration	Engineering	3
Requirements development	Engineering	3
Technical solution	Engineering	3
Validation	Engineering	3
Verification	Engineering	3
Organizational process definition + IPPD	Process management	3
Organizational process focus	Process management	3
Organizational training	Process management	3
Integrated project management + IPPD	Project management	3
Risk management	Project management	3
Decision analysis and resolution	Support	3
Organizational process performance	Process management	4
Quantitative project management	Project management	4
Organizational innovation and deployment	Process management	5
Causal analysis and resolution	Support	5

Source: Chrissis, M.B., Konrad, M., and Shrum, S. 2006. *CMMI: Guidelines for Process Integration and Product Improvement,* Second Edition. Addison Wesley Professional.

Control Objectives for Information and Related Technology (COBIT®)

The IT Governance Institute (ITGI) was established in 1998 to advance international thinking and standards in directing and controlling an enterprise's information technology. ITGI believes that effective IT governance helps ensure that IT supports business goals, optimizes business investment in IT, and appropriately manages IT-related risks and opportunities. ITGI's affiliate organization is the Information Systems Audit and Control Association (ISACA), which publishes the *Information Systems Control Journal,* and offers certification opportunities as a Certified Information Systems Auditor (CISA) or Certified Information Security Manager (CISM). Together ITGI and ISACA focus on the information technology control community, IT governance, and risk, specifically regulatory requirements.

COBIT was developed by a consortium from the worldwide governance community with many contributors and reviewers having the CISA designation. It is intended to provide a framework, an inclusive language for other IT frameworks such as:

- ITIL for service delivery
- CMMI for solution delivery
- ISO/IEC 27002:2005 for information security
- PMBOK or PRINCE2 for project management

COBIT began as a tool for auditors but has grown to include a security component and covers IT governance.

The following text is an excerpt from the executive overview of COBIT 4.1®[5]:

The need for assurance about the value of IT, the management of IT-related risks, and increased requirements for control over information are now understood as key elements of enterprise governance. Value, risk, and control constitute the core of IT governance. IT governance is the responsibility of executives and the board of directors, and consists of the leadership, organizational structures, and processes that ensure that the enterprise's IT sustains and extends the organization's strategies and objectives. Furthermore, IT governance integrates and institutionalizes good practices to ensure that the enterprise's IT supports the business objectives. IT governance thus enables the enterprise to take full advantage of its information, thereby maximizing benefits, capitalizing on opportunities, and gaining competitive advantage. These outcomes require a framework for control over IT that fits with and supports the Committee of Sponsoring Organizations of the Treadway Commission (COSO) Internal Control–Integrated Framework, the widely accepted control framework for enterprise governance and risk management, and similar compliant frameworks.

The business orientation of COBIT consists of linking business goals to IT goals, providing metrics and maturity models to measure their achievement, and identifying the associated responsibilities of business and IT process owners.

COBIT's good practices represent the consensus of experts.

They are strongly focused more on control, less on execution. These practices will help optimize IT-enabled investments, ensure service delivery and provide a measure against which to judge when things do go wrong.

For IT to be successful in delivering against business requirements, management should put an internal control system or framework in place. The COBIT control framework contributes to these needs by:

- Making a link to the business requirements
- Organizing IT activities into a generally accepted process model
- Identifying the major IT resources to be leveraged
- Defining the management control objectives to be considered

The business orientation of COBIT consists of linking business goals to IT goals, providing metrics and maturity models to measure their achievement, and identifying the associated responsibilities of business and IT process owners.

The process focus of COBIT is illustrated by a process model that subdivides IT into four domains and 34 processes in line with the responsibility areas of plan, build, run, and monitor, providing an end-to-end view of IT. Enterprise architecture concepts help identify the resources essential for process success, i.e., applications, information, infrastructure, and people.

Figure 6.1 and Table 6.3 show the overall COBIT framework within the context of an IT organization[6] and a list of the 34 high-level control objectives.

COBIT reinforces the need for IT to provide the information that the enterprise needs to achieve its objectives from a perspective of governance and risk. The COBIT framework promotes managing IT resources from a set of naturally grouped processes in line with the responsibility areas of plan, build, run, and monitor.

Additional information on COBIT can be found at www.itgi.org or the book *COBIT 4.1* by the IT Governance Institute, published by ISACA.

IT Infrastructure Library (ITIL®)

The IT Infrastructure Library (ITIL) was developed by the United Kingdom's Central Computer and Telecommunications Agency (CCTA) in 1987 as a means to establish process standards for U.K. government agencies. Now maintained by the Office of Government and Commerce, ITIL is a series of documents that comprise the "best practices" of ITIL. A non-profit organization, itSMF USA, acts as the official ITIL user organization, dedicated to promoting and helping to advance best practices in IT Service Management.[7]

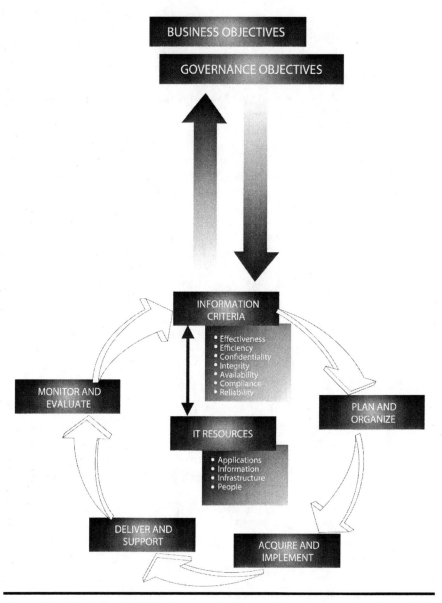

Figure 6.1   The overall COBIT framework. *Source:* **IT Governance Institute. 2007. COBIT 4.1. www.isaca.org.**

ITIL adoption rates have been on the rise. The CIO executive board reported in 2004 that 30 percent of global companies with more than $1 billion in revenues evaluated the potential of implementing ITIL, and approximately 13 percent were moving forward with ITIL implementation. Adoption is expected to increase to 60 percent of global companies with more than $1 billion in revenue by 2008.[8]

Table 6.3   COBIT's 34 High-Level Control Objectives

Plan and Organize		Deliver and Support	
PO1	Define a strategic IT plan	DS1	Define and manage service levels
PO2	Define the information architecture	DS2	Manage third-party services
		DS3	Manage performance and capacity
PO3	Determine technological direction	DS4	Ensure continuous service
		DS5	Ensure systems security
PO4	Define the IT processes, organization, and relationships	DS6	Identify and allocate costs
		DS7	Educate and train users
PO5	Manage the IT investment	DS8	Manage service desk and incidents
PO6	Communicate management aims and direction	DS9	Manage the configuration
		DS10	Manage problems
PO7	Manage IT human resources	DS11	Manage data
PO8	Manage quality	DS12	Manage the physical environment
PO9	Assess and manage IT risks	DS13	Manage operations
PO10	Manage projects		
Acquire and Implement		Monitor and Evaluate	
AI1	Identify automated solutions	ME1	Monitor and evaluate IT processes
AI2	Acquire and maintain application software	ME2	Monitor and evaluate internal control
AI3	Acquire and maintain technology infrastructure	ME3	Ensure regulatory compliance
		ME4	Provide IT governance
AI4	Enable operation and use		
AI5	Procure IT resources		
AI6	Manage changes		
AI7	Install and accredit solutions and changes		

Source: IT Governance Institute. 2007. COBIT 4.1. www.isaca.org

To produce an ITIL baseline, an organization is audited or measured for performance according to ITIL standards according to a process, BS 15000, introduced by the British Standards Institute in 2000.[9] BS 15000 is a formal standard allowing organizations to benchmark the delivery of their IT services. It defines a set of requirements covering ITIL service support and service delivery, security management, and relationship management, and specifies a level of quality that can be audited. As an industry standard, it helps firms qualify and choose suppliers and partner organizations.

The key business drivers for the BS 15000 standard are

- To provide a formal and auditable standard for the delivery of IT services within an organization
- To reinforce and provide accreditation based on best practices as defined by the British Standards Institute

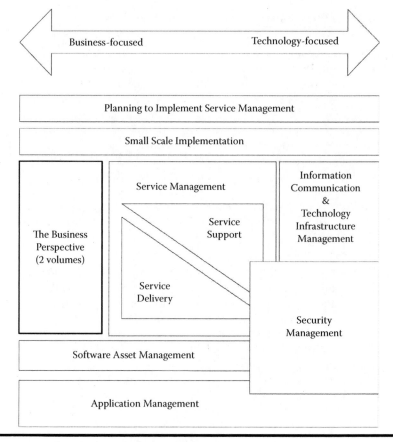

Figure 6.2 ITIL version 2 structure of book titles.

BS 15000 is also aligned with the international standard, ISO 20000 (sometimes known as "ISO20K"). The ISO 20000 is a specification and code of practice for IT service management (ITSM). ISO/IEC 20000 is aligned with the ITIL best practice.[10]

ITIL[11] is a set of best practices built around a process model-based view of controlling and managing IT operations. ITIL is considered one set of best practices in the more general field of ITSM. It is important to remember that ITIL is truly a library of books. The "architecture" of ITIL can be thought of as the structure imposed by the titles of the books that describe the best practices (see Figure 6.2 and Figure 6.3). Alternatively, the architecture can be thought of as the set of practices that make up the life cycle that ITIL describes.

At the time of writing, ITIL is undergoing an upgrade from version 2 (released in 2000) to version 3 (released in 2007). Why the change? The change was not driven by lack of success. Indeed, the opposite may be closer to the truth. As we noted previously, ITIL version 2 has been widely adopted and has demonstrated its business

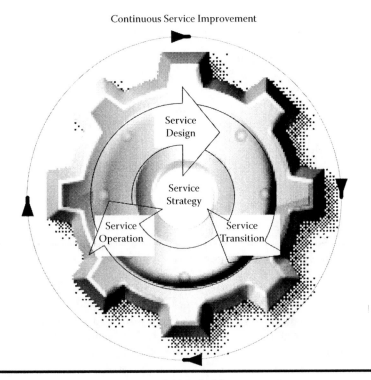

Figure 6.3 ITIL version 3 structure of book titles.

value, particularly in helping organizations to demonstrate their compliance with increasing regulatory requirements around the management of operational business (and hence IT) risk. It was version 2 that led to the national (BS 15000) and then international (ISO/IEC 20000) standards development described previously. In fact, the changes were driven by a desire to make the IT service life cycle (implied by the process defined in version 2) more explicit in version 3 in the form of an integrated process model and to reflect changes in professional practices since 2000. Further, although ITIL generally is quite prescriptive (more so than CMMI, for example), it was felt that even more "how to" information was needed. At the same time, the opportunity was taken to clear up some inconsistencies and add some detail in areas where widespread usage had shown to be light or missing altogether (e.g., return on investment, the supply chain).

Where ITIL version 2 focused on processes, version 3 focuses on business value. This shift attempts to improve the linkage between the business needs of the organization and the IT operational processes that enable them. Hence, version 3 has a more strategic approach than the tactical approach of version 2. Version 3 also acknowledges the value and applicability of other standards. Figure 6.4 summarizes the positioning of version 3 with respect to version 2 and other standards and Figure 6.5 shows, broadly, how the content of the version 2 books has made its way

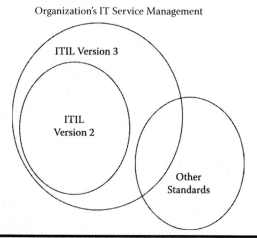

Figure 6.4   Relationships between ITIL versions 2 and 3.

into the version 3 books. Of course, the processes are still important and they are still included in version 3 (with a few added). The content and education associated with version 2 remain relevant but, particularly from a business perspective, using version 3 and updating from version 2 will provide more value.

To establish connectivity between COBIT and CMMI, it helps to have an understanding of the ITIL service management process areas and where they fit in the ITIL version 3 books (see Figure 6.6).

The ongoing relevance of the education elements of version 2 in version 3 is important because the major dissemination technique for ITIL is the education and certification of individual practitioners. The ITIL Foundation course is the starting point if you want to start implementing ITIL in your organization.

Service Strategy Processes

- Financial management is responsible for identifying, calculating, and managing the cost of delivering IT services. Financial management influences user behavior through cost awareness or charging and provides budgeting data to management. Cost accounting focuses on the fair allocation of shared costs and charging for IT services.
- Return on investment (ROI) (new in version 3): In service management, ROI is used as a measure of the ability to use assets to generate additional value. As a process, ROI includes the business case, pre-program ROI, and post-program ROI.
- Service portfolio management (new in version 3): A service portfolio describes a provider's services in terms of business value. It documents business needs and describes the provider's responses to those needs. Service portfolio

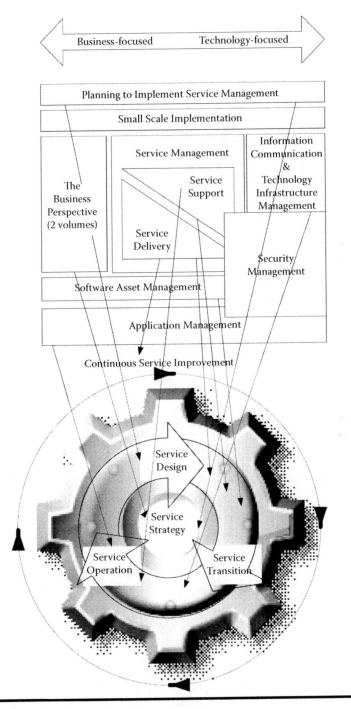

Figure 6.5 Mapping of version 2 to version 3.

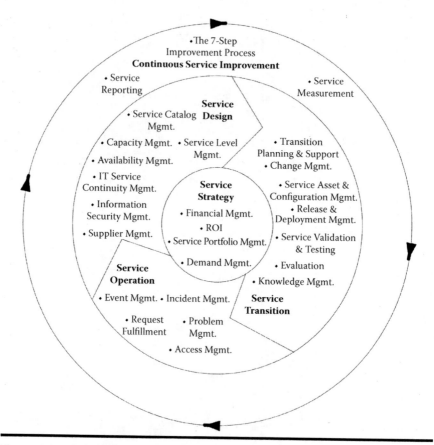

Figure 6.6   ITIL version 3 processes.

management is a dynamic method for governing investments in service management across the enterprise and managing them for value.

■ Demand management (new in version 3): Poorly managed demand is a source of risk for service providers because of the uncertainty of the capacity needed. Uncertainty over demand usually leads to provision of excess capacity ("just in case") which can be financially inefficient. Equally, insufficient capacity can lead to missed service levels and penalties. Demand management techniques include off-peak pricing, volume discounts, and differentiated service levels.

Service Design Processes

■ Service catalog management (new in version 3): Provides a single source of consistent information on all of the agreed services. The services catalog needs to be widely available to everyone who is approved to access it. Service catalog management is the process for ensuring that the information in the service catalog is maintained with accurate, current information.

- Service level management: This discipline manages the quality and timeliness of service delivered by the IT services organization to its customers. The essence of service level management is the service level agreement, a virtual "contract" between the IT organization and customers that articulates in detail which services are to be delivered along with the quality and quantity characteristics, such as performance and availability, for those services. The SLA can serve as a catalyst for establishing other valuable ITSM disciplines in terms of their contribution to fulfilling the SLA.

- Availability management: A discipline that allows IT management to optimize the use of IT resources, anticipate and calculate expected failures, implement security policies, and monitor for targeted service agreements. Availability management includes security, serviceability, recoverability, maintainability, and resilience of IT resources.

- Information security management: Aims to ensure that the security aspects of services are provided at the level agreed upon with the customer at all times. Security is now an essential quality aspect of management. Information security management integrates security in the IT organization from the service provider's point of view. The code of practice for information security management provides guidance for the development, introduction, and evaluation of security measures.

- IT service continuity management: A discipline that covers unexpected IT service losses. IT service continuity management involves the planning for alternate configuration items (CIs) or an entire alternate disaster recovery site with alternate IT resources. Analyzing risks, researching options, planning alternatives, and documenting the contingency plan are all part of IT service continuity management.

- Capacity management: A discipline that ensures cost-justifiable IT capacity always exists to match business needs. Capacity management determines business demands on IT resources, forecasts workloads, and performs IT resource scheduling. One of the major contributions of capacity management is a documented capacity plan.

- Supplier management (new in version 3): Ensures that suppliers and the services they provide are managed to support IT service targets and business expectations. The goal is to provide seamless quality of IT service to the business ensuring value for money is obtained.

Service Transition Processes

- Transition and planning support (new in version 3): Service transition is the management and coordination of the processes systems and function to package, build, test, and deploy a release into production and establish the service specified in the customer and stakeholder requirements. Effective transition and planning support can significantly improve a service provider's ability to handle high volumes of change and releases across its customer base.

- Release and deployment management: Responsible for the storage of management-authorized software, the release of software into the live environment, distribution of software to remote locations, and the implementation of the software to bring it into service. It is also responsible for hardware so that incidents and installations can be performed quickly. Most of the CMMI life cycle takes place within ITIL release and deployment management.

- Service asset and configuration management: Asset management provides a complete inventory of assets and determines who is responsible for their control. Configuration management allows IT management to gain tight control over IT assets such as hardware devices, computer programs, documentation, outsourced services, facilities, job descriptions, process documentation, and any other CIs that are related to the IT infrastructure.

- Change management: Describes the change management best practice and discusses its foundational role in the implementation of many other ITSM best practices. After all, evolution of the IT infrastructure in every sense, whether it is related to capacity management, network services management, or service desk, involves change. Change involves risk and invites a rigorous management approach.

- Service validation and testing (new in version 3): Can be applied throughout the service life cycle quality to assure any aspect of a service. It can equally be applied to quality assure the service provider's capability, resources, and capacity to deliver a service or service release successfully. That said, businesses need to understand that, for IT services, successful testing is not a guarantee but a sign of a particular confidence level. Businesses should ensure that they understand and are comfortable with the confidence level that any particular set of tests assures.

- Evaluation (new in version 3): Considers whether the performance of something is acceptable and worthwhile. This goal is to set stakeholder expectations correctly. This includes consideration of possible unintended effects as well as the intended objectives. Evaluation considers the actual performance of service changes against the planned performance.

- Knowledge management (new in version 3): Relevant to, and referenced by, every part of the ITIL life cycle. Just as knowledge is more than information, knowledge management is about ensuring that knowledge, information, and data are available to help the people involved in delivering a service to respond to "circumstances" or, in the words of Harold MacMillan when asked what represented the greatest challenge for a statesman, "events, my dear boy, events." The creation of a single system for knowledge management for the whole organization and its IT Providers is an excellent method for individuals and teams to share data, information, and knowledge about all facets of the IT services.

Service Operation Processes

- Event management (new in version 3): Monitors all events that occur throughout the IT infrastructure to detect and escalate exception conditions (see Harold Macmillan quote above).
- Request fulfillment (new in version 3): The process for dealing with service requests. Request fulfillment includes the functions of the service desk (which had been treated as a separate process in ITIL version 2).
- Incident management: A discipline responsible for resolving incidents as quickly as possible. This process monitors the IT environment in compliance with those predetermined service levels and properly escalates incidents in service delivery when they arise.
- Problem management: This process is aimed at handling all types of failed IT services. Its main objective is to identify the root causes of those failures and to recommend changes in CIs to change management. The problem-management processes use information collected from a variety of other areas, including incident management and change management.
- Access management (new in version 3): The process of granting authorized users the right to use a service while excluding unauthorized users from that service. It is based upon being able to accurately and, in some cases, uniquely identify authorized users.

Continual Service Improvement Processes

- The seven-step improvement process (new in version 3): This process is best illustrated by Figure 6.7.
- Service measurement (new in version 3): Building, populating, and maintaining a service measurement framework that leads to value-added reporting. Within the ITIL domain, the three basic measurements that most organizations utilize are availability, reliability, and performance. To assess the business performance of IT Providers, organizations may want to go further to measure productivity, customer satisfaction, the impact of IT on functional goals (delivered value), comparative performance against internal or external benchmarks, and business alignment and investment targeting (ensuring that IT spending is aligned with business priorities).
- Service reporting (new in version 3): An ideal approach to building a business-focused reporting framework is to start with a set of policies and rules to define how reporting will be implemented and managed that has been agreed upon

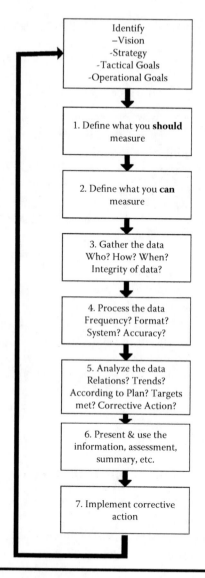

Figure 6.7 The ITIL seven-step improvement process.

by the business and the service design team. The driving force for reporting must be to get the right content to the right audience in a timely manner.

International Organization for Standardization (ISO)

ISO is the world's largest developer of standards and its principal activity is the development of technical standards. ISO began life in the field of electrical engineering as the International Electrotechnical Commission (IEC) which was established in 1906. In 1946, ISO was chartered to facilitate the international coordination and unification of industrial standards. Today, ISO is a network of the national standards institutes of 155 countries. It operates on the basis of one member per country, with a Central Secretariat in Geneva, Switzerland, that coordinates the system.[12] ISO is a non-governmental organization, meaning its members are not delegations of national governments.

ISO has published more than 16,000 international standards. They range from agriculture to construction, mechanical engineering to medical devices, and finally to IT. Due to the number of standards and the range of areas covered, international standards are numbered and named using the format "ISO[/IEC][/ASTM] [IS] nnnnn[:yyyy] Title" where "nnnnn" is the standard number, "yyyy" is the year published, and "Title" describes the subject. "IEC" is included only if the standard results from the work of a joint technical committee.

Adherence to ISO specifications is evaluated through a conformity assessment. This entails checking that products, materials, services, systems, or people meet the specifications of a given standard. To facilitate this, ISO develops ISO/IEC guides and standards to be used to carry out conformity assessments. Similar to the CMMI appraisal, achievement of a specific ISO certification by an organization indicates a level of achievement and implied level of quality or compliance according to the standard achieved. In some industries and situations including IT, compliance with certain ISO standards is a requirement for doing business. However, the ISO standards that we refer to in this chapter are voluntary (unless required by customers) and are more often used for marketing purposes.

The two most recognized families of standards that impact IT are the ISO 9000 and ISO 14000 standards. These families of standards are known as generic management system standards. ISO 9000 is concerned with quality management and ISO 14000 is concerned with environmental management. ISO/IEC 27002:2005 Information Technology — Security Techniques — Code of practice for information security management (formerly ISO/IEC 17799:2005)[13] provides best practice recommendations on information security management for use by those who are responsible for initiating, implementing, or maintaining information management security systems.

ISO/IEC 20000, previously mentioned in the section on ITIL, is the international standard for ITSM, and is generally aligned with ITIL. This standard comprises a "specification" (part 1) and a "code of practice" (part 2). Specifically:

- ISO/IEC 20000-1:2005 Information Technology — Service Management — Part 1: Specification defines the requirements for an organization to deliver managed services to meet its customer expectations.[14]
- ISO/IEC 20000-2:2005 Information Technology — Service Management — Part 2: Code of practice, seeking evidence of performance according to the defined requirements.

Performing an ISO/IEC 20000 conformity assessment indicates the level of conformance with the best practices of ITIL.

Other ISO standards provide internationally developed methods to assess conformance. ISO/IEC 15504:2004 describes the assessment model SPICE (Software Process Improvement and Capability Determination). ISO 15504 SPICE is the international standard for process reference models and assessments. It contains the methodology and structure to perform assessments of system development processes, similar in structure to CMMI. The difference is that SPICE defines a capability level for each process. This is similar to the continuous representation of CMMI but does not afford the same maturity level rating as the staged representation of CMMI.

SPICE and CMMI have been noted by both the ISO and SEI communities as conforming and complementary to each other. Determining which one to choose does not have to be a definitive choice. If an organization is using one to improve, the other can be achieved as well. If acknowledgment by a broader international community is sought, ISO's SPICE is the more appropriate credential. If contracts with the U.S. government are sought, CMMI is more applicable.

Project Management

The need for project management has sharply increased over the last 20 years, evidenced by the number of professionals in the field, universities offering formal undergraduate and graduate degrees in the field, and an explosion of books on the topic. Once a discipline associated mostly with the construction industry, project management is now both a profession and a widely used methodology. The de facto authority on project management is the Project Management Institute (PMI®), headquartered in Newtown, Pennsylvania. Founded in 1969, PMI is a non-profit organization which defines project management as "the application of knowledge, skills, tools, and techniques to a broad range of activities in order to meet the requirements of a particular project."

Since its inception, PMI has grown to become the global advocate for the project management profession with more than 240,000 members in over 160 countries.[15]

An organization can assess its own project management maturity according to the Organization Project Management Maturity Model (OPM3®). At the time of writing, this was the only assessment method for project management similar to the assessment methods linked to the other models described in this chapter. OPM3 does not have the same community or government recognition as the others. However, PMI does offer three types of professional credentials for individuals:

1. Program Management Professional (PgMP^SM)
2. Project Management Professional (PMP®)
3. Certified Associate in Project Management (CAPM®)

The PMI community defines five process groups (or phases) of a project as:

1. Initiating
2. Planning
3. Executing
4. Monitoring and controlling
5. Closing

They also define nine knowledge areas that apply across projects in nearly every industry worldwide[16]:

1. Integration
2. Scope
3. Time
4. Cost
5. Quality
6. Human resources
7. Communications
8. Risk management
9. Procurement

Project management can make or break some of the largest investment decisions an organization can have, including investing in new technology or enhancing existing technology. It is critical to have people who can perform as expert project managers in any organization. Following the discipline as defined by PMI provides an external community of support, standardized expectations for practicing professionals, and again the emphasis on process as being a cornerstone for success.

Six Sigma

Unlike other frameworks, Six Sigma is not owned and maintained by any specific community. Six Sigma began at Motorola in the 1980s. Its roots are in the quality movement of Total Quality Management (TQM), begun by Dr. W. Edwards Deming and Dr. Joseph M. Juran as well as in the statistical process control of Walter Shewhart. Six Sigma is frequently called "TQM on steroids," a tired term referring to the precision techniques of measurement and control introduced by the focus on statistical methods used in the process quality framework. The lack of ownership and governance has fostered the myriad of management consulting firms utilizing this framework according to their own proprietary interpretations.

In the narrowest definition, Six Sigma is a statistical term that translates to 3.4 defects per million opportunities (DPMO) or parts per million (PPM). As Table 6.4 shows, Six Sigma is actually a level of achievement or a metric. Although not all organizations pass through all of the sigma levels, it is likely that they will pass through some on their way to the desired state of Six Sigma. A defect is defined as anything

Table 6.4   Process Sigmas

Process Sigma	Accuracy (%)	DPMO/PPM[a]
6	99.9997	3.4
5	99.98	233
4	99.4	6210
3	93.3	66,807
2	69.1	308,537

[a] Defects per million opportunities or parts per million.

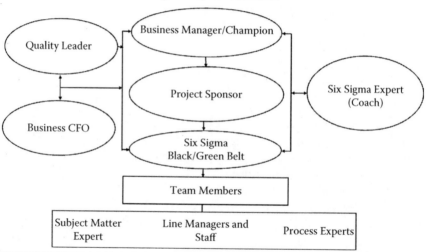

Six Sigma Project Team Roles

Figure 6.8   Six Sigma project team roles.

that does not meet the customer requirement.[17] At GE, a well-known advocate of the model, Six Sigma was defined as a "disciplined methodology of defining, measuring, analyzing, improving, and controlling the quality in every one of the company's products, processes, and transactions — with the ultimate goal of virtually eliminating all defects." Today Six Sigma is a quality movement intended to improve processes to achieve the highest standards of quality, thereby managing cost and reducing defects to improve customer satisfaction while improving process output.

The fundamental contributions of Six Sigma are in the culture shift required of the organization and the statistical but project-focused approach to quality improvement.

The audience for this quality framework is any organization seeking to improve quality and introduce statistical process control as a method for reducing cost and increasing customer satisfaction. The needs of focused leadership and team structure are addressed through the defined roles on Six Sigma teams (see Figure 6.8).

This structure serves to prescribe the roles and the responsibilities of those operating on a team. So, regardless of the company, product, or industry, the Six Sigma project team construct remains the same.

The process model for Six Sigma is called DMAIC (pronounced "deh-MAY-ihk"), which stands for the phases of a Six Sigma project defined as:

- Define
- Measure
- Analyze
- Improve
- Control

The current model was developed at GE Capital and was later adopted by all of GE. It was based on the "Plan-Do-Check-Act"[18] process improvement model of Dr. W. Edwards Deming. Figure 6.9 provides the outline of the DMAIC process and tools.[19] Some acronyms referenced here include

- SIPOC — Supplier, input, process, output, customer (a process modeling technique)
- CTQ — Critical to quality. Customer requirements called conditions of satisfaction
- VOC/VOB/VOE — Voice of the customer/business/employee
- ANOVA — Analysis of variance between groups. A statistical test similar to a t-test
- COPQ — Cost of poor quality
- DOE — Design of experiments
- FMEA — Failure modes and effect analysis

Figure 6.9 is an overview of the Six Sigma framework, DMAIC. It does not cover all of the underlying statistical models and data gathering techniques that are part of Six Sigma. Another similar process also exists for new process design: DMADV (design, measure, analyze, design, validate). DMADV is used when designing a new process to allow for process pilot and improvement loops.

Six Sigma is not a one-size-fits-all solution and can be a challenge to implement well in an IT environment. Pande, Newman, and Cavanagh put it best:

> It's a pretty simple equation, really: well-selected and defined improvement projects equal better, faster results. The converse equation is also simple: poorly selected and defined projects equal delayed results and frustration.[18]

The project selection essentials are

- Executive/leadership training: Teach the senior team how to select projects and launch a reasonable number for the organization

DMAIC Process & Tools

Define	Measure	Analyze	Improve	Control

• Launch the project
• Define project objectives/outcomes
• Develop project charter
• Select team, define responsibilities and launch
• Identify key stakeholders
• Create high-level project plan
	• Create current high-level process map "Current State"
	• Obtain customer input, priorities and CTQs
	• Gather initial metrics
	  – Historical performance
	  – Current performance
	  – Existing ABC (activity based costing) data
	• Determine current process sigma level
		• Identify sources of variation in the process by analyzing data and the process
		• Use benchmarking data to size the performance gap
		• Develop initial value proposition: opportunities & targets
		• Use problem solving tools to get to the root causes
			• Identify improvement breakthroughs
			• Design "To-Be" process map & targets
			• Perform cost/benefit analysis
			• Design dashboard
			• Review & update FMEA
			• Develop storyboard
			• Develop detailed Implementation plan
			  – Execute
			  – Train
			  – Communicate
			• Pilot/measure results
			• Manage change
				• Sustain the improvement
				• Implement continuous measurement systems
				• Report dashboard & scorecard data
				• Document new process and procedures
				• Transfer best practices
				• Reward & recognition

Key Tools:

Define	Measure	Analyze	Improve	Control

• Project Launch
• Business Case
• Project Objective
• Project Scope
• SIPOC
• Project Team
• Project Plan
• Project Charter
• Stakeholder Analysis
• Resistance Analysis
• Communication Plan
	• Process Maps
	• "Current State"
	• Quick Wins
	• VOC/VOB/VOE
	• CTQs
	• Affinity Diagram
	• Kano Analysis
	• Data Collection & Plan
	• Data Stratification
	• Measurement System Analysis
	• Sampling
	• Gauge R&R
	• Data Analysis
	  – Histograms
	  – Run Charts
	• Baseline Sigma Calculation
	• Current Process Performance Metrics
		• Value Added Analysis
		• Data Stratification: Pareto, Scatter Plots
		• Advanced Statistical Tools (Hypothesis Testing, Chi Square, T-Tests, ANOVA, Control Charts, Scatter Diagrams, etc.)
		• Regression Analysis
		• Data Transformation
		• Activity Prioritization Matrix
		• COPQ Assessment
		• Benchmarking
		• Cause & Effect Diagram
		• DOE
			• Brainstorming, idea generation
			• Decision Matrix
			• Prioritization Matrix
			• Decision Making (Multi-voting, consensus, etc.)
			• FMEA
			• "To Be" Process Map
			• Force Field Analysis
			• Cost/Benefit Analysis
			• Dashboards
			• Storyboards
			• Approval Checklist
			• New Sigma Calculation
			• Implementation Plan (High level & detailed)
				• Documentation
				• Control Chart
				• Process Control System-Continuous Improvement
				• Dashboard
				• Best Practices/Replication
				• Capability Studies

Figure 6.9 DMAIC process and tools.

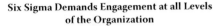

Six Sigma Demands Engagement at all Levels
of the Organization

Figure 6.10   Six Sigma engagement.

- Scope projects properly
- Focus on both efficiency and customer benefits

There are three basic qualifiers for a Six Sigma project:

1. There is a gap between current and desired state performance.
2. The cause of the problem is not clearly understood.
3. The solution isn't apparent or predetermined.

Notice here the pervasive use of the term "project" when referring to Six Sigma. Six Sigma programs are portfolios comprised of improvement projects. Six Sigma is a very specific type of project management process with a strong management framework that demands leadership involvement. The involvement from the leadership within the organization translates to attention from staff, creating focus on the Six Sigma project and the program (see Figure 6.10). Over time this brings organizational change, a cultural shift away from "that's just how we do things around here." Leadership focus and management behaviors translate for the staff into the level of importance of any initiative. The defined expectations of leadership involvement in reviews called "tollgates" and other stages in the project contribute to the success of Six Sigma by creating a change in the focus of what is important to the organization, namely commitment to process excellence, reduction in defects, and focus on customer requirements.

For additional information, read *The Six Sigma Way*, by Pande, Newman, and Cavanagh (published by McGraw-Hill); *A Six Sigma Pocket Guide*, by Rath (published by Rath & Strong); or *Six Sigma: The Breakthrough Management Strategy Revolutionizing the World's Top Corporations*, by Mikel Harry (published by Bantam–Dell Publishing Group).

Summary

According to George Box, "all models are wrong and some are useful." This chapter has provided an overview of the most popular models in use in IT today. Though none are perfect, it is important to begin by assessing the need for improving at all. Understanding how each of the models came into existence and the audiences who use them today provides a comparison point for use in any organization. Engaging in the journey toward process improvement requires commitment from all levels of the organization, regardless of the selected path or paths.

References

1. Chrissis, M.B., Curtis, W., Weber, C.V., and Paulk, M.C., Capability Maturity Model for Software (abstract).
2. SEI, Changes to Policies on SCAMPI A Appraisals in CMMI Version 1.2 and the Sunset Period for V1.1., www.sei.cmu.edu/cmmi/appraisals/cmmiv11-sunset-appraisal-policies.html (accessed Sept. 21, 2007).
3. Chrissis, M.B., Konrad, M., and Shrum, S., 2004, *CMMI Guidelines for Process Integration and Product Improvement*, CMU/SEI–Addison-Wesley.
4. SEI presentation, CMMI Overview 07, www.sei.cmu.edu/cmmi/adoption/pdf/cmmi-overview07.pdf, p. 35, Reporting Organizational Categories, results as of 6/06.
5. IT Governance Institute, May 2007, COBIT 4.1, ISACA.
6. IT Governance Institute, May 2007, COBIT 4.1, Figure 23, ISACA.
7. itSMF USA, About Us, www.itsmfusa.org (accessed Sept. 20, 2007).
8. Corporate Executive Board, March 2006, The ITIL Implementation Process (research brief).
9. CIO Executive Board, May 2004, Trends in ITIL Implementation (research brief).
10. ITIL® v3 Glossary v3.1.24, 11 May 2007, IT Infrastructure Library, version 3 (5 volumes), TSO (The Stationery Office).
11. ITIL® v3 Glossary v3.1.24, 11 May 2007, IT Infrastructure Library, version 3 (5 volumes), TSO (The Stationery Office).
12. ISO, www.iso.org, An overview of the ISO system (accessed Sept. 21, 2007).
13. IT Governance, www.itgovernance.co.uk/products/31 (accessed Sept. 20, 2007).
14. LRQA United Kingdom, 2006, ISO/IEC 20000, www.lr.org/industries/lrqa/ (accessed Sept. 21, 2007).
15. Project Management Institute, www.pmi.org, membership data (accessed Sept. 21, 2007).
16. Project Management Institute, 2004, *A Guide to the Project Management Body of Knowledge, Third Edition (PMBOK® Guides)*, Project Management Institute.
17. Eckes, G., *The Six Sigma Revolution*, John Wiley & Sons Inc.
18. Pande, P.S., Newman, R.P., and Cavanagh, R.R., 2000, *The Six Sigma Way: How GE, Motorola, and Other Top Companies Are Honing Their Performance*, McGraw-Hill.
19. *Rath & Strong's Six Sigma Pocket Guide: New Revised Edition*, 2006.

Chapter 7

Are We Outsourcing Effectively?

If IT governance is about defining what decisions need to be made, who should make them, and how they should be made, then one of the biggest decision areas that business and IT Providers should exercise strong governance over is outsourcing.

Many books and articles have been written about IT outsourcing. The business and social impact of outsourcing and, particularly, offshoring have been huge in the 21st century. It seems that for every success story, there is a story of a painful transition. However, we believe that there is no turning back. The future masters of IT will necessarily be masters of outsourcing. This chapter is an overview of outsourcing from the singular perspective of what the business should expect from its IT Providers.

As has been previously noted, we have used the term "IT Providers" in its plural form extensively in this book. This is a conscious change from the traditional concept of businesses being dependent on a choice of one IT provider, the centralized or local IT department. Today, businesses (and IT departments) must remember that there are many options available for the provision of IT services.

This chapter sets out the considerations a business faces in trying to decide, "Are we outsourcing effectively?" We have taken the path of providing further questions businesses and IT Providers should discuss together. Each business–IT Provider partnership will need to put different weights on these questions depending on their environment, so it is not meaningful to draw particular conclusions. Suffice it to say that the following sections introduce the questions in what we consider to be a reasonable order of priority:

- Why should we outsource or why are we outsourcing?
- What are our competitors outsourcing today?
- What should we be outsourcing?
- Is our governance of outsourcing appropriate?
- Are we engaging with our outsourcing vendors appropriately?
- Are our Service Level Agreements (SLAs) driving the behavior we need?

Why Should We Outsource or Why Are We Outsourcing?

It is very important that the business and IT Providers are crystal clear on why they are starting to outsource or why they are continuing to outsource if they have already started. Choosing the right path requires knowledge of where you want to be and where you are starting from. The key word in this question as a starting point is "Why?" That said, it must be considered together with the question posed in the following section entitled "What Are Our Competitors Outsourcing Today?"

To help identify the reasons and their respective importance, the following are a sample of the most common real or communicated goals for undertaking an outsourcing exercise (also see Reference 1):

- Reducing costs
- Maintaining cost competitiveness while implementing additional revenue generating strategies
- Leveraging resources to achieve increased productivity while maintaining the bottom line (getting more done with less or the same)
- Inability to find resources locally and cost effectively
- Ability to implement a resource center that you would not be able to afford otherwise
- Supplementing your current business processes with additional but less expensive functions
- Re-examining core competencies and value chain to divest all non-critical business functions
- Reduce risk in a "desperation or survival" situation (e.g., bankruptcy)
- Reduce risk associated with inability to retain quality/critical resources
- Contain and replace legacy technologies
- Achieve improved cost/service delivery of commodity IT services
- Rapidly drive standardization or other changes
- Establish a continuous path of IT advancement with reduced internal investment
- Ability to develop an additional prototype of a new product or service
- Outsource non-critical back-office functions
- Customer requests for new product features with which you cannot keep pace

This list should be revisited to ensure that all assumptions are still valid in an annual review meeting between the business and the IT Providers.

In practice, IT outsourcing decisions should be like decisions for outsourcing any other function. The decisions should consider, and weight according to the business goals, an appropriate blend of:

- Expertise availability in-house and outsourced
- Total cost of expertise in-house and outsourced
- Manageability in-house and outsourced
- Corporate philosophy in-house
- Transition barrier to outsourcing

Clearly, the weight applied to each of these considerations and, indeed, the business goals themselves can and will change over the duration of a typical outsourcing contract. Businesses should arrange for regular reviews with their IT Providers to ensure that the sourcing choices are still valid and that the outsourcing is being conducted effectively.

What Are Our Competitors Outsourcing Today?

This question is important and must be considered with the previous section because it may help the business to decide if its outsourcing strategy must be a defensive one in response to its competitors' actions or if there is an opportunity to grasp an opportunity ahead of the competition.

The answer to the question of what it is that competitors are outsourcing is generally "anything and everything," but the specifics are changing continuously and no book like this can hope to provide an answer that is as current as it needs to be to drive the sort of questions and decisions that we hope businesses will generate from the book. Research will be needed to find out what your competitors are outsourcing and monitoring (of press releases, conferences, etc.) will be required to stay in touch with changes. Our advice is to take the ideas in this section and validate them against current information from sources such as the International Association of Outsourcing Professionals (www.outsourcingprofessional.org) or Websites such as www.cioinsight.com annually, at least.

In March 2007, www.cioinsight.com published a survey of companies with revenues spread fairly evenly between the three ranges of less than US$100 million, US$100 to $999 million and greater than US$1 billion. Almost 400 companies provided responses although not all companies answered all questions. Table 7.1 is an extract from those results.

Table 7.1 March 2007 Survey of Outsourcing Practice in IT

	%									
	>0	>10	>20	>30	>40	>50	>60	>70	>80	>90
Roughly what percentage of your organization's total IT spending in 2006 was spent on fees for outsourced activities?										
Compared with 2006, how do you expect the amount your organization spends on fees for outsourced activities to change in 2007? (Only includes companies that outsource)										
Increase										
Remain the same										
Decrease										
Percentage of companies outsourcing IT activities to offshore companies in 2006 or planning to in 2007										
If your company uses offshore outsourcers, what percentage of total 2007 outsourcing budget goes to offshore outsourcing companies?										
In the past 12 months, what percentage of your company's previously outsourced IT activities or applications have been brought back in-house?										

What is the main reason your company uses IT outsourcers?							
To free up people to focus on other activities							
To reduce costs							
To do work we cannot do in-house							
To increase speed, flexibility, or innovation							
In which offshore countries have you outsourced IT activities or plan to in the next 12 months? (U.S. respondents only, only top three countries listed here)							
India							
China							
Philippines							

Source: Adapted from www.cioinsight.com.

The following observations may be helpful for reviewing this type of metric between the business and the IT Providers:

- On average, companies spend 21 to 30 percent of their IT budgets on outsourcing. [Business and IT Providers should discuss: Do we spend more or less? Why?]
- More than 70 percent of companies that outsource appear to have plans to increase their outsourcing spending next year or keep it at the same level. [Business and IT Providers should discuss: What are our plans? Why?]
- Companies spend the majority (greater than 50 percent) of their IT outsourcing budgets offshore. [Business and IT Providers should discuss: Do we? Why or why not?]
- There is a non-trivial amount (11 to 20 percent) of IT outsourced activity being brought back in-house. [Business and IT Providers should discuss: Is this significant? Why is it happening? Does this represent risk management activity that we are/should be engaging in?]

As an aside, perhaps another question to pose is "where" to outsource. In this survey, IT outsourcing to India was far ahead of any other location. As we write this, there are fears that the Indian market is short of suitably qualified and experienced labor and this shortage is driving up the prices of labor and the turnover rates at many companies. Balancing these market drivers are the temporary nature of any labor shortage in India (although nobody knows what time period "temporary" represents) and the continuing (but, hopefully, also temporary) political/legal risks and language difficulties for businesses (particularly small- and medium-sized) trying to set up operations in China.

The list of countries that did not make it to the top three in March 2007 is worthy of further investigation for organizations seeking to take advantage of waxing or waning trends. The next two countries to which U.S.-based IT was outsourced most often were Canada (10 percent) and Israel (8 percent). Five countries were used by 5 to 6 percent of respondents: Brazil, Ireland, Malaysia, Mexico, and Russia. Finally, these countries were cited by less than 5 percent of respondents: Armenia, Australia, Belarus, Bulgaria, Chile, Costa Rica, Hungary, Japan, Kazakhstan, Latvia, Pakistan, Poland, Romania, South Africa, South Korea, Thailand, Ukraine, and Vietnam.

The simple message in this list is that there are a lot of countries out there with the capability to meet some or all of your IT needs. Their absolute and relative strengths will change. Organizations need to perform broad reviews to ensure that their outsourcing decisions are made with global knowledge.

Table 7.1 implies that the candidates for "what to outsource" seem to be any activity where:

- The staff doing it today are enabled to do higher-value work
- Outsourcing costs less than doing the activity in-house for the same quality and productivity

- The required skills are not available (or needed) in-house
- Speed, flexibility, or innovation can be improved by outsourcing

Of course, there are also pitfalls to be avoided. In the same survey, respondents reported the following top five factors that were most likely to lead to a failed outsourcing experience in March 2007:

- Management lacks skill at overseeing outsourcing vendors
- Outsourcing vendors do not share the same culture/language as outsourcer
- Management lacks skill at writing and negotiating outsourcing contracts
- Outsourcing vendor lacks experience with providing outsourcing services
- Management lacks prior experience with outsourcing

Many organizations are developing the necessary knowledge, skills, and above all, experience to address these challenges. From our own experience, for organizations that are not where they need to be yet, we recommend training, consultants, and coaches. The first two of these are well known, if perhaps not yet well enough applied.

The last approach merits a little more explanation because it is not so well understood. Whether hiring independent coaches or assigning suitably trained and experienced internal staff (including line managers if they have the right skill set), providing coaching resources to individual managers or teams newly involved in outsourcing enables the asking and answering of those culturally or managerially difficult questions that arise on a day-to-day basis in the early days of a new outsourcing engagement. Further, the coach can ask the managers or team members the questions that fall into the category "they don't know what they don't know" to help them broaden their perspectives of their roles in the new environment before major cultural clashes emerge. The point here is that coaching is available real-time and is, hence, situationally focused whereas training and "outsourcing consulting" are usually best applied at the start of the engagement.

What Should We Be Outsourcing?

Let's start with the counter-question, "Is there anything in IT that should not be considered for outsourcing?" Everyone has their own opinion. The following list of things that should never be outsourced was extracted from the thoughts of Keil,[1] Lutchen,[2] and Broadbent and Kitsis[3]:

- Problems
- IT leadership/management
- Architecture development
- Business enhancement

- Technology advancement
- Vendor management
- Anything that directly touches a customer (at least at first)
- "Core" competency (at least at first)
- Strategic functions
- Measurement functions

In practice, the authors have seen examples where all of these things have been successfully outsourced. Yes, even problems. Many companies have solved their IT problems by outsourcing their whole IT department to someone who can do a better job for whatever reason. Several global consulting corporations make plenty of money by taking on an organization's inability or unwillingness to execute an offshoring strategy through a less controversial outsourcing contract which often involves taking on some or all of the organization's IT staff.

Broadbent and Kitsis propose an excellent framework for considering the distribution of IT services inside and outside of the central IT department (Figure 7.1). Although we do not necessarily agree with the scope of their proposed distribution, the figure itself provides an ideal framework for the business to discuss the appropriate service distribution strategy with their IT Providers. For example, we would argue that outsourcing software code implementation and retaining all software architectural development in-house can be detrimental to the end product for two reasons. First, the people writing the code need a solid understanding of the architecture and the ability to interact with the architects throughout the development as coding constraints put tension on the architecture; second, it is naïve to expect to establish and maintain a strong group of coders who are happy never to progress to architectural development — recruitment will be difficult and turnover will be high.

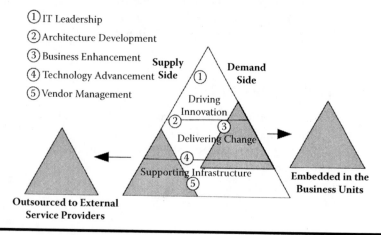

Figure 7.1　A framework for considering IT service distribution.

The value to the business of this framework is as a tool to get the IT Providers to set out their strategy and justify their tactical decisions.

Is Our Governance of Outsourcing Appropriate?

Outsourcing must be an integral part of your strategic planning and review functions. It may be an issue in which the Board takes interest, given the opportunities and risks it presents. For these reasons, it is more appropriate to adopt the term used by Broadbent and Kitsis,[3] namely, "strategic sourcing." As Broadbent and Kitsis state, strategic sourcing asks, "What's the best source for every IT service?"

In a paper written for the Outsourcing Institute in 2007, Casale[4] noted that "nearly one half of the buyers in the outsourcing community reported that they didn't have the time or the expertise to identify and evaluate the kinds of information that would enable them to elevate the outsourcing decision-making process and/or implement best practices on a consistent basis."

The authors have been involved in several engagements where an IT organization has become the victim of unforeseen circumstances in its long-term IT outsourcing contract. The point here is that there will be unforeseen circumstances. The skill is to negotiate into the contract a way of dealing with them. If this means the initial contract costs a little extra, pay it — it's money well spent!

There are many approaches to the governance of outsourcing:

- Direct management of IT providers
- Management through a "Global Sourcing Department"
- Management through Procurement
- Management through M&A
- Captive Investments
- Build–operate–transfer
- Management through CIO and IT Department
- Management through third parties — "outsource the outsourcing"

There does not seem to be one way that works best because, at the end of the day, the results depend on the knowledge, skills, and experience of the individuals concerned irrespective of where they happen to be working.

Choosing a management strategy for the outsourced services will necessarily require consideration of whether the outsourcing relationship will be that of customer–vendor or partner–partner. In the authors' experience,[5] it is very important to be clear on this from the start of the relationship because both sets of behavior will emerge during the operational engagement on both sides of the engagement. Either sort of relationship can be made to work for outsourcing. Indeed, it is even possible for both sorts to work within the same contract but the two options drive different behaviors and it is absolutely critical that all members of the team are working with a clear understanding of whether they are operating as customer–vendor or as partners.

In a white paper[6] written back in the early days of outsourcing (and CMM), Koni Thompson Houston of the David Consulting Group made the case for building the governance framework for outsourcing upon the existing best practices captured in models such as CMMI®. As we have discussed in previous chapters, both CMMI and ITIL® have practice or process areas devoted to best practice in managing suppliers. As Houston states, "Many organizations engaged in outsourcing activities are not focused on such quality activities and may not realize that the rigor found in CMM could be a prescriptive template for success in their outsourcing activities."

Consider that the basis of the CMM model (now CMMI), developed in the mid-1980s, was to provide a sound model to assess sub-contractors for the federal government. So, even if your organization does not wish to become CMMI-certified, you would be well advised to consider this template for your outsourcing activities based on the strength of the model. The strength of CMMI encourages comprehensive planning and governing throughout the life of the outsourcing arrangement and establishes a repeatable process for successful outsourcing.

A prerequisite for successful outsourcing governance is senior management sponsorship in the business, the IT Department, and the IT Provider(s). Senior management has significant accountability for the outsourcing arrangement. Senior management should be expected to:

- Set the expectation that all outsourcing activities will be effectively managed.
- Ensure that a management resource is designated as responsible for establishing and managing the contract.
- Ensure that adequate resources and funding are provided for both selecting the service provider and managing the contract.
- Ensure resources involved in establishing and maintaining these activities are trained to perform the tasks.

Managers also have significant accountability for establishing the outsourcing arrangement which should minimally include ensuring that:

- Client employees who are involved in the outsourcing arrangement receive orientation in the technical aspects of the contract.
- All work to be outsourced is defined and planned (often through a framework of responsibilities).
- The service provider is selected based on an evaluation of ability to perform the work (through a comprehensive request for proposal and evaluation of responses).

Every article and training class on outsourcing recommends, extols, and exhorts you to govern the contract. The requirements include ensuring that:

- The contract is the basis for managing the outsourcing arrangement; it should contain a statement of work and delineation of tasks between provider and client.
- The service provider's plan should be reviewed, approved, and used to track activities and communicate status; this gives you a starting point for communication with the service provider.
- Changes to the statement of work, terms and conditions, and commitments should be documented and reviewed with all affected parties. This gives you additional leverage when approving (or not approving) vendor-initiated changes.
- The outsourcing manager conducts various reviews with the service provider:
  - Periodic status/coordination reviews
  - Periodic technical reviews and interchanges
  - Formal reviews to address the accomplishments at selected milestones
  - Performance reviews
  - Acceptance tests
- Various other quality groups have a requirement to review the service provider's quality tasks, which include monitoring their quality assurance and configuration management activities.
- Measurements are made and used to determine the status of activities for managing the contract.

Tom Cagley, also of the David Consulting Group, takes this last point one step further in his white paper on Metrics and Governance in Outsourcing.[7] He argues that successful outsourcing arrangements require that all parties pay continuous attention to the goals of the engagement. However, the differing corporate cultures, short attention spans, and competing channels of information involved in outsourcing make monitoring difficult. Contracts often contain one or more tools intended to focus the parties' attention, typically as a portion of the governance requirements. There is a chance (that we have often seen played out in practice) that such tools are designed to reduce risk and, almost inevitably, that stifles innovation. Cagley argues that a better practice is to construct governance covenants that build and strengthen the capabilities of both parties. ITIL, CMMI, metrics, and scorecards typically build capabilities and at the same time mitigate risk. The choice of tool and the construction of the governance requirements are as critical as the financial portions of the contract.

All too often, contract personnel with a limited understanding of process or metrics develop governance processes. This lack of process or metrics knowledge is exacerbated when the principles are championed by parties on one side of the table or the other. But if each side of the negotiation does not have a metrics advisor, agreements could be governed by requirements that incent unbalanced behavior, do not add capabilities, and do not strengthen the relationships between parties to the contract. Examples of this inequity range from contracts that pay penalties and bonuses on a single metric (typically indexed productivity or time to market) to contracts with scores of embedded metrics. Soliciting input from your organization's process and metrics personnel (or outside consultants if you lack these capabilities in-house) is a best practice that does not find its way into enough contract negotiations.

You can use many techniques to develop a balanced approach to using metrics in the governance process. Goal-driven metrics techniques are processes for developing useful metrics for the core of contract governance. One technique organizations find useful is the Goal–Question–Metric technique introduced in Chapter 1.

A basic tenet of any goal-driven metrics technique is to begin with an understanding of your business goals (see previous section "Why Should We Outsource or Why Are We Outsourcing?"). A thorough and honest appraisal of the reasons you are outsourcing will allow you to build a set of measures that show you whether those goals have been met. The measures will also provide a filter by which to screen the data that provides useful information from the extraneous noise. This requires a careful and thoughtful data analysis. Without using a goal-driven approach, the contract may reward behavior that does not accurately reflect the goals, targets, and objectives of executive management. As an old adage points out, "you get what you measure."

The two worst-case scenarios typically result from focusing on a single goal (cost reduction, increased productivity, or better quality) or developing scorecards with too many contributors (if you need an econometric model to understand the impact of a metric, you certainly have gone too far). Kaplan and Norton's work on the Balanced Scorecard[10] has driven home the point that a single view of performance is at best not very useful and, more than likely, is dangerous. But balanced does not need to be synonymous with overly complex.

Dashboards and scorecards are excellent techniques to summarize data; however, they are inadequate for developing knowledge or directing action. A more granular level of detail provides organizations with the facility for event-centric and experience-based interactions with their data that generate actionable insights not purely reliant on personnel interactions. Granular, sliceable data allows you to defeat "the tyranny of the average," in which you lose the ability to identify special cases — good or bad.

Sourcing is a process that needs to evolve over time (even within one contract if that contract lasts for more than one year) as business needs and vendor capabilities evolve. As such, it is critical that sourcing contracts are written with both clear accountability for deliverables and flexibility in defining what those deliverables will be and how they will be measured in different phases of the contract. It should be noted that a "balance" between flexibility and accountability is not the goal and will not result in a workable contract. Instead, both flexibility and accountability must be achieved. In practice, this means both sides acknowledging that during the running of the contract it will be necessary to define trigger points that will allow for certain predefined aspects of the contract to be renegotiated. If negotiators from either side believe in the zero-sum game approach to negotiating, this approach can often be difficult to accept. However, all too often an apparently wonderful job done by the company's negotiators in year 0 can turn into a rod for the backs of the operational side of the company in year 2 or 3.

One example of the type of flexibility that should be included is a "benchmarking clause," so called because it gives the customer the right to assess the vendor's prices and performance using an independent benchmarking firm. It has to be said that vendors do not like these clauses because they often structure their pricing to absorb cost at the start of the contract knowing that they can recoup it later in the contract as their knowledge and productivity improves. Hence, a benchmark exercise in the middle of the contract is likely to show higher margins than the customer might expect. In some cases in recent years, when customers have invoked these benchmarking clauses, expensive lawsuits have followed. *CIO Magazine*[8] reported one of the worst cases when Britain's Cable & Wireless sued IBM for more than $200 million after a disputed benchmark. IBM countersued and the parties settled out of court.

Are We Engaging With Our Outsourcing Vendors Appropriately?

The first outsourcing projects are the trickiest because there is the additional hurdle of selecting and working with outsourcing vendors for the first time. When asked about their recent outsourcing experiences, most company representatives say selecting the right vendor is paramount to success. But how can you be sure you have the right vendor to meet your needs?

Whether you're planning a large project (support for all legacy systems) or a small project (an offshore development contract for a new application), the approach for vendor selection should be the same. Establishing a process for vendor selection will not only save you time, it's a required activity in CMMI and ITIL.

The time to establish the planning vendor selection criteria is before writing the Request for Proposal (RFP), not when you have a pile of RFP responses balanced on the edge of your desk! This ensures that the (successful) RFP responses will provide the information needed to make the right choice for the project.

Houston[9] proposes three major activities to the vendor selection preparation process:

1. Establish the project's technical needs
2. Identify and quantify your business strategies
3. Assess the RFP responses based on the pre-established criteria

You're going to be receiving a significant amount of information in response to the RFP. If you plan ahead, you'll be able to consolidate the information quickly and efficiently.

The first step is to identify the critical requirements for the project. What are your technology requirements? Staffing requirements? Architecture requirements? Job experience requirements? Create an inventory of the skills, technologies, platforms, hardware, and experience levels that are required to fulfill the function, project, or area being outsourced. Be as specific as possible, identifying the unique skills needed to perform the job successfully. These requirements will be invaluable in obtaining the correct match for your needs.

Every project has specific business drivers or strategies that are factors in your decision-making process. What are your business drivers, and what are the factors that will come into play when you actually make a decision about a vendor? Each business factor can efficiently be used as a major section in your RFP template. Some examples of common business drivers include

- Cost
- Culture
- Skills and resources
- Turnover
- References
- Supplier stability

The cost factor is too often taken for granted. There are a number of choices to be considered when establishing the pricing structure of the outsourcing contract. The most common pricing options are

- Fixed price — Requires a very precise definition of deliverables and a tightly defined change control process. High risk for vendor and priced accordingly.
- Time and materials — Low risk for vendor so may be cheapest hourly rate but buyer needs to exercise strong metrics and management. High risk for buyer.
- Fixed team — Buyer pays for a fixed number of resources and manages the deliverables according to the team productivity. Although this gives predictable costs, it is not necessarily the most cost-effective way forward because the vendor has no incentive to maximize productivity or quality.
- Hybrid — A mix of the above.
- Risk/reward — For a fixed price, the vendor builds in its own risk/reward by including a contingency buffer. The risk/reward approach can be a way to get low hourly rates on a fixed price contract by adding rewards for successful execution against delivery or quality objectives. For the other approaches, adding a risk/reward factor can provide useful incentives for maximizing productivity or quality.

Table 7.2   Quick Reference Engagement Matrix

	H=High Suitability, M=Medium, L=Low		
	Fixed Price	Time and Materials	Fixed Team
Flexibility for change	L	H	M
Price protection	H	L	M
Up-front certainty	H	L	M
Least risk for customer	H	L	M
Least risk for vendor	H	L	M
Suitable for large, complex projects	L	M	H
Suitable for small, well-defined projects	H	M	L

Source: Keil, S., Outsourcing the SME Way, Sciant AG, www.sciant.com.

Table 7.2 summarizes the suitability of the three main approaches for different types of need. For long-term contracts, it is sensible to include frameworks for projects to be managed against each of these approaches.

After identifying your business drivers, apply a weighting factor to each one. Usually, business drivers are constant but their factors may change from project to project. Qualify these factors in their order of importance to the particular outsourcing deal. Numerically rate them according to their level of importance in your decision-making process. If you have six factors, and cost is the most important factor for this project, rate it as a 6. This rating allows you to apply a weighted factor when you review your RFP responses and assess their applicability to your project. Your final decision will be based on the highest rate factor; other factors will be important but not the tie-breaker in selecting a vendor.

Develop a list of the qualities you are looking for in a business partner for your outsourcing project. These are the actual areas that you will request in your RFP. You are building a selection checklist specific to your project and documenting the detailed areas within each category that will quantify your selection of the best vendor for the deal. These may include proposed schedule, proposed staff, degree of your involvement required (always underestimated), project understanding, methodology, experience in project domain, location of staff, understanding of risks involved, tools/techniques, and pricing. Don't forget to ask for references, and you may want to consider a trip to a prospective vendor's customer site.

With a mountainous stack of RFP responses to review, you and your team can use your customized checklist to quantitatively assess each vendor's RFP response based on various questions. You can assess your satisfaction with their responses using a scaling factor. Focus on your specific needs and determine the following:

- Does the RFP response satisfactorily address your specific project needs?
- Are you satisfied with the suggested resource resumés that are provided?
- Do you have any concerns about the vendor based on the previous project results?

Effective planning before sending out an RFP will ensure that you have the information you need to make the right decision. Plan in advance and follow through with quantitative and qualitative analysis and you will have the recipe for successful vendor selection.

In selecting outsourcing vendors, it is important to consider your company's long-term strategy for outsourcing, particularly if offshoring is being considered as part of the outsourcing. In choosing an offshore outsourcing vendor, organizations are buying (or should be buying) the expertise and local management that the offshore vendor has built up over a number of years. This is real value that should not be ignored or minimized. In return, the organization will pay prices that enable the offshore vendor to make a nice profit on the business. Such organizations also run the risk of the loss of intellectual property over time. Although cases exist of actual theft of intellectual property, these are few and far between. More insidious is the gradual transfer of knowledge about how the organization's IT runs and how it is put together to the point that, although the vendor does not steal or reuse the intellectual property, most of the IT intellectual property is held by the systems and people of the vendor and little remains with the staff of your organization.

Transformational outsourcing is about focusing on corporate growth, not corporate costs, by making better use of skilled local staff and, eventually, local growth (wherever "local" happens to be in the world). Transformations typically involve a team coming in to analyze one or more business process workflows, redesign those processes for efficient outsourcing, design and build/configure an IT system to maximize efficient workflows (given that two organizations will now need to work in synchronization) and, finally, implement using existing and new staff (suitably trained) anywhere in the world.

As an alternative to offshore vendors, organizations tend to resort to one of the following "do-it-yourself" options:

- Captive investments — The organization outsources to an offshore vendor that it owns wholly or partially.
- Build–operate–transfers (BOTs) — The organization outsources to an offshore vendor that agrees to build an offshore capability, operate it for some specified or unspecified time, and then transfer ownership of the working offshore center back to the organization.
- Near-shore vendors — The principle is exactly the same as offshore vendors (skilled resources at lower cost) but the vendors are within easier reach, though perhaps not at the lowest possible cost.
- Low-cost onshore locations — It is possible that your own country has regions with skilled resources at lower costs due to local economic conditions. These resources could be very accessible now that you have a distributed IT infrastructure. This is a particularly attractive option for small organizations whose ability to invest in offshore operations and then compete for scarce resources in those locations can be very limited.

Regardless of the approach adopted, organizations should focus on the following critical success factors for outsourcing partnerships:

- Understand each other's business
- Understand each other's processes
- Set short- and long-term goals
- Define realistic expectations clearly
- Share benefits and risks
- Develop measurable performance metrics across the whole relationship
- Expect changes
- Prepare for the unexpected
- Nurture the relationship

Finally, always compare any potential outsourcing agreement with your best non-outsourcing option before making a commitment. It is too easy after going through all of the above to be left with a set of sub-optimal options that may be worse than what you started with.

Are Our Service Level Agreements (SLAs) Driving the Behavior We Need?

The old adage "if you can't measure it, you can't manage it" has been extended for Service Level Agreements (SLAs) to "if you can't measure it, it won't get done." The job of an SLA is to ensure that everything that needs to get done, gets done and (ideally) nothing else.

Keil[1] provides a simple definition of what a good SLA does:

- Defines the scope of services that are to be covered by the contract
- Describes either acceptance criteria or thresholds for different levels of quality that the included services must meet (or both)
- Defines means to measure and monitor these services
- Describes actions to be taken if service levels fall below acceptable levels

An SLA is one of the most critical components of an outsourcing arrangement. When properly designed and executed, an SLA drives desired behaviors, monitors performance, and guides the governance of contractually agreed upon objectives. Numerous other factors can also contribute to the ultimate success of the outsourcing relationship. For example, consider the importance of establishing clearly defined business goals, or the critical importance of effective communications and contract management. The ultimate success or failure of an outsourcing arrangement cannot be attributed to a single element; but as we will soon see, an SLA can have a significant impact on desired outcomes.

Of course, it is necessary to define priorities within an SLA because, although every customer wants the highest quality ahead of schedule at the lowest cost, it is not possible to maximize performance on all three dimensions of quality, cost, and schedule simultaneously. In deciding these priorities, it is also important to understand that the dimensions are not as independent as is sometimes supposed. For example, poor quality can increase cost and delay schedule. Schedule slip always costs more money.

The problems (and perhaps, ultimately, the failures) associated with outsourcing relationships are varied. Improper business alignment, poor execution, and failure to realize stated levels of improvement are among various contributors. In most cases, causes of failure can be tied directly or indirectly to the fact that SLAs and supporting measures were not properly established. A recent outsourcing survey asked respondents what problems they have faced in current or past supplier relationships. According to the survey results, the following responses were among the top ten (percentages represent the percent to total number of respondents).

- Expectations not met (48 percent)
- Service level agreements not clear (38 percent)
- Poor quality of service (38 percent)
- No measurable evaluation criteria (31 percent)
- Outsourcing agreement not well written (22 percent)

A pattern emerges from these results — service level agreements and measures play a key role:

- Expectations not met — This may be the result of poorly conceived performance targets.
- No measurable evaluation criteria — Perhaps the service levels don't provide quantifiable measures of performance.
- SLAs not clear — This could be the result of inadequate scope definition.

Although not conclusive, the survey suggests that the majority of these problems can be linked directly or indirectly to service level management. What is the right way to approach the preparation of an SLA? ITIL provides a lot of good information in this area in its service level management process (see Chapter 6). However, for the purposes of this chapter, we will consider four key steps:

1. The SLA framework
2. Identifying service level measures
3. Measuring levels of service
4. Monitoring performance

The SLA Framework

Properly framing the SLA does not guarantee success but the process of defining levels of service and creating the proper measures of those services is an opportunity to position expectations of the desired outcomes effectively.

The successful outsourcing arrangement typically has followed a well-thought-out framework for establishing and monitoring SLAs. A basic service level agreement framework includes

- Planning — Identifying service level measures and performance targets
- Executing — Collecting data, analyzing results, and reporting
- Governance — Monitoring performance and making adjustments

During the planning phase, efforts are made to identify service level measures that support the business objectives of an organization and provide meaningful indicators as to the level of service. At this time, baseline data is collected and analyzed, identifying the current levels of performance. Based upon these levels of performance and in consideration of business goals and objectives, service level measures are established. At the same time, the required infrastructure to support future activities that are necessary to support the capture and reporting of service level data is defined. Finally, a detailed implementation plan is developed, preparing the organization for executing the SLAs and measuring performance.

The execution phase begins when the contract is in place and services are being provided. This phase includes the collection of all necessary service level measures. Checks and balances must be in place to ensure data integrity and accuracy. As data is collected and stored in a secured repository the results are analyzed and reports are produced. Ideally, the proper distribution of reports was identified during the planning phase and the various management groups that use these results are now receiving the critical information they need to govern the contract.

Governance, in this context, is the ongoing process of reviewing performance measures and contrasting those results to the stated goals and targets. It's also a standard procedure to conduct periodic audits on the service level data to ensure consistency, accuracy, and completeness. During the life of the contract, it will most likely be necessary to adjust the service level measures. Business opportunities may change or more realistic targets and goals may come to light. So, it's important to incorporate procedures for making changes to the service levels in the outsourcing agreement.

Identifying Service Level Measures

As mentioned earlier, identifying the proper service level measures during the planning phase requires knowledge about the strategic direction of the business.

In addition, it is important to consider the depth and breadth of various categories that may need to be considered. For example, in an outsourcing arrangement that supports the Application Development and Maintenance (AD/M) of an IT Provider, there may be several ways in which service levels are to be evaluated. Measures that support the business may include time to market and product quality. Customer-oriented measures related to levels of satisfaction comprise another typical SLA category. From the technical view of the service delivery proposition, response time and day-to-day performance measures may be included. Finally, from a process performance perspective, issues such as compliance and effective communication may well round out a general outline of service level measures in an AD/M outsourcing arrangement.

Properly framing the service level agreements and the supporting service level measures requires the setting of reasonable and appropriate performance targets for the customer. Once the service level measures are identified, the next step is to establish performance thresholds by asking questions such as "What is the proper level of service that can be expected?" and "What is the appropriate level of improved performance that can be expected year after year?"

These are the fundamental questions that must be properly answered to have a reasonable expectation of performance yields.

Keil suggests the following metrics as a starting point:

- Problem size (as a normalizer for the other metrics)
- On-time delivery
- Cost effectiveness or productivity
- Total cost of ownership
- Service availability
- User satisfaction
- Processing time
- Defect rates
- Technical quality
- Rework rates
- Acceptance rates

Measuring Levels of Service

The answers to these questions come from baseline performance data that reflects the customer organization's current performance level. Performance targets that represent achievable results and best fit customer requirements are established. Ideally, performance targets are established based upon a baseline period that covers a period of 12 to 18 months prior to the final contract. When these targets are established prior to final negotiation of the contract, they can become part of the contractual agreement. Unfortunately, baselines are often developed during the first year of an outsourcing contract, which is not necessarily the ideal time to baseline an organization because it takes 12 to 18 months for a new contract to "settle in," and performance levels tend to be lower during this period.

The ideal baseline scenario requires a precontract activity that includes both a quantitative and qualitative analysis of current practices and performance levels. The quantitative element measures the level of performance and may express this performance in terms of dollars, defects, units of work, etc. The qualitative element, meanwhile, includes an assessment of the current practices that have contributed to high or low yields of performance. This is used to determine current areas requiring improvement, where you can set improvement expectations.

Once established, performance levels provide for contractually defined service levels that will monitor service performance trends over time. For example, if we have identified the need to measure a cost per unit of work and reduce our costs over time, we need to set reasonable reduction targets based on current costs. A contract is sure to fail if unrealistic performance levels are established.

By using industry-accepted measures, such as function points for software sizing, organizations can access and incorporate industry-standard performance levels and best-practice performance levels. These industry benchmarks can be used for establishing annual performance targets, or to compare best-practice levels of performance. They bring a sense of reasonable expectations regarding performance levels to both the customer and the provider.

Monitoring Performance

The reporting of performance levels of service is scheduled on a periodic, pre-defined basis. It's intended to provide a status of performance and used to identify unacceptable variances from the stated standards. This reporting also serves as the basis for initiating changes, which will improve service level performance.

Typically, senior management receives a high-level, scorecard-like summary of performance results. The information on a performance scorecard may contain information relating to each service level measure, including the baseline performance level, the annual target or goal, the current performance level, a trend indicator and, perhaps, information relating to industry best practices performance levels.

As results are reported and assessed, it may be necessary to adjust the SLAs. Procedures for making adjustments should be noted in the contract. Reasons for possible adjustments include scope changes, service level performance changes, or procedural changes. When changes occur, it may be necessary to establish new baseline measures and keep customer expectations in line with current performance trends.

Finally, an annual audit is always key in keeping SLAs on track. Both parties should agree on audit criteria and include them in the contract. Audit criteria may include such topics as data collection integrity, data storage and security, reporting accuracy, and compliance with procedures. A reasonable check on these variables will be particularly helpful during the first year of a contract.

Summary

Outsourcing agreements are negotiated with good intentions and high hopes. However, once the contract is signed and service delivery begins, it is the service level agreements that govern the success of the outsourcing arrangement. They help to set expectations and they are critical to the proper monitoring and governing of the contract. It is important to remember:

- SLAs should follow a proper and well-planned framework.
- Service level measures should focus on the strategic direction of the business and drive desired behaviors.
- An adequate baseline period should allow for both quantitative and qualitative performance measures.
- The accuracy and integrity of the service level measurement data is key to the monitoring of performance.
- Plan for reasonable and fair adjustments.

References

1. Keil, S., Outsourcing the SME Way, Sciant AG, www.sciant.com.
2. Lutchen, M.D., 2004, *Managing IT as a Business: A Survival Guide for CIOs*, John Wiley & Sons, Inc.
3. Broadbent, M. and Kitsis, E.S., 2005, *The New CIO Leader*, Harvard Business School Press.
4. Casale, F.J., Outsourcing 2.0: An Overview, The Outsourcing Institute, www.outsourcing.com.
5. Maynard, A.B. and Harris, M., Managing Outsourcing in a World of Mergers and Acquisitions, The 2006 Outsourcing World Summit. February 20-22, 2006. International Association of Outsourcing Professionals, www.outsourcingprofessional.org.
6. Houston, K. Thompson, A Prescriptive Template for Outsourcing, www.davidconsultinggroup.com/publications/default.aspx#articles (accessed Sept. 21, 2007).
7. Cagley, T.M., Jr., Metrics and Governance in Outsourcing, www.davidconsultinggroup.com/publications/default.aspx#articles (accessed Sept. 21, 2007).
8. Overby, S., Outsourcing — No comparisons, *CIO Magazine*, March 1, 2007.
9. Houston, K. Thompson, Vendor Selection: A Recipe for Success, www.davidconsultinggroup.com/publications/default.aspx#articles (accessed Sept. 21, 2007).
10. Kaplan, Robert S. and Norton, David P., 1996, *The Balanced Scorecard: Translating Strategy into Action*, Harvard Business School Press.

Chapter 8

What Tools Should IT Use?

The authors' interest in the economic benefits of applying tools to IT were sparked by Baetjer's book, *Software as Capital*.[1] Baetjer explains in terms of economic theory (particularly the Austrian school of economics) that knowledge is embodied in capital goods. As he states,

> In virtually all human production (other than gathering berries in open fields, and even there we often bring a pail or a box to carry them in), we employ capital goods — tools — for the purpose. Much of our knowledge of how to produce is found not in our heads, but in those capital goods that we employ. Capital is embodied knowledge.
>
> In particular, capital equipment — tools of all kinds, including software — embodies knowledge of how to accomplish some purpose. Much of our knowledge of how to accomplish our purposes is not articulate but tacit. That is, we can do it but we can't say in detail how we do it.

This suggests, particularly in the IT world, that tools are the organized embodiment of accumulated intellectual property. Tools evolve as knowledge grows and as new technologies emerge for organizing the existing knowledge into new tools.

For a simple example of this, consider the hammer. The hammer is the organized embodiment of centuries of experience of hitting things with rocks. It evolved as new technologies emerged for using wood and metal, not just in the making of the hammer but through the parallel evolution of nails. After thousands of years, different forms of hammers are available for general or specialized purposes.

Too often in organizations, either the ubiquity of IT tools or the problems and costs associated with introducing new tools obscure the business reality that (as embodied intellectual property) the tools and associated data that an organization builds, buys, and uses are valuable assets of the business. Although organizations list the acquisition costs of IT tools on their financial books for depreciation purposes, they do not necessarily acknowledge that these tools, correctly used, could appreciate in value as they embody more and more of the intellectual property of the business. Interestingly, this effect is sometimes better understood in small businesses than in large businesses. When a small IT business is being acquired, the use of tools in that business provides more asset value to a potential buyer because business continuity risks associated with the post-acquisition loss of staff are partially offset by the knowledge encapsulated in good tools.

There is a wealth of useful information on IT tools in the Information Technology Infrastructure Library (ITIL®) which includes the following advice[2]:

> ...good people, good process descriptions, and good procedures and working instructions are the basis for successful service management. The need for, and the sophistication of, the tools required will depend on the business need for IT services and, to some extent, the size of the organization.

The primary goal of this chapter is to provide a starting point for a taxonomy of tools that could be used to improve the performance of IT Providers. It is only a starting point for three reasons. First, it is impossible to capture the whole range of small but immensely useful tools that fulfill a niche utility and are either available to small markets or are built in-house. It is our intent that readers will find value by using the terms in this chapter as keys for subsequent Internet searches. Second, an underlying goal of the chapter is to get businesses and IT Providers continuously to ask the question, "How can we make this process more repeatable or efficient or effective or economical by deploying a tool (from a third party or built in-house)?" Finally, this chapter will concentrate on software tools or, more specifically, tools implemented as software. This excludes a category of hardware tools that are useful in IT (e.g., for monitoring of hardware such as servers and networks in IT operations).

What Are the Business Benefits of Using IT Tools?

Picking up on the theme introduced at the start of this chapter, the prime business benefits of using IT tools are the organization and embodiment of intellectual property. This high-level idea manifests itself in business benefits in two main ways. First, IT tools can be built within the business to capture the business' own intellectual property and provide greater repeatability and enforcement of process through automation of previously manual tasks. Second, IT tools can be acquired from outside the business to allow the business to take advantage of somebody else's solutions to common problems. Reinforcing the idea of the value of good tools, other people's intellectual property naturally comes at a price. Open source and freeware tools are growing in use in IT Providers and can be very helpful but they must be carefully managed. Careful management requires the purchase of maintenance contracts or contracts for commercial use to accompany software that was offered with licensing at no cost. As ever, you get what you pay for.

Even when IT tools are acquired, it is important to remember that as the tools are used, the data captured in them and the choices of configuration or customization create intellectual property that is specific to the business, not to the original tool provided.

IT tools can deliver the following benefits to business:

- Help to meet more sophisticated customer demands — Complexity is the double-edged sword of IT. More powerful IT can meet more complex customer needs but more complex IT is harder to deliver, manage, and maintain. More sophisticated IT tools are essential enablers of more sophisticated customer solutions.
- Reduce the impact of a shortage of IT skills — The power of IT tools to compartmentalize complexity facilitates two things: more complexity and higher productivity. Both of these advantages help businesses to manage with fewer highly skilled staff needed to drive the technology.
- Reduce the impact of budget constraints — People are often the largest expense item in IT budgets. So if fewer IT skills are needed, then using tools should ease budget pressures. Right? Unfortunately, the answer is a strong "it depends." It is certainly true that the authors have seen situations where investment in new tools can (with some pain) solve problems in IT Providers that were costing more than the investment in the tool. Resulting productivity improvements have released staff for new projects (or reductions in force). However, the authors have also seen situations where the acquisition of a major tool by an otherwise healthy IT Provider almost drove the IT Provider into the ground. The cost and complexity of implementing the tool was not fully understood or planned for in advance and, more importantly, the tool distracted the IT Provider from its core purpose of supporting the business.
- Reduce the risk associated with business dependence on quality IT services — IT tools support automation of key business activities and processes. Through repeatability, automation raises the quality of IT services by

minimizing errors and facilitating automated detection of unexpected events. Automation allows
- – Centralization of key functions
- – Automation of core service management functions
- – Analysis of raw data
- – Identification of trends
- – Preventative measures to be implemented

■ Integration of multi-vendor environments — For businesses, the need to integrate multi-vendor environments is usually due to either purchasing decisions or mergers and acquisitions. Historically, integrating multi-vendor environments has been difficult for IT Providers without the loss of some functionality and, in the case of mergers and acquisitions, significant transactional risk. Increasingly, data management and integration tools are available to make this process easier and more reliable.

■ Manage and make visible the increasing complexity of IT infrastructures — As noted above, managing complex IT is all but impossible without appropriate tools.

■ The emergence of international standards — International or national standards can be introduced as an external influence on the business from regulatory or technology sources. Good IT tools can simplify the implementation of the necessary changes as they would for any other IT change but, more specifically, IT tools can be applied to monitor continued compliance with the external standards or regulations.

■ Facilitate an increased range and frequency of IT changes — By improving the reliability of changes, IT tools can reduce the risks associated with frequent changes. The business' ability to change to meet dynamic market requirements should never be constrained by the IT Provider's inertia.

What Are the Business Risks of Using IT Tools?

The risks associated with using IT tools can be broadly summarized as incorrect cost–benefit analysis or business case. Put simply, the risk is that an IT tool is created or acquired, at a cost to the business, to solve problems or deliver opportunities and it either fails to do so or, in doing so, it fails to generate enough benefits to cover the cost.

As an aside, there is also a risk that a poor cost–benefit analysis could result in rejection of a tool that would have been very valuable to the business. There may be many reasons for the failure of the tools to deliver. Some common reasons for failure are

■ The tool was not designed to address the targeted problem/opportunity.
■ The tool was not designed to address all of the targeted problems/opportunities that it was expected to address.

- The full cost of implementing the tool was not included in the budget — missed items often include
  - Training costs
  - Unexpected hardware costs
  - Unexpected extra license costs
  - Unexpected extra maintenance costs
- The tool is poor quality with too many defects in key areas.
- The tool requires much more customization than expected.
- Too much customization of the tool to the needs of the business destroyed its effectiveness, reduced its quality, and increased its maintenance costs.
- People with knowledge about the tool are not available enough to help make it work because:
  - Vendor goes out of business or loses key staff.
  - IT Provider loses key staff.
  - Vendor is overstretched and has too few experienced staff to meet needs.
- Staff resistance because:
  - Value of tool is not clear.
  - Tool may threaten jobs.
  - Tool is too difficult to learn or to use.
  - Managers are unwilling to let go of the staff who are no longer required and whose salary savings justified the business case.

As can be seen, some but not all of the reasons for failure are the responsibility of the tools vendors. All these reasons (and the list could go on) for failure of a tool to deliver benefits should be examined before the decision is made to proceed with the tools. Further, mitigations should be developed, costed, and built into the budget.

As is the case with most software projects, the risk associated with the introduction of a new tool is exponentially proportional to the disruption it brings to the existing processes. Hence, again as for most software projects, the most effective mitigation strategies are those that introduce the new tool gradually in a phased way. Unfortunately, although this lowers risk, it may also increase cost because the phased introduction will take longer (more cost) and may delay the time when full benefits are being achieved and pay back on the investment can be expected.

The right tools will deliver long-term benefits if implemented correctly, so it is worth taking the time and spending the extra money to ensure a successful implementation. If the cost–benefit analysis does not identify clear-cut benefit in implementing the tool, then don't do it!

How Will IT React to Business Questions About Tools?

There are many interesting ideas in Baetjer's book but the small extract quoted in the introduction to this chapter contains a few that are particularly relevant for the use of tools in IT:

- Tools should improve productivity.
- Tools are an embodiment of how to accomplish some purpose.
  - If a tool is custom-built to accomplish the purpose of some part of an existing in-house process, then there is a good chance that the remaining in-house process will not need to change.
  - If a tool is purchased to accomplish the purpose of an existing in-house process, then there is a good chance that it will have been built to accomplish the purpose of some other slightly different external process and so the remaining in-house process will need to be changed to get maximum benefit from the tool. Usually, this does not happen. Rather, the external tool is modified to suit the in-house process. Sometimes this can be effective. Often, it is not.
- Most tools for IT are themselves the product of IT. For example, most software development tools are software themselves. This is sometimes construed as a limitation. If it is a limitation, then it is due to the challenge of producing high-quality software and not because of any philosophical problem of using something to build more of itself. In the field of mechanical engineering, everyone is familiar with the use of robots to build cars.
- Tools allow for higher productivity because they embody knowledge that the practitioner does not then need to be able to articulate. Reducing the number of things that practitioners need to think about improves productivity because it reduces complexity. This is particularly valuable in IT and software development where the complexity of real systems exceeded the grasp of single individual minds long ago.

This last point is particularly relevant for the business–IT dialogue about tools in an organization. Most IT practitioners start in their profession because of a particular competence in, or fascination with, technical subjects and technical details. Yes, the stereotype of the IT geek is too simplistic and as limited as all other stereotypes, but is based on some grains of truth. The value of IT practitioners is based on their knowledge of the details of complex technology. Implementing tools to remove the need for some part of that knowledge evokes the following emotions which business has to try to filter from the resulting proposals (or absence of proposals) for tools:

- Enthusiastic acceptance and implementation due to a quick, clear, and accurate understanding of the benefits of the tool to the business.
- Enthusiastic acceptance and implementation due to a delight in any new technology to play with, but an inaccurate understanding of the benefits of the tool to the business.
- Enthusiastic dismissal due to fear of the reduced need for (or value of) specialist knowledge or the transfer of that need to third-party tool providers. The transfer of dependency from internal IT staff to external tools providers is a real issue but should be a business and IT risk decision.

- Enthusiastic dismissal because of a perception that the abstraction or simplification of part of a process produces a sub-optimal solution. This may or may not be a real issue.
- Reluctant dismissal because there are real concerns that the tool cannot be implemented in a way that will meet the goals (and improve productivity).
- Reluctant dismissal because there are real concerns that the business or IT Providers will not be willing or able to change their processes to realize the potential of the tool to improve productivity.

An IT Software Tools Taxonomy

The following tools taxonomy is based upon the structure defined by version 2 of the ITIL. Although version 3 has now been released and both versions provide extensive coverage of all IT processes, version 2 provided a separation of IT processes that lends itself to a tools taxonomy. The processes added in version 3 can be used to extend the taxonomy if desired. At the highest level, ITIL version 2 provided definitions of IT "service management." Service management was subdivided into service delivery and service support.

Service delivery is the management of the IT services themselves, and involves a number of management practices to ensure that IT services are provided as agreed upon between the service provider and the customer. It includes five disciplines: service level management, capacity management, continuity management, availability management, and IT financial management.

Service support is the practice of those disciplines that enable IT services to be provided effectively. The six service support disciplines are configuration management, change management, service/help desk, release management, incident management, and problem management.

Using this structure, the tools taxonomy is summarized in Figure 8.1.

Service Management Tools

The following tool types are applicable to all other service management processes and so are defined at the top level of the taxonomy:

- Workflow management tools
- Project planning and management tools
- Data management tools
  - Data warehouses
  - Database management tools
  - Data integration tools (e.g., metadata tools)
  - Data analysis and reporting tools.

Tool types specific to particular processes are listed in the following sections.

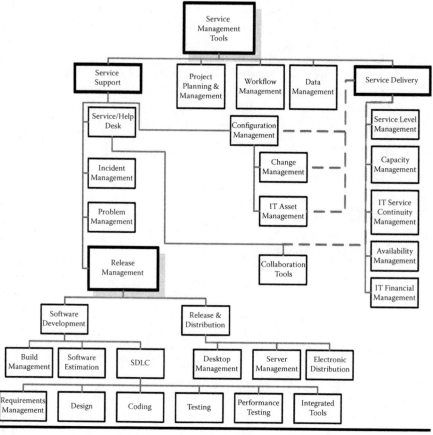

Figure 8.1   IT tools taxonomy.

Service Support Tools

Configuration Management (CM) Tools

■ Configuration management database (CMDB) for storing information about "every" item (configuration item or CI) of hardware, software, or documentation deployed in the organization. It is important to note that "every" refers to every item at the level of granularity chosen by the organization. To quote ITIL, "the target is maximum control with minimum records."

■ IT asset management
  – Asset management tools
    ■ Inventories of hardware and installed software
    ■ Inventories of software licenses
    ■ Document management systems
  – Inventory and auto-discovery tools

- Change management tools or, more likely, change management capabilities on the main configuration management tool:
  - Requests for change (RFCs) and problem records (PRs) on the same system
  - The ability to identify the relationships between RFCs, PRs, and CIs
  - Automatic production of requests for impact and resources assessment to the "owners" of CIs impacted by changes
  - The ability for all authorized personnel to create and process RFCs, PRs, and CIs
  - Clear definition of back-out procedures for each change in case it causes problems
  - Automatic prompting to carry out reviews of implemented changes

Service/Help Desk Tools

- Collaboration tools
  - E-mail
  - Internet
  - Intranet
    - Search engines
  - News group
  - Papers
  - Mail
  - Electronic notebook
  - Telephone
  - Videoconference
  - Chat/white board
  - Shared authoring and applications
  - Instrument control
- Interactive voice response (IVR) systems
  - Call tracking systems
- Self-help knowledge tools
- Case-based reasoning/search systems
- Network management tools (including remote support capabilities)
  - System monitoring tools

Incident Management

- Automatic incident logging and alerting in the event of automated fault detection systems on hardware or software detecting an issue
- Automatic escalation facilities based on the elapsed time of incidents in different statuses together with flexible routing of these notifications to ensure they get to the right staff wherever they happen to be at the time
- Diagnostic tools (e.g., case-based reasoning)

Problem Management

These tools are a combination of the development and testing tools used by Release Management together with access to the services or tools of the Performance Management team. In this area, the tools are important for diagnosis and simulation but the primary driving force is people and brain power.

Release Management

- Software development tools
    - Build management tools — For the automated building of new releases of software to ensure that appropriate versions of all the necessary components have been included.
    - Software estimation tools[3] — By improving the software (or any IT) project estimating process, these tools can provide better predictability and appraisal of options for the business which are always valuable. The tools need to be calibrated with historic data, either for the industry or in-house, in terms of effort in staff months, schedule, in elapsed months and size, in function points (preferred), or lines of code (if desperate). For example, these tools can enable
        - Simulating project outcomes
        - Probability analysis
        - Accounting for diseconomies of scale
        - Accounting for creeping requirements
        - Estimation of less common software issues
        - Calculation of planning options and integration with planning tools
        - What-if? analysis
        - Arbitration for unrealistic project expectations
        - Objective authority when revising estimation assumptions
        - Sanity checking estimates created using expert knowledge or "back of the envelope" techniques
        - Estimation of large projects
    - Software development life cycle (SDLC) tools — These can be delivered in a single development environment or as stand-alone programs (many small ones are available "free" on the Internet), something in between or any combination of the above. Care must be exercised to ensure that IT staff inform the appropriate governance mechanisms about all tools they are using to ensure that licensing, security, and reliability standards are upheld.
        - Requirements management tools — Provide a requirements database and requirements tracing
        - Design tools
            - Diagramming support tools
            - Data management tools

- Modeling tools and languages (e.g., ULM)
- Graphics tools for presenting and manipulating models
- Application integration tools (e.g., Eclipse)
- Coding tools
  - Code or data comparison
  - Code or data "tagging"
  - Prototyping support
  - Incremental code compilation
  - Debuggers
  - Code generation
  - Source code checking tools — These find problems not detected by compilers and, if customizable, can be used to detect and enforce organizational programming standards.
- Testing tools
  - Automated testing tools — Driven by test scripts
  - Unit testing tools — Powerful test runners are available that include support for post-mortem debugging of test failures. Some also include profiling and coverage reporting.
  - Mock testing tools — Enable the easy creation of mock objects that can be used to emulate the behavior of any class upon which the code under test depends. Expectations can be set up about the calls that are made to the mock object, and the history of calls made can be examined. This makes it easier to unit test classes in isolation.
  - Fuzz testing tools ("fuzzing") — A software testing technique that basically attaches the inputs of a program to a source of random data ("fuzz"). If the program fails (for example, by crashing or by failing built-in code assertions), then there are defects to correct. The great advantage of fuzz testing is that the test design is extremely simple and free of preconceptions about system behavior.
  - Web testing tools — (1) Browser simulation tools: Simulate browsers by implementing the HTTP request/response protocol and by parsing the resulting HTML. (2) Browser automation tools: Automate browsers by driving them. (3) Acceptance/business logic testing tools: Work by comparing plaintext logged by programs with a previous "gold standard" version of that text. (4) Graphical user interface (GUI) testing tools
  - Code coverage tools — These use code analysis tools and tracing hooks to detect which lines of code are executable and which have been executed in test runs.
  - Continuous integration tools — These can automate the compile/test cycle required by most software projects to validate code changes. By automatically rebuilding and testing the build components each time something has changed, build problems are

  pinpointed quickly, before other developers are inconvenienced by the failure.

 – Test fixtures — Modules for loading and referencing test data. For example, a test case for a database-backed Website isn't much use if there isn't any data in the database. Test fixtures make it easier to put test data into the database.

 – Miscellaneous testing tools — (1) Metrics generators: McCabe, lines of code, %comments, etc. (2) Code analyzers: Analyze code and compare with programming and design best practice. Can be useful for performance improvement or knowledge transfer when responsibility for code maintenance is being transferred.

- Performance testing tools
  - Load stress tools
- Integrated (or partially integrated) tools that claim to integrate some of the above capabilities in one tool. Computer aided software engineering (CASE) tools fall into this category.

- Release and distribution systems
  - Desktop management tools — In an organization of any size, it is good practice to save standard workstation builds on a server and use some form of automation (scripting languages and/or dedicated installation products) to perform the installation.
  - Server management tools — These include remote monitoring, control, and diagnostic capabilities for operational servers. The remote monitoring should include
    - Event logs
    - Problem logs
    - Processor, memory, and disk utilization
  - Electronic software distribution tools

Service Delivery Tools

- Capacity management
  - Capacity planning tools
  - Performance monitoring and analysis tools
  - Discovery tools — Designed to find hardware and installed software on active networks and collect relevant data on them.
  - Metering tools — Designed to measure active usage of software products (as opposed to the passive existence of the software on a particular machine).
- IT service continuity management tools (including automatic backup capabilities)
- Service level management tools
  - Contract management tools

- Availability management
  - System management or network management tools
    - Infrastructure event monitoring and management tools
    - Activation or deactivation of infrastructure components
    - Diagnostic monitoring, tracing, and analysis tools
  - Environmental management tools
  - Service, application, and database management tools
    - User concurrency monitoring
    - Service, application, and database transaction statistics, volumes, and response times
    - Transaction control, management, processing, queuing times, tracing, and diagnosis
    - Resource utilization levels
  - Scheduling tools
  - Data storage management tools
  - Security monitoring and control tools
    - Password control
    - Vulnerability scanning
    - Penetration testing
    - Detection of violations
    - Virus protection
- IT financial management
  - License management tools
  - Procurement tracking tools
  - Software and hardware auditing tools — For example, organizations can often save a lot of money by having good information about the usage of their licenses for third-party software.
  - Financial allocation tools — Used to allocate hardware and software costs between different business profit and cost centers.

What Criteria Should We Use for Evaluating Software Tools?

The following criteria are a useful summary of considerations to apply to any new tool purchase:

- Does the tool meet more than 80 percent of our operational needs?
- Is the tool compatible with our IT environment?
- Does the tool completely fulfill 100 percent of the mandatory requirements upon which the business case was based?

- Are the ongoing administrative, maintenance, and training costs consistent with the budget in the business case?
- What impediments are there to full usage of this tool by the target staff? Can these impediments be removed?
- Does this tool require significant customization to meet our needs?
- Does the tool have a strong data structure and good data-handling capabilities?
- Do we have other tools with which this tool must work? Can it be integrated with them? If so, how much cost and effort will be involved? If not, is it more economical to change the other tools?
- Is the tool ITIL- or CMMI-compliant or compliant with any other applicable standards?

Additionally, Chapter 7 contains some useful advice on selecting outsourcing vendors that can be applied to the selection of tool vendors.

What Are the Best Options for Delivering IT Tools to End Users?

The evolution of information technology has been characterized by surges in productivity for IT workers driven by the availability of more computing power, centrally and locally, and the introduction of more sophisticated software to take advantage of that computing power. As this evolution has occurred, there have been shifts in the emphasis of where applications are "best" implemented (centrally or locally or in some combination of the two). These shifts continue to occur right up to the present day. The problems of maintaining application software on local desktop computers drive organizations increasingly to implement browser-based solutions with a very limited presence on the local computer. However, an enhanced browsing experience that can be facilitated by having some capability on the desktop makes the pendulum swing back in the other direction somewhat.

For IT tools, it is important to remember that they represent an embodiment of intellectual property. It is as important to centralize the embodiment of that intellectual property as it is to acknowledge that intellectual property creation usually occurs at the desks of the users. To reconcile this tension, tools must be selected and implemented to provide full power to the individual users but enforce centralized storage and sharing of data. It may be surprising how few tools on the market today can enable shared access to data across an organization in one location, so the increasingly typical distributed organization can suffer significant constraints if it does not insist on distributed capabilities in its tools.

Discovery tools should be implemented to ensure that staff are not misusing tool licenses or introducing unlicensed or unapproved tools onto their desktops.

The best option for delivering IT tools to end users is browser-based access, central data storage, and local processing for complex problems. This capability can be delivered over an organization's internal network (physical or virtual) or, by some tools providers, over the Internet.

Summary

Businesses should expect their IT Providers to use some of the huge range of IT tools because this is the only way they will remain competitive. However, businesses must be diligent in the oversight of the acquisition and use of tools by IT Providers to ensure that cost and risk to the business is minimized and focused on business needs.

References

1. Baetjer, Howard, 1998, *Software as Capital: An Economic Perspective on Software Engineering*, IEEE Computer Society Press.
2. TSO (The Stationery Office — United Kingdom), *Service Support*, 13th Impression, 2006 (first published 2000).
3. McConnell, S., 2006, *Software Estimation: Demystifying the Black Art*, Microsoft Press.

WHY SHOULD WE MEASURE IT PERFORMANCE?

Chapter 9

How Do I Measure IT Performance?

The need to measure IT performance varies from organization to organization. It can be based on the need to understand the IT value contribution to the business. It can include the need to evaluate current IT development practices and improve those practices so as to improve the ability to make strategic business decisions (e.g., outsourcing). In this chapter, we discuss how to measure IT performance. Once IT has realized that they need to measure performance, the next step is to determine what performance means to IT and to the business. What are the desired outcomes? Accordingly, we are going to take an in-depth look at key measures and focus on how to address IT's value contribution to the business, and how to identify the key performance measures, the key "missing measure," and the attributes of a successful measurement program. For this chapter, the context for our view of IT performance is primarily within the application development and maintenance (AD/M) domain.

IT Providers are faced with the common challenges that come from managing any major business unit within an organization. There are budgets to manage, resources to plan, and customers to satisfy. In addition, IT Providers are expected to provide services at an acceptable level of performance (often subjective) or they will be faced with the prospect of losing some or all of their work to alternative sources. The success and optimum performance of IT is critical to the success and competitive positioning of the business. The ability to effectively measure IT performance can safeguard against making uninformed strategic decisions. Measurement is the key to the continued effective and efficient operation of IT.

An IT Provider, or any software development group for that matter, is in the business of defining, designing, developing, and deploying software for (and with) a customer. That customer may be a business unit within the company or it may be a customer external to the company. When measuring IT performance, there are two points of view to consider:

1. From an external customer's point of view, performance will mean issues of speed (the timely delivery of software), cost (seeking the lowest cost provider), and quality (the right functionality performing efficiently and effectively). From this external perspective, IT Providers should focus their attention on measuring performance relative to speed, cost, and quality.
2. From an internal customer's point of view, these same measures of IT performance (speed, cost, and quality) are equally important but can take on a different perspective relative to the level of performance that is needed to satisfy the business goals and objectives. Perhaps compromises have to be made with regard to level of performance. For example, there is no argument that speed (timeliness of delivery) is important. Or perhaps timely modifications to a transaction-based claims processing system are critical to the Claims Department so they can process their work more effectively and efficiently, but at what cost? Questions may arise such as "Are all the features and functions necessary to satisfy the basic needs of the user?" "What is the cost–benefit of a particular software release in terms of a return on investment?" "What about quality? Is a Six Sigma level of quality really all that necessary, after all (as they say), we're not putting a man on the moon!"

Whether from an internal business point of view or from an external customer point of view, what gets measured (speed, cost, and quality) may be the same. However, the specific measures may vary and the perspective of what constitutes acceptable levels of performance may vary. For example, the cost of performance needs to be balanced with the cost of running the business.

IT Value Contribution

IT Providers perform services. They are responsible for the effective and efficient operation of day-to-day computer systems ensuring system reliability and data integrity. They are responsible for making enhancements to production software. They are responsible for developing new software and delivering technical responses to help the business stay competitive. They are also responsible for maintaining fiscally sound organizations. Measuring IT performance should address the commonly asked question, "What value does IT bring to the business?" Are IT Providers providing business solutions that will have the appropriate functionality and quality of data, and will the solutions be delivered on time and within budget?

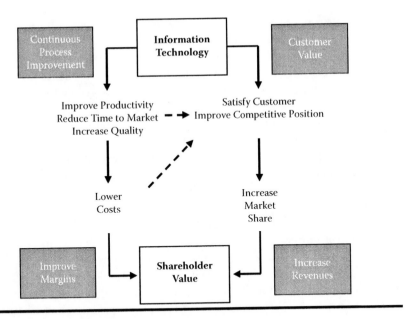

Figure 9.1   IT value contribution.

The business value of IT can be measured based on value delivery and development efficiency. Value delivery deals with the question, "Does IT provide value that has a bottom-line impact on the business?" Development efficiency addresses the question, "Has the software been developed in a cost effective way?" The good news is that both aspects are measurable. The greatest IT expense within the AD/M domain is labor. The majority of that labor is focused on developing and supporting software. So the question, "Is the company getting the most out of the monies spent on labor?" is the key question for most IT Providers. This includes, "Are they operating efficiently?" and "Are they producing a deliverable that has value to the business?"

Figure 9.1 shows the two perspectives: on the left-hand side, there is the IT focus with continuous process improvement resulting in greater efficiencies, lower costs, and improved margins; on the right-hand side, the IT deliverables that provide value to the customer, ideally resulting in increased market share. Each perspective is measurable.

Are IT Providers responsible for measuring both aspects — improving IT operating efficiencies as well as delivering value to the business? The answer is "yes" and "not entirely." In the area where IT Providers have the most control (i.e., internal IT improvements), "yes," they are responsible for performance in that area. With regard to delivering value to the business through the delivery of software solutions, the answer is "not entirely"; it is a shared responsibility with the business.

On the business side of the equation the responsibility of IT Providers is to properly define, design, develop, deploy, and support the software. They need to do this in a timely and cost-effective fashion. They have to deliver software that meets the business requirements and that functions properly. When they fail to deliver on these expectations, then they have failed to provide value to the business. We know they have to get the software right, but is IT responsible for delivering the right software? In other words, who is responsible for designing the right software solution for the business problem at hand?

Solving business problems is the primary responsibility of the business units. Certainly IT Providers have a responsibility with regard to determining the right software solution. They need to be familiar with current business operations. They have to be aware of available innovative solutions which could technically enhance the proposed business solution. But the bottom-line impact the software solution will have on the business is ultimately the responsibility of the requesting party, the business unit. The business unit needs to determine the value contribution to the business — will the software solution result in increased sales or more efficient operations?

Here is where IT Providers can have a significant impact on the value question and can also take responsibility for their performance. Looking again at Figure 9.1, we see an opportunity for IT to impact the bottom line by lowering costs. The IT Providers can be empowered to set expectations properly, and measure their performance so that the organization can make more informed and intelligent decisions. This will allow them to set proper goals and objectives that focus on providing levels of service that improve the delivery of software and, ultimately, the bottom line.

The objective is to improve the overall performance so that IT Providers can reduce expenses. This means that the labor force needs to operate more efficiently (see the discussion on IT tools in Chapter 8). The alternative may simply be to make use of cheaper labor but that decision depends upon a proper analysis of the current performance measures. For example, the current labor force may be twice as costly as the cheaper alternative but three times as productive!

So what do IT Providers need to measure to determine their level of performance? Remember, measurement is all about providing answers to the questions. So the primary question that the IT Providers need to consider relative to providing value to the business is, "Is IT producing a high-quality product in a timely and cost-effective manner that functions according to the requirements?"

Four Key Performance Measures (+ One)

There are four primary performance measures that are most effective when measuring IT performance: cost, quality, duration, and customer satisfaction. For software development, cost is mostly a measure of the cost of labor. Quality is a measure of how well the delivered software satisfies the business requirements and a measure of the number of problems in the software (defects). Duration relates to the length of time from project initiation to software delivery. Customer satisfaction measures the success of the software from the user's perspective. Is the software fit for use? Is it user friendly? Does it support the way the user conducts his business? We will explore each of these measures in greater detail.

Cost

Collecting cost data is a standard operating procedure for most IT Providers. The IT budget process requires a general accounting of all IT expenditures. Businesses should ensure that their IT Providers are gathering and reviewing cost data on a monthly basis. For the purposes of measuring IT performance, it will be important to collect and measure expense data related to the cost of developing and maintaining the portfolio of applications at the business or organizational level. The most effective means of measuring performance based on cost is to evaluate the cost (mainly labor) for each of the individual work products produced by IT. By assessing expenses at the product or project level, the organization will be in a better position to look at outcomes specific to each unique development activity and determine which projects were the most cost effective.

Additionally, the cost of maintaining and supporting the portfolio of applications should also be considered part of the IT performance measurement. The organization needs to be aware of what it costs to fix problems introduced because of poor process or poor execution within the development shop.

Quality

As an IT performance measure, quality relates to the level of defects found in a product or application. Measuring defects is often performed during the testing phase of the development life cycle. Unfortunately, this takes place when it is the most costly to discover and remove defects. Defect removal should be done throughout the project life cycle, not just during testing. There is enough evidence to show that removing defects early on is far more cost effective than waiting until the later phases of the development life cycle.[1] By removing defects early in the life cycle you can apply a more effective performance measure such as defect removal efficiency. Defect removal efficiency measures the effectiveness of removing defects throughout the life cycle. For example, if the majority of the defects are discovered in the later phases of development, then either the front-end defect removal activities are flawed or defects are being introduced late in the life cycle, perhaps by poor coding.

Duration

Measuring duration includes measuring how long it takes a project team to define, design, develop, and deploy a software solution. There is no standard definition of duration. Many organizations define the beginning of a project as the time when a feasibility study is performed; others define it as the time when a project code is first set up. If a project starts, gets put on hold, and then restarts after several months, the duration may be measured from the initial start of the project request or begin again when the project is restarted. How an IT Provider decides to measure duration is up to that individual IT Provider. Once established, this defined standard needs to be adhered to across the organization consistently. Businesses need to be aware that different IT Providers (including the in-house IT Department) may be using different standards.

Customer Satisfaction

Part of any IT performance measurement activity needs to include the customer's perspective. One of the most effective ways to find out how your customers view the value proposition relative to IT is to ask them. A customer satisfaction survey is one of the most economical vehicles for measuring IT performance and yet is seldom performed on a consistent basis. Several factors should be considered when performing a customer satisfaction survey. It is often best to use a third-party organization to develop and conduct the survey. This helps to eliminate any biases and provides a more objective survey. The question set that is developed needs to be well thought out with a clear understanding of the objectives of the survey. Finally, the IT Providers must be willing to respond to the results of the survey. If you are going to ask people what they think, you need to acknowledge that you are listening and be prepared to react positively to major issues that are raised from the survey.

Most measures need to be applied at a project level. The project is the work product for which IT Providers are responsible. Therefore, that is where the level of IT performance should be measured. This holds true for costs, quality, and duration. Customer satisfaction, depending upon the situation, can be executed on a project basis but, more often than not, it is executed from an overall IT performance perspective. However, it is recommended that some form of customer feedback is obtained for large project initiatives.

The Missing Measure: Size

As stated earlier, these forms of measurement are not new. Many organizations use these measures. However, they have not necessarily positioned these measures to be used as an effective means to evaluate their performance. In fact, a key measure is often missing. Although an IT organization may be collecting measurement data, there may not be a good basis for evaluating and comparing levels of performance. How do we know if one deliverable or one project performed better than another? If 15 defects are discovered on one product and 115 defects on another,

Table 9.1   Sample Project Data

Project	Cost ($000s)	Quality (Major Defects Released)
PO special	500	12
Vendor mods	760	18
Pricing adj	80	5
Store sys	990	22

Table 9.2   Sample Project Data With Size

Project	Size	Cost ($000s)	Unit Cost ($)	Quality (Major Defects Released)	Defect Density
PO special	250	500	2000	12	.048
Vendor mods	765	760	993	18	.023
Pricing adj	100	80	800	5	.050
Store sys	1498	990	660	22	.014

is there enough information to assess which product has better quality? These are the questions IT Providers and businesses will ultimately want answered. So far, the measures we have reviewed do not provide the information needed for realistic comparisons.

So what is the missing element? Table 9.1 shows a sample set of project data which includes cost and quality information. Assume that these projects were deemed to be successful, having been delivered on time and within budget. But what about performance levels? Are they all performing consistently? Even more important, are these projects performing at a level that maximizes efficiency and is cost effective? We actually can't tell from the data presented in Table 9.1. But with one additional measure — size — the picture becomes clearer (see Table 9.2).

Assume for the moment that size is a measure of the functionality (or unit of value) being delivered to the user. Calculated in Table 9.2 is a "unit cost" based on size and it is expressed as a "cost per unit of work" (unit cost). Also noted is a defect density measure based upon the number of defects and the size of the deliverable.

The "Store sys" project has the lowest unit cost and the lowest defect density. In contrast, the "PO special" project has an extremely high unit cost and an equally poor defect density level.

Here is the moment of truth — size does matter! Size is the key element that adds value to measures that may already be in place and being used within an organization.

A good sizing measure should have the following attributes:

- Meaningful to the IT Practitioner and to the user
- Defined and recognized as a standard in industry
- Consistent and follow a documented methodology
- Easy to learn and apply
- Accurate and statistically based
- Available when needed early in the life cycle

In the next section, we consider a very important technique for measuring the size of software. We use this useful metric for expanding our discussion in the rest of this chapter but it must be remembered that the most important thing is to have some sort of size metric for normalizing comparisons of IT projects.

Function Point Analysis

The most effective sizing technique used today for software is Function Point Analysis (FPA), an industry accepted sizing technique that has been adopted worldwide.[2] The methodology is supported by the International Function Point Users Group (IFPUG), which maintains the defined FPA methodology, supports the current counting practices, and certifies professional counters. The advantages of FPA are

- Statistically demonstrable repeatability
- Speed of implementation
- Availability of expertise

The FPA method is dependent upon the identification of five elements of a software design: inputs, outputs, inquiries, internal stores of data, and external references to data (see Figure 9.2). The definition of these elements is logical and

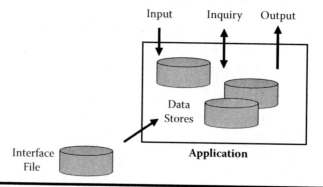

Figure 9.2 The five functional elements.

therefore aligned to the user's requirements. After identifying all occurrences of the five elements, the next step in the methodology requires a detailed examination of each of the individual elements to determine a "true value" of its size.

Each element carries a specific "complexity" value as determined by a defined set of variables. To calculate a total value, all of the elements are evaluated, assigned a value, and then totaled to derive a total function point size. The size of a project varies from the very small enhancement (50 to 100 function points) to the very large application (thousands of function points).

With this basic knowledge of how to compute size, we can further explore the advantages of adding a sizing metric to a base of performance measures. As noted above, size will serve as a normalizing factor. Assuming that function points represent a unit of work, we have the basis for evaluating each work product based on its level of performance. Now the key performance measures (cost, duration, quality) are enhanced by adding size into the equation.

Combing the Key Performance Measures

Cost and Size

A common measure using functional size and cost is a "cost per function point." This measure identifies the cost for each functional unit developed, and can be applied at the project and organizational levels. Project and organizational baseline values can be established and used as a point of comparison for performance. A cost per function point value may also be used to compare the cost of developing an internal solution to the cost of purchasing a commercial package solution, or to compare internal cost to external industry (benchmark) costs. The cost per function point metric is computed as follows:

$$\frac{\text{Total project cost}}{\text{Total function points delivered}}$$

Another important view of IT costs is the cost for software fixes or repairs. A "cost to repair" measure can be used to track the costs to repair applications that are currently running in production. This metric can be used to measure how effectively systems are repaired. Historical values can be applied before project implementation to predict defeat levels and, hence, repair effort. It can also be used to monitor project expenses directly related to the repair of defects that have occurred during the life cycle. The function points can either represent the total number of function points for a project or product release or they can represent only those function points associated with a specific repair. The "cost to repair" metric is calculated as follows:

$$\frac{\text{Total hours to repair} \times \text{Cost per hour}}{\text{Release function points}}$$

In concert with the "cost to repair" measure, a reliability measure can be used to measure the number of failures an application experiences in relation to its functional size. This measure is used to track system performance and to monitor service level measures associated with the application. The metric is calculated as follows:

$$\frac{\text{Number of production failures}}{\text{Total application function points}}$$

Of course, if failures cause system downtime, then metrics can be expanded to include measures of lost revenue or productivity.

Duration and Size

"Time to market" measures calendar time to deliver the required software solution to the end user. As discussed earlier, it is essential that the definition of "elapsed calendar time" be created and used consistently throughout the organization. The duration metric is calculated as follows:

$$\frac{\text{Number of function points}}{\text{Elapsed calendar time}}$$

Quality and Size

"Defect density" measures the number of defects identified across one or more phases of the development project life cycle and compares that value to the total size of the application. It can be used to compare density levels across different life-cycle phases or across different development efforts. Defect density is calculated as follows:

$$\frac{\text{Number of defects (by phase or in total)}}{\text{Total number of function points}}$$

One of the most powerful performance indicators is "defect removal efficiency." It measures the total number of defects found prior to release of the software and compares it with the total number of defects found both before and after delivery. Function point size is not part of this equation. This defect removal metric is calculated as follows:

$$\frac{\text{Total number of defects found prior to delivery}}{\text{Total number of defects}}$$

The total number of defects represents a specified period after delivery. Defect removal efficiency can be calculated by life-cycle phase, or by comparing front-end development defect removal efficiencies to back-end defect removal efficiencies. Typically, defect removal efficiency measures only include the most severe defects, severity levels 1 and 2.

"Test case coverage" measures the number of test cases necessary to support testing of a development project adequately. This measure does not indicate the effectiveness of the test cases, nor does it guarantee that all conditions have been tested. However, it can be an effective comparative measure to forecast anticipated requirements for testing that may be required on a development system of a particular size. This measure is calculated as follows:

$$\frac{\text{Number of test cases}}{\text{Total number of function points}}$$

Note that this is an aggregate measure for comparison purposes only and, as such, it is different from the metric generated by some software development tools which calculated the "code coverage" of test cases based on the amount of code exercised by all of the test cases. In later chapters we will discuss how these measures can be used to compare internal levels of performance with industry benchmarks. Once again, it is the use of size (in our case, function points) that allows an organization to gain this level of information and insight about their performance.

Effort and Size Productivity

Productivity is about the efficiency with which inputs are transformed into outputs. This can vary in different IT Projects but in a typical software development project, the input is effort and the output is working software (size). It is in considering productivity that the limitation of using effort as a proxy for size becomes apparent. Productivity is calculated as:

$$\frac{\text{Size}}{\text{Effort}}$$

For software, this rate is typically inverted and productivity is measured in hours (effort) per function point (size).

A Successful Measurement Program

The final discussion point in this chapter on measuring IT performance addresses the issue of establishing and maintaining a measurement program. There is no need for, and little value in, making the measurement process overly complicated. For the organization that is just beginning to consider why and how to measure their IT performance the task can be a daunting one. For the more mature, process-oriented organization, sustaining their measurement activity can also present many challenges.

Performance measurement programs vary, depending upon the unique needs of the organization; however, basic elements are fundamental to the success of any measurement program. The basics are well defined in several best practices measurement frameworks. The best practices framework that we will refer to in this chapter is the Software Engineering Institute's (SEI) Capability Maturity Model Integration (CMMI®).[3] The SEI states the purpose of a measurement activity is "to develop and sustain a measurement capability that is used to support management information needs."

The framework builds upon an initial statement of goals and objectives. For IT performance measurement the objective is to collect meaningful and reliable data points that allow for the analysis and reporting of IT performance. The first step is to agree on the measures being used and how they will be analyzed. Clear measurement definitions need to be developed and must be in line with the needs of the organization. A clear vision of how these measures will be used is necessary to ensure that the information will be used and that it will potentially benefit both the IT Providers and the business.

There is no magic formula for determining how to best measure IT performance. The most practical place to begin is to consider the customer's expectations. As a reminder, these customers may be internal or external. What aspects of their IT services do these customers value? In addition, IT Providers have a fiscal responsibility to operate in an efficient manner. Finally, IT Providers are responsible for technology and IT innovation; therefore, they are expected to bring solutions to business problems that will help the organization maintain their competitive position.

Once you have established what you are going to measure, the critical next step is to establish a well-founded and sustainable measurement program. Using the CMMI as our best practices model, we will expand upon a few aspects of a measurement program that are critical to sustaining that program. The following discussion points from our own client experiences are aspects of a measurement program that can result in barriers to successful implementation.

Determining the Source of the Data

It is easy enough to determine that size, cost, quality, and time to market are all areas that need to be measured and monitored. These high-level measures can easily be linked to customer expectations and business requirements. However, the likelihood that you have the level of detailed data you need to analyze your performance properly is not very high. For example, do you have data about the quality of your software releases? Problem reports are useful but not sufficient. In addition, defect-tracking data points should be used to analyze performance pertaining to each release, your development practices, and the work effort associated with responding to defects released to the field. Few organizations have this information available. Another example is cost. If you have determined that performance needs to be monitored and analyzed at the project level, do you have the detailed project level data available?

The data you need to monitor IT performance may not be readily available and it will most likely require an additional investment in time and resources to make that data available.

Ensuring the Integrity of the Data

There is no point in collecting, analyzing, and reporting on performance data if no one believes the data. Many IT Providers do not have the mechanisms in place to ensure that the measurement data being collected is accurate. Many organizations track time for their projects, but fail to have the mechanisms in place to ensure the integrity of the data.

We often suggest to clients that they establish an internal audit process for measurement data. That process usually consists of the following steps:

- Agreeing on what is being audited
- Scheduling the audit to coincide with performance evaluations
- Developing the audit criteria
- Accumulating evidence
- Assessing the results
- Reporting the results
- Making adjustments and corrections

Once again, additional resources may be required to audit the data you will be using to measure performance. This investment pays back quickly because the improved data integrity benefits other functions such as invoicing and cost accounting. For example, we often find that effort is being misallocated to projects and tasks and the true picture reveals opportunities for savings.

Reporting the Data

The process of defining and collecting data may have been well planned and executed, but when it comes time to produce the periodic report, you may realize that not enough thought has been given to what the report should look like or how you will display the information. The first step is to consider who the audience will be for the information. Will they need to see details or will a summary be enough? Will they want both? Also, what is the message that you are trying to communicate? Is it enough simply to report the information or should a face-to-face presentation be scheduled?

Data can be misunderstood and it can be misrepresented. Similar to the discussion earlier about the integrity of the data, it is important to build credibility around the reporting of that data. The analysis and the representation of the results need to produce an honest view of the data.

Of course, a number of other aspects to operating a successful measurement program will require careful thought and planning. The CMMI model references the following steps for institutionalizing a well-managed measurement activity:

- Establish an organizational policy
- Plan the process
- Provide resources
- Assign responsibility
- Train people
- Manage configurations
- Identify and involve relevant stakeholders
- Monitor and control the process
- Objectively evaluate adherence
- Review status with higher-level management

A reasonable approach to defining the metrics to be gathered is to work with the eventual report users to set the goals for the measurement plans by outlining the reports first. Even when this approach is adopted, expect that the report users will want changes, and so an agile approach is recommended.

Summary

This chapter discussed IT performance measurement from an external customer's perspective and from an internal IT perspective. Key performance measures include cost, quality, duration, and customer satisfaction. The use of a sizing measure such as Function Point Analysis will allow for the enhanced use of these core measures by serving as a normalizing factor.

IT performance should be measured at the project level. The software product or software release is the end product produced by IT Providers and represents the value deliverable being provided to the business or to the customer. The outcome or performance of each deliverable is going to vary and it is important to note those variances in performance. From that level of detail, further analysis can be performed that will provide insight as to the causes of those variances. Additionally, by analyzing performance at the project level, a more complete view of the overall IT performance can be realized.

Finally, the key to defining, collecting, and reporting on IT performance data successfully is centered on the establishment and sustainment of a measurement program. Following a best practices framework such as the SEI's CMMI model will provide the basic building blocks for a successful initiative.

References

1. Wiegers, K., 2002, *Peer Reviews in Software: A Practical Guide,* Addison-Wesley.
2. International Function Point Users Group, www.ifpug.org (accessed Sept. 20, 2007).
3. Software Engineering Institute, www.sei.cmu.edu (accessed Sept. 20, 2007).

Chapter 10

Is IT Operating Effectively?

In Chapter 9, we identified the primary measures (productivity, duration, cost, and quality) for measuring and monitoring IT performance and we learned the importance of including a size measure as one of the primary measures. This chapter builds upon that information and expands into the area of measuring the effectiveness of IT. The focus of this chapter is on measuring the software development and maintenance component of IT. We will discuss how to measure IT effectiveness through the collection and analysis of quantitative and qualitative data. We will examine what data needs to be collected, how it should be analyzed, and some of the ways in which it can be reported effectively. One of the keys to measuring IT effectiveness is to establish a performance profile. Performance profiles are comprised of key attributes that influence the effectiveness (productivity and quality) of IT practices. Once a baseline of performance is developed these profiles become a valuable tool for measuring effectiveness and for predicting outcomes. Furthermore, from this baseline of information IT Providers can begin to develop estimating capabilities that will increase their ability to estimate workloads more accurately and develop and deploy software more effectively. Again, as in Chapter 9, we will focus on application development and maintenance for our discussion and examples.

Introducing the Measurement Model

The key to successful IT performance management is performance measurement. As the IT industry evolves into a more mature set of processes, technologies, and development practices, the inclusion of performance measurement to manage and direct decisions is becoming a more mainstream practice. Senior managers acknowledge the need to establish strategic goals and objectives; equally important, however, is the identification of an appropriate set of measures that provide quantitative evidence that those goals and objectives have or have not been achieved.

An IT Provider must share the business' strategic goals and objectives. In addition, the IT Provider will most likely have strategic objectives of their own. It should not be assumed that these are compatible, and regular review is appropriate and necessary. Although these goals and objectives can vary from company to company based on their unique business drivers, a relatively common set of objectives remain that tend to be associated with IT Providers when measuring the effectiveness of their performance. These objectives include the ability to:

- Improve decision making capabilities
- Improve productivity
- Measure performance
- Increase IT transparency

Improving decision-making capabilities means making decisions based on quantitative data, thus providing an opportunity to make more informed decisions regarding the impact that various technologies, tools, and practices have on productivity and quality.

Improving productivity requires IT Providers to identify opportunities for improved productivity ideally based on a quantitative analysis of process strengths and weaknesses. The key is having the ability to identify those areas within IT where improvements can be made which will result in higher yields of cost effective software delivered on time.

Measuring performance involves identifying and tracking the measurable impact of improvement initiatives within IT. Ultimately, this creates a knowledge base of data to monitor and control future continuous improvements.

Increasing IT transparency means increasing visibility into IT both at a macro and micro level. Achieving meaningful levels of transparency into outsourced IT Providers is both more challenging and more important.

To assess whether or not IT is operating effectively and meeting the stated business objectives, a model needs to be developed that will provide data that measures the level of performance and will allow for the causal analysis of high or low performance levels. The model must provide performance measures that are based on quantitative data as well as qualitative data. Therefore, the most effective measurement model will include the collection and analysis of both quantitative and qualitative data elements (see Figure 10.1). Once again, this data should be collected at the project, product, or release level.

Quantitative Data

The quantitative data elements include a minimum of four basic measures: the size of the deliverable; the effort required to produce the deliverable (cost); the overall

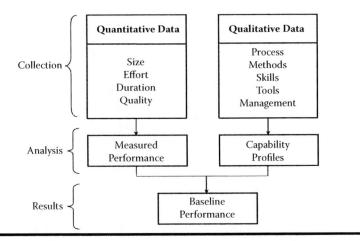

Figure 10.1 Baseline measurement model.

duration required to define, design, and develop the deliverable; and the quality — the number of defects that were removed prior to delivery and the number of defects that were discovered after delivery.

As mentioned in the previous chapter, the best measure used for software size is function points. Function Point Analysis is a measure of the functionality delivered to the end user. The function point methodology is an industry standard and serves as the basis for numerous performance calculations. Source lines of code (SLOC) has been used in the past as a measure of size; however, it does not lend itself as a consistent source of comparative analysis. There is no industry standard definition for source lines of code, making it difficult to compare the effectiveness of one development effort over another. An effective size measure must be well defined, meaningful to both IT and the user, easy to learn and apply, and statistically sound. Function point analysis meets that criterion. Function Point Analysis is a well-defined standard supported by the International Function Point Users Group.[1]

The level of effort required to produce the software deliverable is basically a measure of IT labor. Measured at the project level, level of effort accounts for all labor expended on a project. Although there is no industry standard for measuring level of effort, the common practice is to measure effort in person hours. This includes effort for all members of the project team including the project manager. It does not typically include end-user effort.

Duration is the measure of calendar time beginning with the start of a project through delivery. There are several considerations when measuring duration. When does a project start? What happens when a project starts and is then put on hold? Typically, the start of a project begins when IT resources start recording time attributed to a project. The end of a project is when the software is fully tested and is "fit for use." If a product or a piece of software is being rolled out to the organization, then the end time of the project is measured when the first rollout occurs. In those organizations where there are occurrences of projects starting, then stopping, and starting again, it is reasonable to suggest that the entire duration be measured and include the entire time period from the project's first inception until its final delivery. Under this scenario, a lag-time measure may be derived to show the non-productive time as a percentage of the total duration.

Measuring of defects includes the measurement of pre- and post-release defects. There are varying degrees of complexity regarding how defects may be measured. At the simplest level, defects are often recorded as problem tickets or problem reports that have resulted from user-discovered errors. At a more comprehensive level, post-release defects can be classified based on their point of discovery, severity, and origin. In addition to post-release defects, pre-release defect tracking and analysis can begin at the requirements phase and carry through each phase of the development life cycle. When defects are discovered as a result of a design review or code inspection, the defect is recorded with information relating to its location and origin, thus providing the opportunity to analyze pre-release defect removal efficiency.

Qualitative Data

The qualitative elements in the measurement model include a variety of data points that are used to evaluate levels of competency regarding process, methods, skills, automation, technology, management practices, etc. Although this data can be organized and collected in many ways, many organizations develop their own proprietary process to collect and organize this data. For example, an organization may first collect information relating to the technical aspects of a project. These technical assets may include general category information about the business/industry (telecom, manufacturing, finance), application type (new development, enhancement, maintenance), technical platform (mainframe, PC, client/server, Web based), and language (or language generation). These categories are used to analyze the data based on selected groupings of like projects. For instance, a selection of projects to be analyzed may include enhancement projects developed on a client/server platform.

In addition to this general data, our proprietary method includes the collection of detail data in six major categories (Table 10.1). Those categories include information relating to project management, definition, design, build, test, and environment. There are approximately 80 different variables that make up these six categories (a sample of which is listed in Table 10.1).

The management characteristics deal with issues relating to how the project is managed, how experienced the project managers are, and what management tools are deployed. The definition, design, build, and test categories are organized to collect information regarding the skill levels of individuals working on each phase of development, the processes and techniques used as well as the level of

Table 10.1 Qualitative Data

Management	Definition	Design
☐ Team dynamics	☐ Clearly stated requirements	☐ Formal process
☐ High morale	☐ Formal process	☐ Rigorous reviews
☐ Project tracking	☐ Customer involvement	☐ Design reuse
☐ Project planning	☐ Experience levels	☐ Customer involvement
☐ Automation	☐ Business impact	☐ Experienced development staff
☐ Management skills		☐ Automation

Build	Test	Environment
☐ Code reviews	☐ Formal testing methods	☐ New technology
☐ Source code tracking	☐ Test plans	☐ Automated process
☐ Code reuse	☐ Development staff experience	☐ Adequate training
☐ Data administration	☐ Effective test tools	☐ Organizational dynamics
☐ Computer availability	☐ Customer involvement	☐ Certification
☐ Experienced staff		
☐ Automation		

automation. Environment data relates to general issues about training, the organizational environment, and the culture.

The goal is to collect data points for those characteristics that have a measurable impact on productivity and quality levels of performance. Furthermore, because the data needs to be analyzed, a historical baseline of data needs to be collected to determine which factors have the most significant impact. David Consulting Group has developed and maintains their own proprietary database which contains up-to-date data for over 7000 projects. This data has been used to analyze performance levels within selected industries as well as to identify those variables that have a known influence on performance.

There are numerous commercial tools available to aid in the collection and analysis of similar types of performance indicators or attributes. Tools such as QSMs SLIM, SPRs Knowledge Plan, and Galorath's SEER product all collect a variety of data for analysis. However, no single tool collects all the relevant data points. The reason for this is simple. The organizations that built these tools have collected and analyzed a finite amount of data. Each organization considers their own version or subset of the available data and collects those attributes they deem to be most relevant. Although the tools do contain some unique and useful data points, there is a great deal of overlap in the data elements collected among the various products. This overlap of data elements does not define a "standard" set of attributes but does point to a level of consistency with regard to those attributes that have an impact on performance.

At the time of writing, there is an initiative under way at the Software Engineering Institute (SEI) involving a significant number of industry participants, which seeks to standardize the parameters of a data set (see the section "Software Engineering Institute Data" in Chapter 11).

Collecting the Data

Numerous organizations already collect many of the data points mentioned above. For example, level of effort and start and stop times for a project are typically gathered and reported as part of the project management activities. However, collecting measurement data such as size and defect data, particularly pre-release defect data, is not performed as frequently.

The collection of function point data is thought to be complex and time consuming. Clearly, if an organization is not currently involved in collecting size data, then any new activity designed to collect size information will be considered an additional effort (and burden) and therefore more time-consuming initially. However, the reality is that the collection of function point data is no more time-consuming than the effort required to collect detailed level of effort data on a weekly basis from all the project teams in a department.

Advances have been made in the function point sizing arena making it easier and quicker to collect function point data. By having highly experienced and dedicated individuals responsible for functional sizing, the effort to collect the size data can be significantly reduced. This capability can be built in-house or outsourced to experienced providers such as David Consulting Group. In addition, the advent of counting practices such as FP Lite® can further aid in the timely and accurate counting of functional size.[2]

Defect data collection is another area that organizations struggle with primarily because it can add effort and cost to the project. This perspective is short sighted for several reasons. By collecting and analyzing defect data during the project life cycle, defects can be found earlier, thereby reducing overall project costs. Further, the final deliverable results in a higher-quality product being delivered to the end user. An easy point of entry for an organization to begin collecting defect information is to incorporate the practice of conducting document reviews and code inspections. Part of this practice should include the collection and analysis of defects. Once again, an initial investment is required, but the return on that investment is significant.[3]

Any time an organization is collecting and analyzing data, the issue of data integrity is always present. As we will discuss in later chapters, the accuracy and integrity of these data points are critical. A great deal of effort goes into the collection of performance data. If that data is suspect, or lacks integrity, then the entire database of information may become suspect and the data labeled or perceived as useless.

Several approaches may be considered when developing a baseline of performance. If an organization already has a practice in place of collecting, analyzing, reporting, and auditing certain data elements, then it may not be all that burdensome to add one or two of the additional data points that we have mentioned here. For an organization with little or no data collection activity, a specific baseline initiative may be the best approach for collecting the data necessary to establish present levels of performance.

Creating a baseline involves the selection of a representative set of projects. Not all projects need to be candidates for data collection and analysis of performance levels. The projects selected should be recently completed and represent a subset of the total project portfolio. For example, if 80 percent of the work is comprised of small enhancements, then the baseline should have a similarly representative portion of small enhancement projects.

Quantitative Data Collection

Collecting quantitative data is usually done as part of project management activities. Because many of the same measures are used to manage the project, it only stands to reason that the project manager (or an assistant) would be the individual responsible for collecting the data. As noted earlier, effort data is most likely going to be captured on a weekly basis as a means of managing project plans and schedules. The beginning and ending of a project are likewise recorded with the beginning and ending of project time reporting. Sizing can be done as an independent effort; usually by someone outside of the development team. As for defect data, if it is not currently being collected as part of the development life cycle, it is not something that can easily be done after the project has been completed. Nor is it a task that can be quickly and easily instituted for the purposes of a baseline study. In our experience when conducting baseline studies, we usually discover that organizations are not tracking their defects and they quickly realize that they have no real handle on their quality control activities. Although this is a serious problem, it is also a tremendous opportunity to make proposed improvements.

For baseline purposes, once the data is collected it can be displayed in a chart or table similar to Table 10.2.

Qualitative Data Collection

Collecting qualitative data is not something that is typically done as part of standard project management activities. Several approaches may be considered

Table 10.2 Project Baseline Data

Project	Start Date	End Date	Platform	FP	Effort (Months)	Schedule (Months)	Cost	Delivered Defects
Replenishment tracking	8/18/03	1/19/04	Mainframe	122	24.08	4.75	$375,600	17
Vendor solution	3/15/03	12/10/03	PC	111	8.63	8.75	$134,640	1
Merchandise reporting	5/27/02	5/9/03	PC	83	25.77	11.50	$401,958	3
End cap alignment	8/15/03	10/19/03	Mainframe	52	5.50	2.25	$85,800	0
Buyer solutions	12/1/02	4/1/03	Mainframe	20	1.34	4.00	$20,880	6
POS tracker	2/19/04	3/4/04	PC	19	1.23	0.50	$19,200	0
Vendor approved	8/1/03	8/22/03	PC	19	0.92	0.75	$14,400	1
Sales forecast	3/12/03	5/28/03	Mainframe	12	1.27	2.50	$19,800	2
Financial analysis	9/15/03	2/9/07	Mainframe	12	6.15	4.75	$95,880	0
Reversal automation	8/27/03	1/5/04	Mainframe	9	1.64	4.25	$25,560	4
Ad magic	8/5/03	1/5/04	Mainframe	8	3.43	4.50	$53,460	1
Store systems	8/1/03	9/15/03	PC	7	0.77	1.50	$12,000	0
Pre-sale inventory report	11/13/02	1/19/03	Mainframe	7	0.35	2.00	$5,400	1
PO redesign	12/22/02	8/18/03	Mainframe	6	0.69	5.00	$10,800	2
Creative colors	2/2/03	2/13/03	PC	3	0.25	0.40	$3,960	0

when collecting qualitative data. Organizations with a mature project estimation process in place are most likely already collecting some qualitative data. A mature estimating process involves the assessment of various risk factors for a project. Information regarding the risk factors may also be gathered by developing a project baseline. For purposes of a baseline, the organization may need to develop its own set of unique project attributes to analyze. Alternatively, an organization can make use of an independent consulting group that specializes in baselining and performance measurement.

The qualitative data is usually collected as a series of questions that can be answered by the project team. The format of these questions varies depending upon the collection vehicle. We use an interview/survey approach with questions presented in a yes/no format. Questions are segmented into the six categories as noted in Table 10.1. An example of how the questions are presented is as follows:

Full agreement on project deliverables, methodologies and schedule	Yes	No
Project management activities are fully automated, integrated, and effective	Yes	No
Development staff experienced with type of application being developed	Yes	No

A weighted value is applied to each question. The values are totaled by category and by project total. The information can be shown in several different formats.

For example, Table 10.3 shows the total score for the project (Profile Score) and the six category scores are displayed. The profile score is on a scale of 1 to 100 with 100 representing the level at which optimum performance may be achieved. The individual category score represents a relative value within each category on a scale of 1 to 100. The shadings represent varying levels of performance. The darkened boxes are areas that need improvement, the gray areas represent average performance, and the white boxes represent optimum performance. Those areas marked "na" were deemed not to be applicable areas of concern for those particular projects. It is interesting to note that the "na"s consistently show up in the design category, indicating that perhaps design efforts are not necessary — ignored — during those projects.

At an individual project level the data display may be formatted as noted in Figure 10.2. Each individual diamond represents the value of the general category for the project. This display represents the project's overall profile.

Analyzing the Data and Reporting the Results

The quantitative and qualitative results come together to form what is commonly viewed as an organization's performance profile. The profile values are usually

Table 10.3 Qualitative Project Data

Project	Profile Score	Management	Definition	Design	Build	Test	Environment
Financial analysis	55.3	47.73	82.05	50.00	46.15	43.75	50.00
Buyer solutions	27.6	50.00	48.72	11.36	38.46	0.00	42.31
Creative colors	32.3	29.55	48.72	na	42.31	37.50	42.31
Store systems	29.5	31.82	43.59	na	30.77	37.50	42.31
POS tracker	44.1	31.82	53.85	34.09	38.46	53.13	42.31
PO redesign	17.0	22.73	43.59	na	15.38	0.00	30.77
End cap alignment	40.2	45.45	23.08	38.64	53.85	50.00	34.62
Merchandise reporting	29.2	56.82	28.21	22.73	26.92	18.75	53.85
Pre sale inventory report	22.7	36.36	43.59	na	30.77	9.38	30.77
Sales forecast	17.6	43.18	23.08	na	26.92	9.38	26.92
Ad magic	40.6	56.82	71.79	na	38.46	43.75	38.46
Reversal automation	23.5	29.55	48.72	na	38.46	6.25	26.92
Replenishment tracking	49.0	38.64	56.41	52.27	30.77	53.13	53.85
Vendor solution	49.3	54.55	74.36	20.45	53.85	50.00	38.46
Vendor approval	22.8	31.82	38.46	na	11.54	25.00	46.15

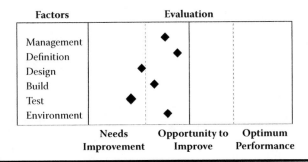

Figure 10.2   Qualitative project profile data.

compiled from a selection of measured projects and serve to represent the overall performance level of the organization.

As an example, let's focus on two contrasting projects, "Vendor Solution" and "Merchandise Reporting," from the data displayed in Table 10.2 and Table 10.3. Vendor Solution delivered more functionality (111 versus 83 function points delivered) with a more efficient rate of delivery (12.8 versus 3.2), a speedier time to market, and cost a lot less money. Both projects were PC-based.

Obviously the Vendor Solution project is operating more effectively. We can analyze the qualitative data to see why (at a high level). There are many more positive indicators in the Vendor Solution profile than in the Merchandise Reporting profile. Upon further analysis, the IT Providers could discover which specific factors contributed to a more positive outcome. They could then promote these practices going forward.

Another useful analysis is to look for any trends across the entire selection of projects (Table 10.2). One simple observation to make is that the qualitative data reveals a rather alarming trend with the performance of the testing attributes. Almost half of the projects performed well below normal. This is an obvious place to evaluate further and look for improvement opportunities.

The compilation and analysis of the data are typically driven by the goals and objectives of the organization. Common objectives include focus on opportunities for improving productivity, having the ability to track progress, and improving decision-making capabilities. The displays of data that will be most useful to the organization should focus on providing insights into the stated objectives.

Tables 10.4a–d represent possible examples that an organization may use to measure performance. These four tables display data relating to productivity, speed (time to market), cost, and delivered defects. The values are calculated based on function points. So, for example, the productivity values (Table 10.4a) are expressed in terms of function points per person month. Consider function points as a value of functionality delivered to the end user. We can observe that the overall rate of productivity (average) is six units of functionality delivered per month.

Table 10.4a Productivity Results

	Productivity		
	Low	High	Average
Overall	2.0	20.6	6.0
Platform			
PC	3.2	20.6	6.4
UNIX	2.0	20.2	5.6
Organization			
Business Unit 1	2.0	20.2	5.4
Business Unit 2	2.3	5.1	4.0
Business Unit 3	5..5	20.2	11.5
Use of SDM			
Used SDM	2.0	12.9	5.3
No SDM	5.5	20.6	12.1

Table 10.4b Time to Market Results

	Time to Market – Months		
	Low	High	Average
Overall	0.40	11.50	3.83
Platform			
PC	0.40	11.50	3.90
UNIX	2.00	5.00	3.78
Organization			
Business Unit 1	0.40	5.00	2.48
Business Unit 2	4.50	11.50	6.92
Business Unit 3	0.50	8.75	3.46
Use of SDM			
Used SDM	2.25	11.50	6.08
No SDM	0.40	5.00	2.32

Time to market data (Table 10.4b) is relative to calendar months. The average delivery time for an average project is 3.83 months.

Cost (Table 10.4c) is expressed as a cost per function point. Delivered defects (Table 10.4d) are calculated as the number of defects per 1000 function points.

In this selection of tables, there is also a breakout of performance levels for each of three organizations or business units within the development environment. There is also a display of data depicting the experience when using a Software Development Methodology (SDM) (e.g., Waterfall, Agile, Spiral, etc.).

Table 10.4c	Project Cost Results		
	Cost per Function Point		
	Low	*High*	*Average*
Overall	$758	$7,990	$2,611
Platform			
PC	$758	$4,843	$2,422
UNIX	$771	$7,990	$2,795
Organization			
Business Unit 1	$758	$7,990	$2,916
Business Unit 2	$3,079	$6,683	$3,901
Business Unit 3	$771	$2,840	$1,353
Use of SDM			
Used SDM	$1,213	$7,990	$2,957
No SDM	$758	$2,840	$1,294

Table 10.4d	Delivered Defect Results		
	Delivered Defects		
	Low	*High*	*Average*
Overall	0	17	2.50
Platform			
PC	0	3	0.83
UNIX	0	17	3.67
Organization			
Business Unit 1	0	2	0.60
Business Unit 2	1	17	7.00
Business Unit 3	0	6	2.00
Use of SDM			
Used SDM	0	17	3.67
No SDM	0	4	1.78

Taking a different view of the data we first saw in Table 10.2 provides us with even more information.

Displayed in Figure 10.3 is the distribution of all the projects. We can note that the projects are typically small in size (expressed in function points) and, in fact, the majority of the projects are small. Within the size range of 0 to 20 function points we see a wide range of performance levels (productivity). Further analysis is called for to determine what the contributing factors are to this wide variation in performance levels. Also, from the data we have presented here, we see an apparent

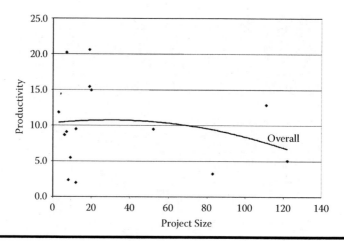

Figure 10.3 Project productivity graph.

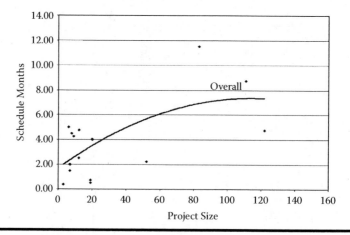

Figure 10.4 Time to market graph.

decrease in performance as projects increase in size. If this trend continues it would be worth analyzing why this is occurring. Perhaps there is a natural "sweet spot" whereby at a particular size range the organization performs at an optimal level.

In the time to market graph (Figure 10.4), we see a similar result among the small size projects in that the duration covers a wide range. The overall trend line appears to be relatively normal, showing an increase in duration based on the size of the project deliverable.

It might be interesting to analyze the two largest projects in this selection to understand why one project took almost nine months and the another project of a similar size took about half that amount of time.

This is a good time to point out one of the key elements in these types of analyses. The data we are examining is the quantitative data. The questions we begin to ask ourselves about the varying performance levels and the reasons for that variability may be best answered by analyzing the qualitative data simultaneously. For example, from our industry database, we know that project size influences performance results. We also know that the type of development work (new development versus enhancement versus maintenance) can influence performance along with platform type and language complexity. However, when we begin to see variations in like groupings of data (in other words, when we hold some of these variables constant), then we need to go to the qualitative data to understand "the rest of story." There we will find what the impact of such things as skill levels, development practices and procedures, management techniques, etc. have on the overall levels of performance.

Another perspective is analyzing the impact of technology on performance. For example, platform type can cause variability in performance. In Figures 10.5a–d, we see four views of data relating to different operating platforms. These graphics include applications by size, by cost, by assignment scope, and by age. In this example, the IT Provider has focused on a selection of applications that have been determined to be among their most critical business applications.

Figure 10.5a (Function point size by platform) identifies that client/server supports the greatest number of function points. If you recall, function points can be viewed as being representative of functionality provided to the end user.

Figure 10.5b (Cost per function point by platform) identifies that the mid-range platforms are the more costly of the four platforms. Of greater interest is the cost per function point with regard to the PC applications. This would suggest that the IT Provider and the business might want to consider additional opportunities to develop in the PC environment.

Figure 10.5c (Assignment scope by platform) introduces a new measure: assignment scope. To simplify this measure, one can think of assignment scope as the number of function points maintained per full-time equivalent (FTE) member of staff. It is calculated by dividing the number of function points for each application by the FTEs supporting the application. Here we can see that the PC environment is not only less expensive to develop in, but also cheaper to maintain.

Figure 10.5d (Aging analysis by platform) displays the average age of the applications for each platform type. Aging software suffers from degradation of the original architecture/structure, and some of the functionality of the older applications tends to become obsolete as technology and business operations evolve.

Any number of analyses can be performed on the data that the organization is collecting. We have demonstrated here the essential basics with some observations about relationships and impacts.

An organization can determine when the data they are reporting is having an impact because people in the organization will start asking questions about the data they see. They will want to understand the meaning of the data and may begin to request different and more meaningful (to them) displays of data. We have already stressed the importance of highly accurate data. There is no value in displaying data

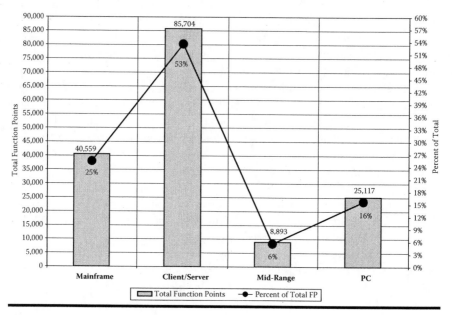

Figure 10.5a   Function point size by platform.

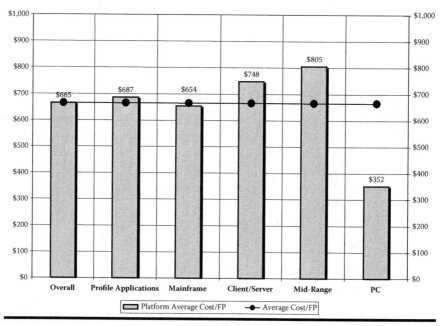

Figure 10.5b   Cost per function point by platform.

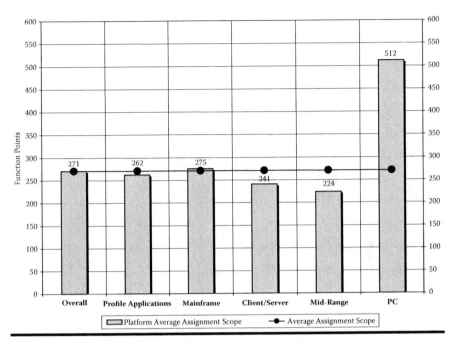

Figure 10.5c   Assignment scope by platform.

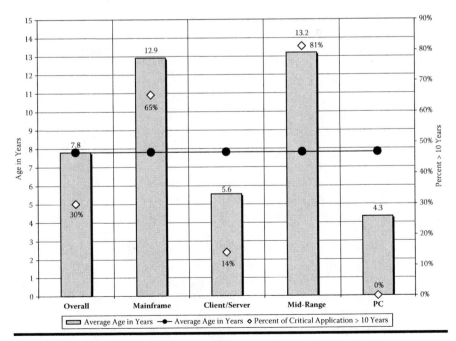

Figure 10.5d   Aging analysis by platform.

if that data is going to be questioned or if the possibility exists that the data collection processes could lead to the corruption of data. But progress can be made and improvement can really start once individuals start asking questions about the data and wanting to know why certain results are occurring.

The more data you collect (in volume and over time), the more you will be able to develop statistically sound models that reflect current levels of performance. Trends can be analyzed and the IT Providers can achieve a greater level of transparency relative to their end user. Armed with this information, IT Providers and businesses can make more informed decisions regarding the types of projects that will be most productive. They will be able to more accurately predict outcomes with regard to cost and schedules. IT Providers' credibility will improve significantly.

Measuring Effectiveness

How should IT Providers measure their overall effectiveness? How do IT Providers know if they are operating effectively? The answer most likely is that IT management already knows how it is currently performing — inconsistently.

As we have seen in the sampling of data in this chapter, results can vary significantly. Some projects perform very well (i.e., low cost and high quality), and other projects do not perform nearly as well. The quantitative data provides management with an objective view of current performance levels. The qualitative data provides the opportunity to examine the attributes of the projects to determine why certain projects have outperformed others.

IT management understands that there is variability in performance outcomes. They have celebrated the successful projects and they have lived through the horror stories of project failures. With measurable data points they are now armed with information that can aid them in their decision making. They can analyze their top-performing projects and learn from the qualitative data what those top-performing projects are doing that is lacking from the lower-performing projects. They can learn which key attributes contribute to higher quality, lower cost, and shorter delivery times. Based on that information they can move forward with improvement initiatives aimed squarely at creating a development environment capable of operating more consistently and optimally.

Consider the IT Provider that has put into effect a new framework for developing and maintaining product releases. Perhaps it has invested in a variety of automated development tools, support software tools, skills training for the staff, etc. Obviously it wants to improve the overall level of performance as a result. Now imagine that it has been collecting some of the key baseline data points that we have been discussing and it now has a solid performance baseline. As it rolls out the new development framework, it will be able to determine the impact it has on performance. If the trends are positive, it can continue to proceed with the rollout. If the trends are less than positive, then the data is available to analyze where the deficiencies may be. Those deficiencies may include lack of training, non-compliance to the new practices, etc. Once known, corrective action can be taken and the initiative put back on track.

Improved Estimating Practices

Software estimating has been an ongoing problem for programmers, project managers, and senior level IT managers. Like most issues in IT, there are a number of perspectives on the topic of estimating. Most organizations consider their estimating practices to be ineffective and they have no real sense of how to make it better. However, if an IT Provider is serious about improving its estimating practices and it wants to estimate more effectively, there are solutions available.

The process of estimating should be viewed as a means to managing customer and management expectations, not a black-box magic process from which the perfect (or absolute) answer appears.

Estimating is a disciplined process that requires quantitative data and qualitative knowledge with regard to the expected outcomes. We need to reframe our thinking about estimating and view it as a vehicle to manage expectations based on best available information at that point in time. If a project ends up being late because the user changed the scope of work or the project manager is called off to work on another project, there is no way to produce an initial estimate that would have considered those unforeseen delays. However, once a change has been introduced, it is perfectly reasonable, indeed essential, to re-estimate and to set expectations anew.

The basic components of an estimating model are well defined and easy to understand. A software project estimating model is comprised of three components. To achieve a reasonable estimate, the model needs to solve for (1) the size of the problem, (2) the complexity of the problem, and (3) the capacity (ability) of the software development team to design, develop, and deploy a satisfactory solution (see Figure 10.6). Within each of the three components, a number of variables are analyzed to create a reasonable value for that component. Additionally, the interrelationship among the components needs to be considered. The resulting estimating model can therefore become highly complex.

Each of these three components is required for any project that needs an estimate. Without a clear understanding of each of these pieces and how they fit together, any attempt at creating a reasonable and responsible estimate will fall short.

Figure 10.6 Basic components of an estimating model.

Two of these three components have been discussed earlier in this chapter. Sizing the problem is a function of applying a functional sizing measure such as function points. Solving for the problem of capacity is a function of analyzing the qualitative data and determining how the various attributes affect the planned outcomes.

The complexity of a software problem is varied. The various estimating techniques and tools on the market today have a wide variety of complexity definitions. These may require analysis of such variables as logical and mathematical algorithms, data relationships, reusability, memory and performance requirements, code structures, etc. These variables and many other risk factors are certainly important and will affect the outcomes of your software solution. The difficulty is in determining what elements to evaluate and having a proper method for consistently evaluating the selected elements.

IT Providers that are effective at estimating their software projects are using either a commercial software estimating tool or they have historical data that they use to develop an accurate set of algorithms to compute a complexity value. Alternatively, you can develop a simplistic complexity evaluation method whereby you evaluate an appropriate list of complexity factors and assign an overall complexity measure of low, medium, or high. Associated with each of the three designations would be a variable that you would apply to your estimating model. By doing this you have accomplished two things — you have raised the level of sensitivity regarding the complexity level in the software problem domain and you are using a consistent method to create an estimate based upon the experience gained from actual outcomes. In addition, you can adjust the complexity factor over time as project characteristics or development environments change.

To further support the benefit or the "correctness" of the estimating model expressed above we need only look to the SEI's requirements for good estimating to underscore the value of these options. The SEI lists the requirements for good estimating to involve the following:

- A historical database
- Structured processes for estimating product size and reuse
- Mechanisms for extrapolating benchmark characteristics of past projects
- Audit trails
- Integrity in dealing with dictated costs and schedules
- Data collection and feedback processes to foster correct data interpretation

Prior to establishing good estimating practices, IT Providers may have gone about their business of estimating by trusting the project manager's "gut feel" for how long the process would take, or the project team would burn extra unaccounted hours trying to fit the actual work load into the originally estimated time frame. Once best practices for estimating are established, project managers reference historical data points for similar project types and then calculate estimates based on known parameters and statistical calculations of risk. Actuals are recorded and stored for use in future estimates.

Summary

In this chapter we have learned about measuring the effectiveness of IT and the importance of capturing both the quantitative and the qualitative data. The quantitative data is necessary to report the "facts" and the qualitative data is used to analyze the variations in the results. These data points make up the IT performance profile. The data collected and reported needs to be accurate and representative of the current environment. From this baseline of data, selected analyses can be performed that support the established goals and objectives for the IT organization and for the company. Once the baseline is in place it can be used to measure and monitor performance trends as well as provide vital data to improve estimating accuracy. In subsequent chapters we will discuss how to use this data to make comparisons to industry baseline data and to measure ourselves against the competition. We will also explore how to move forward and use the measurement data to improve the overall efficiency and effectiveness of IT.

References

1. www.ifpug.org (accessed Sept 21, 2007).
2. Herron, D., 2006, FP Lite™ — Is It a Statistically Valid Method of Counting?, IFPUG Conference, Boston.
3. Jones, C., 1991, *Applied Software Measurement*, McGraw-Hill.

Chapter 11

Where Are We in Relation to Industry Peers?

There is much to be gained by learning from the successes and failures of others. It is not unusual for CIOs and IT senior-level managers to join various industry groups and organizations to develop a network of contacts willing to share information. It is also common practice for organizations to look for ways in which they can compare their IT performance levels with performance indicators from other similar industries or technical environments. The previous two chapters addressed how to measure IT performance and how to measure IT effectiveness. Improving performance means improving the level of productivity and quality. In this chapter, we will build upon that information and learn how key performance data points can be used to make comparisons to industry benchmark data. Once again, in this chapter we are using application development, enhancement, and maintenance (AD/M) functions for our examples. We will explore how to develop a representative baseline of performance using common industry indicators. In addition, we will look at selected sources of industry data and learn more about how they can be used as an effective tool to improve performance. IT Providers use their performance data results to make strategic and tactical decisions. Therefore, it is of paramount importance that the data and the results be reliable and accurate. Towards that end, we will also discuss the need for auditing.

Comparing to Industry Data

One of the first questions that comes to mind is, "Why would anyone be interested in comparing their performance to industry performance benchmarks?" A good follow-up question is, "What data points would be used as the basis for comparison?"

IT Providers need to achieve optimal levels of performance to remain competitive and profitable. Over the past several years IT performance has become increasingly scrutinized from both a financial and a strategic business perspective. There are two very important reasons why IT Providers may want to compare themselves to industry performance benchmarks. The first and probably most obvious reason centers on strategic decisions to outsource. As an organization studies the pros and cons of outsourcing or switching some or all of their functions to a third-party provider, one of the very first steps that should be undertaken is to develop a baseline of current performance levels. Performance indicators similar to the data points shown in previous chapters are used by senior IT management to determine where there are opportunities for possible improvements through the use of a (different) third-party provider. By determining current levels of performance and then analyzing where there are performance weaknesses, the IT leadership can use this information to position those functions or applications that would benefit most from outsourcing. Of course, all IT Providers (incumbents and competitors) need this information to argue for or against new contracts.

The second most noted reason for comparing to industry benchmark data is to establish objective and reasonable performance goals. Take, for example, the IT Provider that is embarking on a Capability Maturity Model Integration (CMMI®) process improvement initiative or a Six Sigma quality initiative. What is the measure of success? What performance gains should it expect to achieve as a result of a successful implementation from these types of programs? Having access to industry data points can provide information relative to levels of performance from similar-sized shops that have successfully deployed a productivity or quality improvement program. Armed with this information and a basic knowledge of its current level of performance, the IT organization can properly set expectations as to the rate and amount of improvement that can be achieved from the improvement initiative.

Where Does the Data Come From?

When researching what data are available for industry comparisons, several factors need to be considered. First of all, how do you define your industry? Second, what data do you need to make reasonable comparisons to industry benchmark performance data?

Identifying your industry type is straightforward and will be the basis for establishing your industry profile. Typical industry performance data is aligned with industry segments such as finance, manufacturing, retail, pharmaceuticals, etc. More importantly, when making comparisons to industry data, it is important to understand that the data you are comparing are representative of your industry and, probably as important, that the data are representative of a technical environment that is similar to yours.

Establishing a realistic and representative industry profile is important and should include a few key attributes. For example, be sure to identify what types of applications you develop and support. Are they business-centric applications or mathematical/scientific-based applications? What is the mix of work regarding new development versus enhancements versus maintenance? What are the various technologies being used by the IT Providers? These characteristics form the basis for creating slices of data that are comparable and most likely will represent differing levels of performance. This will be important when analyzing and comparing specific levels of performance.

The types of industry data available basically come in two "flavors." One is the analytical industry benchmark data that comes from in-depth analysis by firms such as the Gartner Group[1] and Compass America.[2] These are very good sources of information that provide various profiles of performance based upon data that the companies have collected and analyzed. Compass states,

> Benchmarking provides initial positioning information on key metrics, in relation to a peer or reference group of companies. Benchmarking does not provide detailed explanations of performance, nor does it provide a basis for improvement programs. However, benchmarking provides an initial set of high-level metrics and an indication of relative performance.

Gartner produces a Worldwide IT Benchmark Report on IT Spending and Staffing. According to their Website,

> This report contains fundamental enterprise-level IT benchmarks and business productivity ratios. It also contains trending for key enterprise spending, staffing, and business ratios. Understanding year-over-year trends is essential to establishing and understanding the pressures and drivers of both IT and the business.

These sources of analytical data have been very popular in the past and have worked well for organizations wanting to get a better understanding with regard to their position in the marketplace.

Another source of industry performance data includes organizations that have collected data and are willing to make the actual data available to the interested party. This offers IT Providers a more detailed level of data which allows them to perform their own independent analysis of data relevant to their specific needs. In addition to a handful of organizations that offer this data, there are several consulting companies that collect industry benchmark data and from time to time make it available to fee-paying clients. Companies such as Software Productivity Research, David Consulting Group, and QSM have data available for their clients. More often than not, the data is available through the use of one of their commercially available software products. When you purchase one of these products you have access, at some level, to their data.

Additionally, there are sources of data that will actually sell you the specific data points that you can use to do your own analysis and make very specific points of comparison to various levels of performance. The most popular source of this type of data is from the International Software Benchmarking Standards Group (ISBSG).[3] More information about ISBSG appears later in this chapter.

Comparative Data Points

What data are typically used to make industry comparisons with regard to performance productivity in the application development and maintenance space? The answer is both simple and complex. The complex answer is that there are numerous performance data points that one may consider. The first step is to determine what is most important to an organization and then to determine what analytics will be available to support the information needs of that organization.

The simple answer is to keep the data collection and the resulting analysis simple. The more complex and detailed the analysis becomes, the more difficult it is to find reasonable, accurate, and representative data points. Using a few simple performance measures for comparative analysis is more economical, leads to a more accurate and realistic picture, and has a greater opportunity for finding available and reliable data.

One of the major stumbling blocks in finding, using, and comparing to industry benchmark data is the fact that there are no industry standards for defining these performance measures or the metrics that support the measures. Therefore, when accessing industry data, it is of paramount importance that you understand how the data are defined and to ensure those data definitions are in line with your organizational definitions.

Developing a Baseline

Version 1.2[4] of the SEI's Capability Maturity Model Integration (CMMI) for development describes the purpose of a baseline as establishing and maintaining "a quantitative understanding of the performance of the organization's set of standard processes in support of quality and process-performance objectives, and

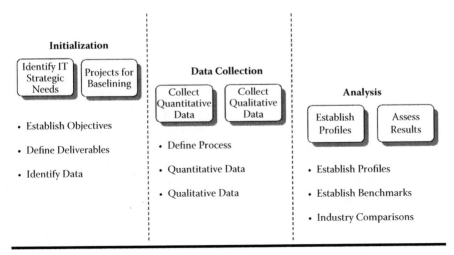

Figure 11.1   The baseline process.

to provide the process-performance data, baselines, and models to quantitatively manage the organization's projects." The CMMI Maturity Level 4 process area, Organizational Process Performance, defines a baseline as "derived by analyzing the collected measures to establish a distribution and range of results that characterize the expected performance for selected processes when used on any individual project in the organization." The focus is on analyzing quantitative data and understanding levels of performance. Note that performance is measured and evaluated at the project level.

A typical process for developing a baseline includes the steps shown in Figure 11.1.

Initialization

Establishing Baseline Objectives

The IT organization that is initiating an effort to establish a performance baseline is focused on achieving identified goals and objectives centered on its current level of performance. The organization wants to gain an understanding of where it fits relative to industry norms and best practices. The objectives of the organization will ultimately determine what data is to be collected, analyzed, and compared to available industry data points. For example, if improved productivity is an organization objective, then data relating to productivity must be collected.

Defining Baseline Deliverables

The deliverables must meet two criteria. They must be meaningful to the organization and they must be in a format that will be compatible with industry standard data. By defining the deliverables early in the baseline process, all parties have a shared expectation as to what they will be viewing when the results are reported.

Identifying Key Data Elements

The data to be collected is defined by the objectives and the deliverables. Continuing with productivity as an objective, the organization must first define what they mean by productivity. Productivity can be expressed as a unit of work measure based on labor rates (costs) or hours. Also, the unit of work that will be used must be defined. Because we are concerned with making comparisons to industry data points it will be necessary to determine what industry data are available for comparison and the format of that data.

Data Collection

Defining the Data Collection Process

The process to collect, analyze, and report the data and the results must be well defined and documented. This includes a detailed description of the data elements and where they are located. Additionally, the data collection methods should be described and any tools that will be used to authenticate the data must also be identified. Organizations are often surprised to find just how disorganized their data is and how susceptible it is to corruption.

Collecting Quantitative Data

The quantitative data elements include those tangible data points that are available, accurate, and represent the true picture. Measures such as the size of the deliverable, the cost of a project, the level of effort (labor), the duration of a project, and the defects associated with a piece of software are all considered to be quantitative data points. This data is collected at the project level.

Collecting Qualitative Data

The qualitative data elements include characteristics attributed to a project regarding the skill levels of the project team, the project management tools being utilized, the development tools and techniques deployed on the project, the software development practices, the involvement of the users, the technical environment, etc. It is often referred to as soft data because of its subjective nature. The data are also collected at the project level.

Analysis

Establishing Performance Profiles

Performance profiles represent the performance levels of an organization. The profile values result from an analysis of the quantitative and qualitative data. The quantitative-based profiles are comprised of such measures as productivity, time to market, quality, cost, and staffing levels. Qualitative profiles are geared toward an analysis of the project attributes and may describe the development processes' strengths and weaknesses relative to their impact on the quantitative data.

Establishing Internal Benchmarks

Internal benchmarks are established that support the objectives of the organization. Rate of delivery (productivity), time to market (speed), and delivered defects (quality) are benchmarks in which organizations are frequently interested.

Comparing Findings to Industry Data

The IT Provider will first determine what sources of industry data are going to be used. Comparisons must be made on an equal basis; if the industry data uses function points as its size measure, then the organizational baseline profiles must reflect values expressed in function points. Additionally, the format of the data should be properly aligned such that data elements collected have been similarly defined. For example, how a particular view of industry data defines defects may be different from how your organization defines defects.

Project Performance Baseline

The following is an example of a baseline process for an IT Provider. The example includes a set of objectives, a description of the data collection process, and a comparison of internally collected data to industry benchmark data. The client profile includes work done on new development projects and enhancements. Work is performed in both mainframe and client/server environments. The data depicted here is sample data and is not meant to represent an actual client.

The stated IT objectives include the following:

- Establish a performance baseline for selected new development and enhancement projects. Analyze and report on productivity rates, time to market performance, cost, and quality performance levels.
- Generate performance profiles and compare to industry average and best in class performance levels.

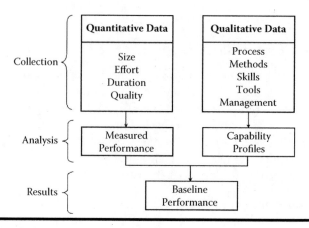

Figure 11.2 Baseline measurement model.

■ Identify contributing factors that influence performance productivity. These performance factors (attributes) should include such things as skill levels, methodologies, technology, and quality practices.

The Baseline Process

The baselining activity consists of two parts: a quantitative analysis and a qualitative analysis (see Figure 11.2). The quantitative analysis will be used to collect and analyze the factual quantitative data. Among these measures, we include size (function points), effort months, project costs, duration (calendar months), and quality. The qualitative portion of the baseline study will include the collection of project attribute data. This data is used to analyze the factors that contribute to high or low yields of productivity.

The Collection Process

Quantitative Data

■ A representative selection of recently completed projects (within the last six to twelve months) is identified. The projects must have the required data available including level of effort, beginning and ending dates, labor hours for the duration of the project, and defects. The selection of projects should also reflect the mix of work as currently represented by new development and enhancement activities within the department.

■ To determine the size of each project, function point analysis will be used; therefore, up-to-date systems documentation must be available as well as access to project team members for questions and answers.

■ All data captured will be stored in a data repository specifically for the baseline initiative.

Qualitative Data

■ Performance profiles will be created from a set of predefined project attributes.
■ Members from each project team will be interviewed in a consensus-driven session and a complete profile questionnaire will be completed during the one- to two-hour session.
■ The profile data will consist of various questions including the software processes used, the tools and methods deployed by each project, the skill levels of the project team members, and the overall management of the project.

Baseline Deliverables

The primary deliverables consist of four charts (see representative Tables 11.1a–d), showing productivity, cost, duration, and quality. For each category, information is displayed for the client, industry average, and industry best practices. The information is further segmented by categories including overall values, new and enhancement projects, and mainframe and client/server projects.

Productivity is calculated using function points and level of effort values. The computations are expressed as function points per effort month (EM). For this example, one person month is equivalent to 130 hours but this can vary and needs to be checked for consistent comparisons. The cost per function point simply reflects labor costs divided by the number of function points. Project duration is expressed in calendar months and represents the time period from the start of the project to when it is delivered. Finally, the quality data reflects the number of defects per function point.

Analyzing the baseline data in this example we see that the client's overall level of productivity, expressed as function points (FP) over effort months (EM), is lower

Table 11.1a   Productivity

	FP/EM		
Categories	Client	Industry Average	Industry Best Practices
Overall	3–12	6–18	42–98
New	6–12	6–14	42–77
Enhancement	3–10	10–18	56–98
Mainframe	3–8	6–12	42–86
Client/server	6–12	9–18	51–98

Table 11.1b   Cost

	$$/FP		
Categories	*Client*	*Industry Average*	*Industry Best Practices*
Overall	535–2345	629–1692	158–473
New	712–2345	823–1692	305–473
Enhancement	535–1660	629–1300	158–289
Mainframe	650–2345	930–1692	216–473
Client/server	535–1245	629–1154	158–420

Table 11.1c   Duration

	Months		
Categories	*Client*	*Industry Average*	*Industry Best Practices*
Overall	5–12	8–17	3.0–7.8
New	5–10	8–14	4.0–7.8
Enhancement	7–12	10–17	3.0–6.2
Mainframe	9–12	8–17	3.8–7.8
Client/server	5–10	9–14	3.0–7.5

Table 11.1d   Quality

	Defects/FP		
Categories	*Client*	*Industry Average*	*Industry Best Practices*
Overall	.0478–.7060	.0333–.0556	.0000–.0175
New	.0478–.6664	.0333–.0556	.0095–.0175
Enhancement	.0873–.7060	.0400–.0556	.0000–.0098
Mainframe	.2568–.7060	.0357–.0556	.0095–.0175
Client/server	.0478–.5566	.0333–.0526	.0000–.0098

than the industry average (3–12 versus 6–18 FP/EM). A further detailing of the data shows that enhancements are far less productive than new development projects for the baseline selection of projects. In addition, it looks as if client/server projects are more productive than mainframe projects. Two areas of concern come to light from looking at this data: mainframe and enhancement projects. This is further supported when we look at the cost data and see that enhancement projects are more costly than new projects, and that mainframe projects are more costly than client/server projects.

Interestingly enough, duration values in all sub-categories look good when compared to industry values. However, the trade-off may be that the client is utilizing more resources, thereby driving up the cost of the project and lowering productivity. This may be an acceptable trade-off if the nature of the business is extremely dependent on getting software delivered in a shortened time frame.

Finally, we have the defect data to complete the story. Unfortunately for this client the story doesn't get any better. The overall defect rate varies significantly, and even more discouraging is the fact that two categories, mainframe and enhancements, appear to be the biggest culprits when it comes to releasing poor-quality software.

One final observation: The data shown in this example are displayed at a high level. A further breakdown of the data is necessary to determine a true picture of the state of performance. For example, looking at these same data points and categories by size would help to pinpoint further where the trouble spots are, relative to poor performance.

Analysis of Process Strengths and Weaknesses

Analysis of contributing factors that have a reasonably significant impact on productivity and quality varies depending upon the data collection vehicle chosen. For our purposes in this example, we have used a survey-based questionnaire. Responses to each question are in a "yes/no" format. Each response is assigned a predetermined value based upon the impact it has on performance. For example, a question relating to the experience level of the project manager will likely have a high impact score because the project manager can have a significant impact on the outcome of the project.

When analyzing input from a number of projects selected as part of a baseline study it is important to look for trends. Patterns typically develop which show common features in those projects that achieved higher levels for productivity and quality. Similarly, those projects that did not perform as well also have common characteristics attributable to levels of poor performance.

Additionally, organizations looking for specific data regarding a new technology or new development practice can use the performance profile to determine what additional actions need to occur to maximize the productive utilization of the particular technology or new process. For example, a new defect-tracking process and tool has been purchased and installed; however, quality does not seem to have improved. Analysis of the profile could reveal issues relating to skill levels that indicate a need for additional training or poor compliance in using the tool.

An example of how qualitative data may be displayed is shown in Figure 11.3, which is an overall view of the qualitative data profile for a range of baseline projects. The horizontal bar represents the range of scores for all projects in the baseline in each of the six categories. The diamond shape in the middle of the bar

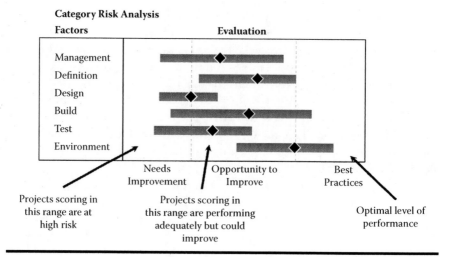

Figure 11.3   Display of qualitative data.

represents the average value for each category. The value range is segmented into three parts: "needs improvement," "opportunity to improve," and "best practices." For example, all attributes analyzed within the "Build" category show a wide range of scores from "needs improvement" to "best practices." The average score for that category is just slightly to the right of center.

To apply this same graphic to our sample baseline, we developed qualitative profiles for enhancement and new development projects (Figure 11.4 and Figure 11.5). As you may recall from the analysis of the quantitative data, enhancement projects did not typically perform as well as new development projects. In all categories except design, the average score for new development projects was better. In other words, most of the diamonds (average scores) are further to the right on the new development chart than on the enhancements chart. These profiles show a consistency between the quantitative data and the qualitative data.

Let's assume for the moment that comparing the practices associated with "enhancement" projects and "new development" projects is not a fair comparison. Perhaps the nature of these two groups of projects is so different that there is no basis for equal comparison. If that were the case, could we learn anything from the "enhancement" set of projects to help us improve their performance? Notice that in each of the sub-categories there is a range of scores (identified by the horizontal bar) and that the average value (represented by the diamond) falls somewhere short of the extreme right-most position of the horizontal bar. This picture suggests that there is at least one project in each category that performed better than the average for that category. By examining those projects and their attributes, one could learn what factors contributed to those higher scores. The next step is to take a look

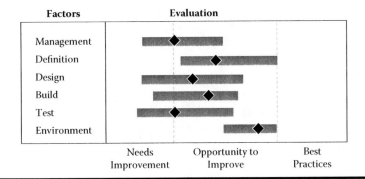

Figure 11.4 Category risk analysis: Enhancements.

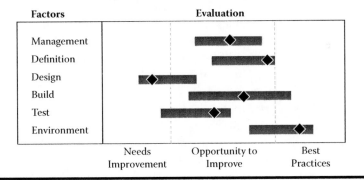

Figure 11.5 Category risk analysis: New developments.

at the quantitative data and see if those higher profile projects in fact had higher performance values for their category.

The example baseline data shown in Figure 11.4 and Figure 11.5 is somewhat limited in scope but it serves to demonstrate the knowledge that can be gained from even a basic high-level analysis of the data points.

Not-for-Profit Industry Data Sources

ISBSG

The International Software Benchmarking Standards Group (ISBSG) is a not-for-profit organization based in Australia that provides commercially available industry data to its worldwide customer base. It has a distinct advantage over many of the other well-known companies that offer industry performance results in that ISBSG provides their customers with the actual project data. This allows for customized analysis from selected views of project data.

ISBSG is committed to improving the management of IT resources by providing public repositories of software engineering knowledge. The available data is standardized and verified, and represents current technologies in the IT environment. ISBSG continually collects and analyzes data related to software project and maintenance and support applications.

The member base includes participants from all over the world, including Australia, China, Finland, Germany, India, Italy, Japan, Korea, the Netherlands, Spain, the United Kingdom, and the United States. The database contains over 4000 projects and represents a wide range of organizations, application types, and development types.

The ISBSG collects data based on a data-collection questionnaire. It will accept data entered into the questionnaire or in an electronic form, for example in Excel. The data is collected on a project-by-project basis and includes the development type, software size, total effort, duration, business sector, development language/tool, and platform along with a host of other project attributes. The data is validated and rated as to its validity and integrity. The collection process also ensures that the data is entered in a consistent format, and definitions for all data elements are made available.

Participation as a contributor of data is rewarded with a free project-benchmark report. There are additional incentives for the submission of multiple projects. In addition, ISBSG offers a wide variety of benchmark analytical reports, CDs, books, research reports, and of course, the data repository.

One of the unique opportunities provided by this repository is the availability of application maintenance and support data. The database contains over 140 applications from nine different countries. The information available includes overall productivity values, staffing capacities, and defect density values.

Customers using the ISBSG repository and various tools now have the capability to:

- Estimate software projects including size, effort, cost, and duration
- Verify completeness of software requirements
- Manage risk
- Make more informed buy-versus-build decisions
- Manage resources more effectively
- Conduct comparative analysis relative to industry benchmark values

Further information about ISBSG can be obtained at www.isbsg.org.

Software Engineering Institute Data

Another potential source of industry data is the SEI's Performance Benchmarking Consortium (PBC). This collaborative project was launched by the SEI in April 2006.

The consortium is comprised of industry notables such as Lockheed Martin and Motorola and experienced consulting groups such as Software Productivity Research and David Consulting Group. The end result will be a performance benchmark repository that will be available on a subscription-fee basis. It is scheduled to go live in early 2008 with a fee-based subscription allowing access to the repository and an annual Performance Measurement report.

Their stated objectives are "to combine benchmark data from multiple repository sources thereby creating a superset of information for benchmark and/or performance comparison and to provide tools and data for goal-setting and performance improvement." Their value proposition includes establishing specifications for the data collection and comparative analysis of benchmark data among various vendor sources and to allow organizations to use the data to establish and achieve their business goals.

The concept of the repository is to allow for Website access via the SEI home page. When accessing the site, users will be encouraged to submit their project performance information, thus making a contribution to the repository. If they do submit a project or two, they will be rewarded with a profile indicating where they are relative to an industry-standard performance indicator. Access to the repository will be based upon the type of subscription service they have purchased (e.g., annual or one time). There may also be the option to engage with an experienced measurement analyst from one of the member organizations.

Initial work focused on the data specifications. This was critical to the success of this endeavor. The software industry lags behind in their efforts to define and standardize common terms such as "a defect" or "start" and "stop" milestones for a project. To normalize the data that will be collected from various sources, it requires a common format and definition.

The PBC is an extremely worthwhile endeavor and should be successful based upon the SEI's history with process improvement initiatives and its reputation as a well-respected world leader in software process frameworks and best practices.

The Importance of Auditing

Once established, you will have a lot invested in your performance benchmark data. Your business objectives and performance standards have been quantified into specific performance goals and are perhaps now being monitored on a periodic basis. You are managing your IT performance levels and potentially making strategic decisions based upon the values being monitored through periodic reviews of performance measures. Critical business decisions are dependent upon accurate and timely data collection, reporting, and analysis. If you do not have the proper checks and balances in place to ensure the integrity and accuracy of that data, you could very well be directing IT resources in the wrong direction or, worse yet, making an invalid assumption that all is well. One very important check and balance activity, too often overlooked, is the audit.

The Oxford American Dictionary defines auditing as "an official examination of accounts to see that they are in order." If we put this definition in terms relating to IT measurement, we can modify the definition to read: "an audit is an examination of metrics to see that they are in order." When an IT Provider has invested in the long-term collection, analysis, and reporting of data being used to track performance and to make periodic comparisons to industry standards, there needs to be a vehicle in place that provides for the assurance that the data being collected, measured, and reported are accurate and reflective of what is actually taking place.

Several key components comprise the audit function. They include audit objectives, scope, process, and adjustments.

Objectives of an Audit

The objectives of an audit are basic in nature. They include

- Ensure the accuracy of the data collected, analyzed, and reported
- Continually improve the consistency of the collection process
- Maintain the integrity of the data (credibility)
- Protect current investments in IT technology

These objectives should be recognized by senior management as important factors in the successful execution of an audit. It should never be taken for granted that these objectives are being satisfactorily achieved.

Scope of the Audit

The scope of an audit includes an examination of the data being collected and reported as defined by the measurement program, or perhaps by internal service level agreements. A more complete view of what should be included in the scope of an audit includes all measurement program activity and all sources of data, some of which originate externally to the organization, such as the industry data points. In those situations where industry data is being used, those data elements and their accuracy should also be included in the audit examination.

The scope of the audit will normally include an examination of:

- Data (source)
- Processes (compliance, roles and responsibilities, collection, reporting)
- Results (computations, analysis)
- Reports (content, format, audience)

- Baseline data
- Industry data
- Repositories
- Definitions

The Auditing Process

The auditing process should be a well-defined and formally documented activity. Here we have outlined six suggested steps of an auditing process:

1. Agree on what is being audited with all stakeholders; the scope of the audit should be evaluated and well defined. The audit would include all data points that are relevant to the performance data measures.
2. Schedule the audit — It is common for an audit to coincide with scheduled performance evaluations. The results of the audit will provide management with a clear statement of the validity of the results. Any performance rewards or penalties should be determined after the completion of the audit.
3. Develop the audit criteria — It needs to be clearly stated what audit criteria are acceptable to all stakeholders. Such things as tolerance levels, thresholds, financial targets, and how the audit will be conducted need to be mutually agreed to and documented.
4. Accumulating evidence — The first actual activity in the audit process involves locating key data elements, retrieving those data elements, and ensuring that a representative sample of data points is available. If an organization does not have a well-defined measurement program in place, it is likely that this crucial step will be more difficult than anticipated.
5. Assessing the results — What should be looked for in an audit? The following is a checklist of issues we address when performing an audit:
   - Verify compliance to the data collection processes and policies
   - Search for patterns that may suggest a consistency in the results (or not!)
   - Uncover any inconsistencies in the collection, analysis, and reporting process
   - Test for completeness of the data being collected and ensure that it is representative of the activities being serviced
   - Ensure the proper classification of terms and definitions
   - Review the mechanical accuracy of the data being collected
   - Review the analytical accuracy of the data being analyzed
   - Assess the reporting accuracy of the results
6. Reporting the results — To ensure an effective and efficient reporting process, the following practices should be followed:
   - Identify the audience
   - Create an executive summary
   - Document the specific audit criteria
   - Describe the scope of the audit

- Detail the approach taken to collect and analyze the data
- Define any necessary adjustments
- Make it official; affix some formal sign-off or "stamp of approval" to the final report

One final note about the auditing process is the issue of who performs the audit. From an organizational perspective, there are two considerations: internal resources may be used to conduct the audit, or an external service may be contracted. Internal resources may use the services of the IT auditing department or the software quality assurance team or may establish an ad-hoc committee for the sole purpose of conducting the audit. External services may include IT or software measurement consultants familiar with the dynamics of an industry baseline initiative.

When performed internally, the individuals used for the audit should possess the proper skill levels, have credibility within the organization, possess good communication skills, and ideally will have previous audit process experience.

Problem Resolution

During any audit activity it is possible that corrective action (adjustments) will be required based upon the final findings of the audit. These adjustments are a natural part of the process and should be anticipated. Given the likelihood of adjustments being required, the following should be considered:

- Procedures for making adjustments must be well defined
- Adjustment may be necessary based upon
  - Scope or mix of work changes
  - Errors in data collection and reporting
  - Errors in the computed results
- If major corrections are required, schedule more frequent (less formal) audits during the following 12-month period
- Establish grace periods that allow adjustments to be made in a timely fashion
- Define dispute resolution and arbitration activities

Summary

Comparing internal IT performance levels to industry average and best in class performance levels can provide an organization with valuable knowledge-based information for improved decision making. Whether it is intending to improve current levels of performance or to determine the strategic and tactical benefit to outsource to a (different) third-party vendor, a performance baseline is a key ingredient in that decision-making process.

Creating an internal baseline of performance is a well-defined process that requires a clear vision of the baseline objectives and expected deliverables. Based on accurately represented quantitative and qualitative data, the results are analyzed and formatted for comparison to industry data points.

Selecting a source of industry data is based on the objectives and expected deliverables. High-level views of performance results are available through research firms such as Gartner and have been very popular with CIOs. An internal baseline, developed as an accurate and detailed view of the performance levels of the various practices within the IT organization, should also be compared to industry data points of the same nature. In other words, access to project-level data and specific, representative comparisons result in a greater understanding of IT performance.

Finally, we discussed the importance of periodic measurement audits. These are too often overlooked as an essential part of an effective IT measurement program.

References

1. www.gartner.com (accessed Sept. 21, 2007).
2. www.compassmc.com/about/index.htm (accessed Sept. 21, 2007).
3. http://www.isbsg.org (accessed Sept. 21, 2007).
4. Chrissis, M.B., Konrad, M., and Shrum, S., 2006, *CMMI for Development, Version 1.2. Second Edition: Guidelines for Process Integration and Product Improvement*, Addison-Wesley, p. 261.

Chapter 12

How Can We Do
IT Better?

In previous chapters, we discussed measuring IT performance and the value of collecting, analyzing, and reporting on data that would allow IT Providers to make comparisons to industry performance data. In this chapter, we explore how we can use some of this same data and performance information for the purposes of improving IT performance. Measurement is going to play a key role. After a brief discussion on best software practices we examine how IT Providers can identify opportunities to maximize their performance and improve productivity and quality. At the end of this chapter, we introduce a technique referred to as "performance modeling." Performance modeling positions IT Providers to maximize the performance of their current practices to gain insights into what is working well and where their weaknesses exist.

The IT Industry Context

What is a best software-development practice and how does an IT Provider ensure that it is performing at optimal levels? The answers to these questions are relatively straightforward. Although there is no industry-defined set of best practices, experience and history provides us with some meaningful insights. Commonly "defined" best practices in the software industry include such things as formal design reviews and code inspections, project management techniques (including accurate time capture and estimating), requirements-gathering methods (including Joint Application Design [JAD] sessions), and agile development. These and numerous other processes and techniques have been labeled as best practices through the collective experience of software developers over the years. They are generally well understood although they are not always practiced consistently or in a disciplined way.

It is an interesting dynamic that within the IT industry there are defined and quantified best practices; however, their use is not widespread and often times even the most well-intending IT Providers will abandon these "best practices" during a project either implicitly or explicitly in the supposed interest of speed. So why don't IT Providers use these best practices more consistently? The reasons are many but too often the business must take some of the blame. Simply, IT Providers are not held accountable for following a standard set of common practices. Schedule and budget pressures may dictate short-cutting some of these practices. There is no doubt that you can get away with this once or twice, but in the long term, avoidance will catch up with you. If these best practices are well known and have demonstrated positive results in the past, why aren't more IT organizations rigorously engaging in these practices?

Best IT practices do not necessarily align with what is considered to be best for the company, at least not in the short term. Best practices take time and they take resources. The utilization of best IT practices can appear to add to the cost of a project and seem to cause a project to take longer to define, design, develop, and deploy. The short-sighted view is to question why anyone would subscribe to a set of practices that cause a project to cost more and possibly take longer to deliver. A huge part of the problem here is the difficulty in overdoing the quality of IT, and particularly software, "just by looking at it." In other engineering disciplines, a body of knowledge has evolved where there are certain ways to do certain things (e.g., build bridges, manufacture engines, etc.). This repeatability is present but not as advanced or accepted in IT and software. The insightful manager would assert that a project that follows best practices is well defined and delivers the right functionality. The project would be relatively free from defects and properly documented. Time reporting would reflect an accurate historical picture of the project. All of this would equate to a longer-term view that would suggest that the resulting implementation would have fewer change requests, would be easier to maintain, and would operate at an efficiency level that was looked upon most favorably by the user. In other words, the total cost of ownership (TCO) for that piece of IT would be less. However, longer to deliver and more expensive to build (in the short run) is not how most IT Providers plan their project activities. Businesses need to be aware of this and consider carefully their needs before driving the behavior of their IT Providers.

With competitive market demands, the focus of IT Providers is to get the software released to the customer as quickly and as cheaply as possible. This becomes obvious when we consider how outsourcing has evolved to meet the demands for lower cost and better performance. Offshore resources are marketed as being less expensive and therefore attractive to companies seeking to reduce expenses or get

more built for the same costs. The de facto best practice models such as CMMI®
are heavily used by the leading offshore providers allowing them to achieve reduced
expenses and high performance. This provides an interesting and powerful option
for businesses. Why pay for in-house process improvements to strive for CMMI
Maturity Level 3 when the same money could be applied to buying more resources
from an offshore IT Provider who already has CMMI Maturity Level 5?

There are, in some cases, other factors to be considered. Not all organizations
are willing or able to send their high-profile applications and software development
work offshore. The geographically distributed working environment, along with
political, cultural, and communication barriers, add to the overall costs and therefore the financial outcomes with some outsourcing deals are not as cost effective as
originally planned. More specifically, government contractors are increasingly being
required to demonstrate compliance with best practices to win or keep government
business. So can an IT Provider seek alternative ways to become more cost effective
and still meet the demands of the business?

Case Studies

We know there are techniques available that allow IT organizations to benchmark
their current levels of performance. We have also learned that they can analyze
the critical data points and ascertain what current practices are contributing to
high or low yields of productivity. To look at this dynamic in greater depth we will
examine three client case studies that used various benchmarking techniques to
assess their current capabilities and identify improvements in their development
practices which are projected to yield greater return on their IT investment. They
have used these techniques to learn how they can do IT better.

In each of our three client case studies, the manager championing the initiative identified the needs of the organization. Our involvement with these clients
began with a request to help the organization select the appropriate measures and
to create a measurement model that would result in the quantification of process
performance levels. Furthermore, we were called upon to utilize a measurement
model that would provide the ability to compare internal performance measures
to industry benchmark levels of performance. Armed with this information, we
could then analyze the data and build performance models that would allow us
to identify current practices that were producing high-quality software effectively
and efficiently.

These case studies demonstrate how three different organizations used a combination of quantitative measures and qualitative values to identify their best practices.
Based on the knowledge gained, the organizations used the results to improve their
development practices and to advance their process improvement programs.

In each case, the desire to identify best practices was driven by senior-level
management. Management wanted results that would have a direct impact on

stated business goals and objectives. A summary view of their business goals included the following:

- Reduce project costs (typically labor)
- Improve time-to-market delivery of software
- Minimize defects delivered
- Improve performance relative to industry benchmark data

In many companies, the IT strategy to achieve these goals centers around quick-fix approaches. Cost reduction frequently tops the list and is usually the driving force behind the decision to outsource software development to an offshore provider who can provide cheaper labor. Time to market is often managed by delivering fewer features to the end user, thus reducing the development work load. However, the end result is often a dissatisfied customer. And all too often, the extra effort necessary to minimize defects is compromised. We know too well that quick-fix remedies are not usually effective. However, the alternative to achieving sustained and measurable improvement can be a hard pill to swallow. To achieve the findings and the results noted in the cases that follow, senior management had a well-defined vision of what they wanted to accomplish, and they had the ability to marshal the resources necessary to realize the desired results.

The ability to set management expectations properly and to gain their support was enhanced by the introduction of a measurement model that objectively and quantitatively generated meaningful results.

Each of the case studies used a performance baseline approach as discussed in previous chapters. The approach was tailored to meet the specific needs of each organization. The presentation of the results for each of the case studies varies due to the nature of each unique engagement and how the client wanted the information displayed. Basic measures, applied through a practical baseline model, provided senior management with the information they needed to make more informed decisions.

Case Study 1 – Large Financial Institution

Objective: Identify the common characteristics of high-performing projects.

Scope: Conduct an organization-wide baseline study.

Collection and analysis: Data (quantitative and qualitative) were collected on 65 completed projects. Productivity rates were computed and expressed in terms of function points per staff month. In addition, three other base measures were calculated — duration, resource utilization, and cost. The results were divided into two categories: high-performing projects and low-performing projects. Finally, an average was computed for each category.

Table 12.1   Case Study 1: Average Values

Client Performance Measures	High Performers	Low Performers
Average project size in function points (FPs)	148	113
Average duration (in calendar months)	5.0	7.0
Average rate of delivery in FPs/person month (PM)	22	9
Average number of resources	2.4	1.8

Table 12.1 summarizes the average values for each of the two groupings. The quantitative data demonstrated that high-performing projects produced (on average) more functionality (148 function points compared to 113 function points) in a shorter time frame (5 months versus 7 months) with a modest increase in staffing.

The qualitative data (attributes about each project) collected and profiles of performance developed identified characteristics consistently present in the higher-performing projects but limited or absent from the lower-performing projects. The resulting set of attributes was then considered to be the leading factors that contributed to higher-performing projects.

Findings: The following listing indicates the attributes and their frequency of occurrence (%) in the high- and low-performing projects. For example, in the higher-performing projects there was full agreement on the project deliverables 100 percent of the time as compared to only 33 percent of the time with the lower-performing projects.

	%	
	High	Low
Full agreement on project deliverables, methodologies, and schedules	100	33
Development staff very experienced with the design methods used	100	33
No staff turnover during the project	100	50
Project management experience high	100	50
Formal processes used to gather requirements	100	67
Requirements clearly stated and stable	100	67
Fully automated source code management	100	67
Projects were not impacted by legal or statutory restrictions	67	33
Structured data analysis performed	67	33
Highly experienced analysts and designers	67	33
Significant reuse of code	67	33

Table 12.2 Case Study 2: Client Summary

Measures	Client	Industry Average	Industry Best Practices
Function point size	567	500–750	500–750
Productivity (FP/PM)	6.9	7.3	22.7
Duration (months)	12	14	10
Defects/FP	.24	.12	.02

Case Study 2 – Mid-Size Insurance Company

Objective: Identify best practices opportunities and perform a benchmark comparison to industry averages and best practices.

Scope: Conduct a baseline study using 25 selected projects.

Collection and analysis: Measurement baseline data was collected and analyzed to produce performance indicators similar to those in the first case study. After determining the current level of performance, a comparison to industry average and industry best practices benchmarks was conducted. A summary of the results is shown in Table 12.2.

About the measures

> Function point size represents the average function point size of the delivered product. Some organizations use this as a measure of value (functionality) being delivered to the end user.
>
> Duration represents the overall calendar duration of the project from requirements through to customer acceptance.
>
> Defect density is a function of defects per function points. A lower number represents fewer defects per function point in the delivered product.
>
> Industry data (average and best practices) was obtained from David Consulting Group's database of productivity performance measurements for over 7000 software development projects (from 2001 to 2003).
>
> We examined these data points and analyzed the underlying profile data. Within this sampling of projects, the client's productivity rate was close to the industry average (6.9 versus 7.3); however, plenty of opportunity for improvement still existed as evidenced by the best practices benchmark. The client was actually delivering products (on average) in a shorter time frame than industry average, and again there was opportunity to improve as the organization moved toward best practices thresholds. Finally, the level of quality (defect density) was significantly below industry data points.

Findings: By analyzing this data, we observed an organization that was getting its software product out the door quickly by increasing staffing levels and short-cutting quality practices. This was further substantiated by evaluating the project attributes. By contrasting attributes on the selected set of projects that were present a majority of the time (common occurrences) with those attributes that were limited or absent altogether (infrequent or absent) we could assess what attributes had the greatest influence on performance.

Common occurrences	Infrequent or absent
Historical-based estimating	Formal reviews and inspections
Experienced project managers	Defect tracking
Highly skilled engineers	Effective requirements gathering
Good user involvement	Formal test plans
Formal methodologies	
Rigorous testing	
Well-defined training curriculum	
Effective SDLC	

Case Study 3 – Large Service Organization

Objective: Identify the impact of moving to CMMI Level 3.

Scope: Perform baseline measures on a sample set of representative projects.

Collection and analysis: This case study involved an organization that wanted to evaluate the impact on performance of a currently planned process improvement initiative. The organization was interested in obtaining a higher level of maturity through the successful attainment of the SEI's CMMI Level 3 rating. They equated the process areas associated with the Level 3 CMMI model to best practices. First the organization wanted to determine its current baseline of performance and establish a composite profile of contributing attributes. Next, it would use industry performance data to determine the impact of advancing to a Level 3 maturity.

Project data was collected and analyzed. Averages for size (function points), productivity (function points per effort month), duration (calendar months), and cost (labor) were computed. Using a composite profile, a mapping of the current project attributes for the organization was developed. In parallel, another model was developed for projects of a similar size with a mapping of attributes that matched a CMMI Level 3 organization. A summary of the results is shown in Table 12.3.

Findings: The projected impact of CMMI Level 3 practices for this organization was significant. For the same size project, productivity (function point/effort month) was projected to increase by 132 percent, time to market reduced by 50 percent, cost reduction by 40 percent, and defect density reduced by 75 percent. This modeling technique helped this organization to evaluate the potential benefits of CMMI process improvement before making the investment.

Table 12.3 Case Study 3: Findings

	Baseline Productivity	CMM Productivity Improvements	Impact (%)
Average project size	133	133	
Average FP/EM	10.7	24.8	+132
Average time to market (months)	6.9	3.5	−50
Average cost/FP	$934.58	$567.29	−40
Projected defect density	0.0301	0.0075	−75

The potential impact may appear to be dramatic, but that is a matter of perspective. Certainly, this significant gain in productivity and reduction in defects would exceed most expectations. When baseline productivity is dramatically below industry averages, based on the nature of the process profile, clearly large gains can and should be expected.

Performance Modeling

As noted in the third case study, the practice of performance modeling can be very useful in projecting or forecasting future outcomes based on current history and industry data.

Figure 12.1 shows the added modeling components (opportunities for improvement and best practices) in a standard baseline measurement model. The IT organization collects the necessary quantitative and qualitative data to determine its measured performance and to develop its capability profiles. These two data points are used to determine the organization's performance baseline. Once established, parametric

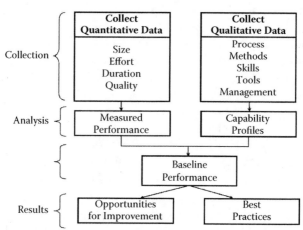

Figure 12.1 Performance modeling.

models can be developed which utilize historical data points for purposes of analyzing the impact of selected process improvements (opportunities for improvement). The results provide a knowledge base for improved decision making by identifying areas of high impact (e.g., productivity and quality, and best practices).

As noted previously, the IT industry suffers from a lack of standardization and consistency with respect to how it defines its operating attributes and measures. We do not have a common definition for a defect. We don't have a defined guideline for when a project has officially begun and when it has completed. If we are attempting to capture cost information for a project, we are not at all consistent with the reporting of labor hours. The list goes on. The simple truth of the matter is that we don't have a standard set of measures like other, more mature industries. Can you imagine what the state of the medical profession would be if we didn't have medical benchmarks for normal ranges for cholesterol, heart rate, blood pressure, etc.? This lack of standardization often impacts the effectiveness of performance measurement efforts based upon perceived inconsistencies in the data analysis. It is of paramount importance that IT Providers perform their measurement activities in a consistent and transparent fashion.

Summary

We explored three case studies that exhibit a variety of ways in which measurement data may be used to learn more about:

- An organization's level of performance
- Key factors that contribute to high or low yields of productivity
- The level of performance as compared to industry data points
- The potential impact of strategic initiatives through the use of performance modeling

Utilization of a measurement model that includes both a quantitative perspective and a qualitative perspective is most important. It is from this vantage point that an organization can assess both the measured performance profiles along with an understanding of the process profile elements that contributed to the results. Process profiles have the added advantage of recommending a direction for future improvement strategies.

In reviewing the experiences and results from these three client case studies, readers should not assume that similar outcomes will be achieved in their organizations. The prudent action is to take your own measures and create your own organizational performance baseline. Utilizing industry-accepted measures, such as function points, will allow you to perform the necessary comparative analysis. The investment in a baseline study is relatively insignificant in comparison to the value of the information gained. Of course, the return on that investment can be fully realized only with the proper execution of improved IT practices.

HOW SHOULD
WE CHANGE?

Chapter 13

How Can We Manage IT Changes?

The Need for Change Management

IT executives today are faced with many challenges. Those challenges include global competition, economic constraints, and increased customer demands for service and quality. These challenges require constant attention and action on the part of the organization. IT executives are called upon to implement new technologies, reduce costs, implement process improvement initiatives, and promote an atmosphere of creativity and innovation. More often than not, organizational and operational change is part of the ongoing strategy to remain competitive. It calls for a dynamic culture that is constantly evolving to stay successful and competitive.

Even though change has been relatively constant within the IT world, many IT Providers do not have a long-standing history of change management on which to rely. Systematically managing change is something that has been easily avoided in the past and so many senior executives are unfamiliar with the change management challenges they face. For those IT managers with experience of change, the strategic and technical side of change management will most likely be more comfortable than the more intimate human dimension. The alignment of a company's people, culture, behaviors, and values is critical to the long-term and sustained success of managing change effectively.

In this chapter, we will focus on how IT Providers can more effectively accommodate change and manage their changing environment. Getting people to change work habits and to adopt and adapt to new business models presents many challenges. We will define and explore some of the basic elements of change management. Examples will be presented along with some important keys to success. We will discuss how to deal with resistance and we will explore the benefits of having a change agent or a coach.

Types of Change

Organizations do not typically change for the sake of change, nor should they. Change is usually part of a strategy to achieve some stated business goal. It is often the result of an outside force demanding that the organization change to meet shifting market demands, introduce a new line of product or services, or make adjustments with dramatic cuts in resources or funding levels. This often involves organizationwide changes where the company finds itself in a state of transition moving to a new business model. However, not all change is organizationwide.

In the IT environment, management and personnel must conform to the external pressures that accompany the changing business climate. Change also occurs frequently within IT Providers without organizationwide change. Indeed, IT changes can drive organizational change. For example, transitioning to a new IT architecture can provoke organizationwide changes in business processes.

Two sources of change challenge and impact IT Providers:

- **Internal** changes may be the result of program changes such as CMMI® or resource shifts to meet the growing demands of competitive pricing such as outsourcing. These changes may be necessary to stay current with the state of the art in software development such as moving to a more agile approach to developing software. These types of changes are largely managed from within IT in a well-planned and orderly manner. However, they can have an impact on other parts of the organization and therefore the impact of that change needs to be managed beyond IT.
- **External** changes come from outside of IT and may even come from outside the organization. The IT Providers have little control over these types of changes. Factors such as new competitors or products, government regulations, global shifts in the economy, or major technology advancements may dictate that a company responds quickly to remain competitive.

Understanding the distinction between these two sources of change is important in a number of ways. The changes will impact the way you establish and manage expectations. The controls you establish for managing change will depend upon how much influence you have over the change. And the measurable outcomes will vary depending upon the nature of the change. Regardless of the source, all change needs to be managed.

Change management is comprised of processes, tools, and techniques focused on successfully introducing change. Successful change can be managed and measured and therefore should not be thought of as simply resulting in a subjective set of outcomes. Managing change can be measured in the satisfaction of customers, speed of delivery of a particular action or service, improved time to market, or increases in productivity. It should be considered a proactive process with a designed program for change, a plan of execution, and predictable outcomes that, when met, can ensure that change was successful.

Change management provides a systematic approach to dealing with change. It includes both an organizational perspective and an individual perspective. The dynamics can be viewed from different vantage points including adapting to, controlling, and effecting change. A successful approach for dealing with change is to be aware of, and to manage, all three perspectives. For IT Providers, change management involves defining and implementing procedures and technologies to deal with changes in the technical or business environment and to realize improvements or changes that impact productivity and quality.

Seven Principles of Managing Change

Changes within IT are often the result of process improvement initiatives such as CMMI, ITIL®, Six Sigma, or COBIT®. These programs represent a significant investment and will most likely impact the entire organization. With change, there is a certain amount of risk. The benefits of a sustained IT process improvement program are well documented but not all improvement programs or change initiatives succeed.

Interestingly enough, the causes of failure are surprisingly consistent among the various cases we have observed. Therefore, it is reasonable to suggest that the causes of failure are definable and the knowledge gained can be used to predict potential risks of failure, or perhaps more importantly, help to avoid future failures. By increasing the overall level of organizational awareness with regard to the pitfalls one may encounter, an organization can assess its current culture and evaluate potential for success or failure. Top-performing organizations are successful at initiating and managing change. They are not afraid to execute bold initiatives nor fearful of making mistakes. They have learned that the road to success is characterized by a few failures along the way.

No single approach fits every company but a set of guidelines and techniques can be used in a variety of situations. The following seven guiding principles provide a framework that executives, change agents, and coaches can use to manage change more effectively.

Principle 1: Two Levels of Management Support

Given the choice to change, people will more often choose the "business as usual" model. The CIO and senior staff must be quick to embrace the "new way" and take on the responsibility of leading and motivating the rest of the department or organization. It is common knowledge that if senior management is not engaged, then the intended change is unlikely to have a long shelf life. The CIO and senior staff must present a united front in their positioning and support of change. For senior managers in IT and the business, the key point is to recognize that being engaged means more than simply providing the resources necessary to execute the change initiative. Being engaged means being aware of what the resulting improvements will yield relative to the benefits to the organization and letting everyone know that you care about these results. Expectations need to be aligned properly with all aspects of the program. You need to model the change; "walk the talk."

Interestingly enough, as important as upper management's buy-in is, it is easy to underestimate the critical role that the middle tier of management plays in any process or organizational change initiative. Typically, middle management is assigned the responsibility of executing the program initiatives and action items. To the extent that these people become the "face" of the program, it is essential that they are highly regarded and respected throughout the organization, and also model the requisite changes.

Organizational transformation introduced by change will naturally affect different layers within the organization in different ways. Beyond the senior-management level, leaders must be identified and take responsibility for introducing, promoting, and managing change. These change leaders must assume a position of ownership to make the planned changes a reality.

Principle 2: Proper Funding

Because change is constant, process improvement is also a constant. This is similar to ongoing maintenance of technical environments. Process improvement initiatives need to have the proper resources available to be successful. Obviously the budget needs to support the current operating plan for the improvement program. However, it must be understood that this is not a one-time budgeting event. Process improvement takes time and needs sustained funding over a period of years. Many organizations make the mistake of not properly setting expectations with regard to what will be required to sustain the initiative. Usually in the second or third year of the program the budget comes under greater scrutiny and funding may be cut back so severely as to significantly impact the program and its chances for success.

The best way to prevent this dynamic from occurring is to take a proactive position by creating a multi-year budget right from the start. It is best to determine what the budgetary needs will be over an extended period of time and to then make a persuasive case for the total amount to be budgeted. If the organization isn't willing to accept this approach, then it may not have the appetite for process improvement over the long haul.

In addition, plan for a contingency fund. For example, process improvement is a big project, and big projects have a way of incurring expenses that weren't initially planned for. Be prepared.

Principle 3: The Business Case

It is natural for people to question proposed changes, why change is needed, what impact it will have on the company, and most importantly what impact it will have on each individual. Therefore, a formal case needs to be made which includes a vision statement, a realistic cost–benefit analysis, and an implementation strategy that clearly defines roles and responsibilities. All of this must be done in the light of reality. The possibility exists that certain barriers will be self-evident and that the planned change will fail without some additional intervention. For example, moving to a more agile development environment may necessitate the hiring of experts, general education among the user community, and a restructuring of the IT departments. A sound business case needs to be supported by a framework that will foster its success.

Writing the business case provides an opportunity to consider and define the risks. Effectively managing change requires a constant assessment of the risks and potential course corrections. A well-designed risk management strategy will prove to be invaluable as changes are introduced into the organization.

Principle 4: Setting and Managing Expectations

Properly setting expectations is one of the single most important factors having the greatest impact on the success of a process improvement initiative. Setting expectations covers the usual categories of estimating cost, determining how long the effort will take, and articulating what the benefits will be. Because this is an initiative that is quite possibly going to affect many parts of the organization, it is important to address the costs and benefits and the impact to each of the business units likely to be impacted by the improvement program. Organizational education and awareness are key. Frequent "all hands" sessions as well as small group sessions directed at informing people about the progress and the anticipated benefits of the program are essential.

A major factor in managing expectations is to understand the cultural environment properly. Change programs have a tendency to take on a life of their own. An organization must consider the impact the change will have on the culture as well as the influence the culture will have on the program. There are organizational readiness assessment vehicles that can be applied to identify the company's values, behaviors, leadership influence, and general perceptions that must be taken into account for successful change to occur.

Principle 5: It's About the People

Change affects people. Depending on the resources available, a well-planned change initiative may require people to shift their priorities. Even more importantly it may require them to change their relationships and develop new ones! Individuals may be assigned tasks that now take them away from some of the more challenging and interesting business plan projects. Similarly, as priorities shift, the cooperation and involvement of the business will be essential. There is going to be resistance and being prepared to manage that resistance is key.

New positions may be created and individuals filling those new positions will have to climb the learning curve of their new job responsibilities along with managing change. As an approach to managing change is designed and deployed, the organizational leaders and managers must engage their assigned resources in the change activities and continuously assess the ability and the progress of the people to accept and become comfortable with the change.

It is important to involve everyone in the process of change — the champions and the skeptics. Allow both to contribute to the redesigning of procedures. By making everyone a part of the change, they will better understand and more naturally accept those changes. There will be less effort required in the future on "selling" them on the new solutions.

Principle 6: Communicate, Communicate, Communicate

Effective communication — up, down, and sideways — is essential for any strategic program to be successful. CIOs and the senior leadership team all too often assume that others in the department understand the reasons for change and share their perspective. Effective communication begins with the creation of a detailed communication plan. It is important that communication includes all levels of the organization. Depending upon the audience, different operating units are going to have different interests in the progress and outcomes of the program. Make sure they are addressed.

Part of the communications plan needs to address how the process improvement programs will impact individuals as well as the overall impact on the organization and the business. In the communications plan, consideration should be given to providing a forum whereby people can express their views and concerns, and ask questions. Ideally, there should be a mechanism for submitting non-attributable or anonymous feedback. Otherwise, some people will suppress valid criticisms that could improve things, perhaps for fear of being wrong or of not conforming.

Principle 7: Measurement Is Key

The ability to measure and monitor progress quantitatively throughout the program will improve your ability to manage the initiative as well as to set and manage expectations properly. The key question here is, what should be measured? Assuming that the organization is seeking performance improvement in the three main areas of lower cost, shorter delivery time frames, and increased quality, the key is to demonstrate progress in those areas in a way that is meaningful to the business. The best place to start is by creating a baseline of current levels of performance. This will serve as your basis for comparison.

Another primary consideration is to make sure that everyone understands that the change initiative will not yield benefits on day one. It is more likely that it will be months before the first measurable progress is realized, so it is virtually important to set those expectations properly. Treat change as a project, just like any other project!

While waiting for tangible benefits to be realized, there is still an opportunity to measure aspects of the process improvement program even in its early stages. Making progress relative to the completion of new procedures, training of staff personnel, and monitoring compliance to new development practices are all signs of progress leading toward planned improvements.

Managing Resistance

Predictably, when change is introduced, resistance to change will be present. It is natural. People are concerned and fearful of the unknown and often tend to assume the worst. People feel comfortable with what they know and with the habits that they have formed over a period of time. Typically, people somehow convince themselves even in a chaotic situation that things are fine, that there is no need for change, or that they are too busy for change. Others may be cynical or even hostile about the suggested changes (e.g., why are we adding new hires to the resource pool when at the same time we are cutting costs to remain competitive?).

Resistance to change is predictable but what form it takes and who it comes from can be less so. Leaders and managers need to understand and address the resistance or it will most likely undermine the chances of success. Response to resistance should not be one of over-reacting. Management should persevere, listen to complaints and concerns patiently, and consider these issues as additional opportunities for growth and maturity. Continued management support is needed and must be sincere. That said, management is paid to lead and too much accommodation of the concerns of a few can kill progress toward the benefits for many. This is a difficult but essential balancing act for managers.

The reasons for resisting change are well documented. Accepting change means accepting the risk (perceived or real) associated with the proposed change. When making the case for change, clarify what the risks are and how they will be managed. Additionally, when change is introduced and there are no models for the new situation or activity, engaging a change agent can be most useful. Getting some person or group of persons involved in the change helps others to "view" the change in a more realistic and positive light. Others will see what the change represents and realize that they possess the skills to participate in making the change a reality.

There never seems to be a good time for change. People are overworked and overwhelmed as it is. The idea of change only adds to the emotional burden of the work force. It is common for people involved in change to feel tired, even lethargic. If productivity was already decreasing, there seems to be a self-fulfilling prophecy that the change is bad, that it will slow down production. This is mostly an emotional response. To gain people's commitment they need to become involved. Also, "before" and "after" measurements are very powerful here to remind people that things were not as great and rosy as they seem to remember.

To effectively manage resistance, get people involved in the process. Facilitating involvement and working together will bring greater success and quicker acceptance of the changes at hand. You can create an advisory group of respected peers who will provide advice on implementation decisions. A suitable mix of champions and skeptics works well. Create surveys or blogs which allow employees who are adopting the new changes to voice their opinions and experiences. Another option is to gather a select group of employees together to create a focus group where ideas and change status information can be openly discussed and experiences can be shared. Finally, encourage managers to hold feedback sessions so people can express their concerns and help with problem solving.

Managers must act on feedback. This includes admitting mistakes. We recommend instigating a process change request system as early as possible. This has the twin benefits of improving the processes and letting people know that they can and do contribute to making things better.

Educating people who are not fully on board will help them to understand the need for the change as well as providing them with the context of their role in making the change a reality. The more involved people become, the more they will understand and accept the change. If new skills are required, then it is critical that the involved resources be properly trained in a timely manner.

Be honest when introducing the reasons for the change. Ordinarily changes are introduced for the betterment of the company. Ultimately, this should be positive for all employees or, rather, all remaining employees. Show people what's in it for them, and whether it is of immediate impact or something that will prove to be beneficial over the long haul. People will care about the risk of losing their jobs. A powerful response to this is that by improving their understanding of best practices, and their ability to implement them, they are improving their value in the job market, internally and externally.

For situations where resistance needs to be dealt with on an individual basis, or within a functional group such as the project-management level, then setting up change agents or coaches may be the best strategy.

Using a Change Agent or a Coach

Utilizing a change agent or a coach is a positive step toward ensuring that the changes being introduced into the organization will have a higher likelihood of success. Any time change is being introduced into an organization, there are change agents (intentional or not) at work.

A change agent is a person who has the power, the belief, and the personal skills to make change a reality and keep people actively involved in the change process. Done effectively, a change agent is able to adapt and to assimilate the issues, while working to manage resistance. The change agent must actively build consensus and manage the impact of change within the organization.

Change agents must master a number of techniques and tools and have the personal skills necessary to manage the transitioning organizational change. They need to be sensitive to the political climate while not taking sides. They must fully understand the current business model and be able to know precisely how and where the changes being introduced will impact existing business processes and assigned resources. They must be able to defend their position without sounding defensive. They must be well respected by senior managers throughout the company. Finally, they need to have the ability to provide oversight to the action teams that are involved in the day-to-day implementation of desired changes.

Coaching is another way in which change can be successfully introduced into an organization. The general principles of coaching include the creation of an ongoing partnership designed to help executives and leaders produce the desired results. Coaching will improve an individual's or team's ability to focus on what is important and be able to communicate more effectively. A coach motivates individuals and groups to set goals and take action toward reaching them. Most importantly, a coach creates a high level of personal accountability.

There are basically two types of coaching: individual and team. Individual coaching typically involves executive- and managerial-level personnel. Executive and senior leadership coaching helps executives become more adept at dealing with and eliciting best performance from their employees. The coaching experience helps to develop a higher level of emotional intelligence. Emotional intelligence involves becoming more emotionally literate and taking responsibility for one's feelings. This creates a general respect and validation of others feelings. Executive coaching also develops a higher level of social intelligence, including social awareness and empathy for others. It creates a greater social recognition of how the world (and the organization) works.

Team coaching is an economical way to have a large impact in an organization. It helps align teams around their common purpose by applying the "power of positive peer pressure." It gets team members out of their individual silos and creates greater cohesion and motivation. It can also generate a climate that promotes a higher level of personal accountability for each team member's actions so they can make and meet important commitments more easily. Perhaps most importantly, it helps team members communicate more effectively.

Summary

In this chapter we learned how to manage change. Change can be the result of external factors that are out of our control but need our response or they can be the result of internal initiatives that necessitate organizational change. Effectively managing change is critical to successful outcomes. The seven principles discussed in this chapter provide insight regarding how to manage change. And with all change comes resistance. Resistance is predictable and manageable. A good change agent or coach can be instrumental in supporting an organization and helping it to manage through the change.

Further Readings

Argyris, C. and Schon, D., 1995, *Organizational Learning II: Theory, Method and Practice*, FT Press.

Harvard Business School Press, 2003, *Managing Change and Transition*, Harvard Business School Press.

Hiatt, J., 2006, *ADKAR: A Model for Change in Business, Government and the Community*, Learning Center Publications.

Kotter, J., 1996, *Leading Change*, Harvard Business School Press.

Kotter, J. and Cohen, D.S., 2002, *The Heart of Change: Real-Life Stories of How People Change Their Organizations*, Harvard Business School Press.

Senge, P., Scharmer, C.O., Jaworski, J., and Flowers, B.S., 2004, *Presence: Human Purpose and the Field of the Future*, Society for Organizational Learning.

Watzlawick, P., 1974, *Change: Principles of Problem Formation and Problem Resolution*, W.W. Norton & Company.

Worren, N.A.M, Ruddle, K., and Moore, K., 1999, From organizational development to change management: The emergence of a new profession, *The Journal of Applied Behavioral Science*.

Chapter 14

How Should IT Manage Risk?

Risk is best defined by *Webster's Dictionary* as "exposure to the chance of injury or loss; jeopardy." Although there can be the potential for an upside or an opportunity, risk is most commonly held in business as the potential for unintended, negative events or consequences. The business of wager-driven gaming (gambling) is driven by the optimism of the player and the odds of the game being played. The potential for risk to the player is the amount being wagered. The potential for risk to the casino is represented by the odds such as 2:1 for blackjack or 35:1 for roulette. If only all business decisions came with stated odds.

In the last decade, IT Providers have become more responsible for managing and reporting on corporate risk. Many factors have influenced this shift:

■ The importance of customer data and consumer privacy; its storage and use is governed by IT Providers' execution of business directives.
■ The increase in automation of many business functions position IT Providers as the guardians of critical assets.
■ New legislation has required many companies to invest in information systems to monitor compliance.
■ Internet transactions and worldwide operations present new threats to systems daily.

Routinely made business decisions often do not require statistical evaluation and risk planning. However, when operating in new or unique situations, it is wise to consult an existing risk assessment to guide decision making. These plans of consolidated information provide the dimensioning necessary to quickly evaluate the potential exposure. These assessments in essence represent the organization's tolerance for pain. What pain might be endured to achieve the potential for benefit? What vulnerability will be exposed to a threat? Is it worth moving forward? If so, what can be done to mitigate or transfer the risk if realized?

The goal of this chapter is to review the categories of risk to form the lens for evaluating the different types of risk. Assessment tools and processes are provided as points of reference for assessing the impact and likelihood of triggering events. The authors do not endorse one assessment technique over another; the important elements are executing a risk assessment and then creating a plan. The influencing factors and legislation introduced in the last ten years have changed the way companies operate and treat risk. In this chapter, we will review the more influential ones, the events that led to their development, and the changes they have instantiated.

Common terms tightly related to risk include security and disaster recovery. The use of the term "risk" indicates a potential future event. "Security" (both physical and systems) needs to be implemented to mitigate certain risks. Security standards are unique to each organization based on elements like governing legislation, physical location, and threat level. Use of the term "security" will always refer to the standards being deployed. Disaster recovery planning is specific planning for the recovery of systems following a large disruption in normal operations. This unique planning usually covers catastrophic events, like a natural disaster, loss of a specific site location, or major system outage. Disaster recovery focuses on regaining access to systems for critical business processes following a catastrophic event.

Why Perform Risk Planning?

"CYA" … cover your assets! The goal of any risk plan is to protect assets, whether it's hardware, software, or access to company data (primarily employee and customer data). High-profile breaches in security have resulted in the loss of large amounts of data residing on stolen laptops and hard drives. Included in these ranks are some of the largest organizations like JPMorgan Chase Retirement Services, MasterCard International, and even the Internal Revenue Service. Not just data losses but other breaches, like the "pretexting" scandal by a now-former member of the board of directors of HP, have changed the landscape of business today. In this information age, identity theft is a major concern for the public. Relationships with companies are based on trust; once trust is broken, it is most difficult for a company to regain its reputation.

A recent case of data theft involved retail stores T.J. Maxx, Marshalls, and Home Goods, owned by The TJX Companies. In December 2006, they found thousands of transactions containing customer credit card data had been accessed by an unauthorized intruder. Upon further investigation, they found the security breach extended as far back as January 2003, according to the press release from

TJX. Although the company's response was swift, once the breach was identified and they openly disclosed all information as they knew it, many people were critical of the chain of events leading up to the incident. Why did detection take so long? Why weren't controls in place to prevent such an attack? Why wasn't the data encrypted?

The incident has been a huge distraction for the company, consuming substantial amounts of time and resources. TJX announced a new CEO following the events in January 2007 and has taken measures to strengthen the security of its internal systems. This, as well as external initiatives including consumer education and hotlines available in three countries to allay the concerns of shaken consumers whose data was compromised. As of July 2007, a link from the Website to a letter from the CEO is still active, extending apologies for any inconvenience to customers and outlining the steps being taken to enhance security further.

Though all impacts are not known, the TJX stock price has been relatively flat since the breach occurred. In the six months prior to the incident, the stock was on a steady climb, increasing about 20 percent from July to November 2006. Can your organization afford the time and effort to address an event like this one? Does senior management take an active role in reviewing existing risk plans and assessments?

This case represents several key lessons about the importance of risk planning, security controls, risk reviews, and management. In most cases, the execution of risk assessments, risk planning, and security measures have meant avoiding a major risk event.

How to Begin Risk Planning

A risk plan begins with a risk assessment. A risk assessment is a detailed evaluation of many dimensions to assess the impact to the organization if an event were to occur. It determines the level of protection against unavailability, unauthorized access, or other breaches in security.

Types or commonly used categories for evaluating risk include the following:

- Financial risk represents the potential for monetary loss. In 2007, Microsoft reserved over $1 billion dollars to cover the anticipated costs of correcting a common hardware failure in the Xbox 360 video game console.
- Legal risk represents the potential for litigation, law suits, arbitration, etc. It is almost impossible to purchase a cup of coffee without the warning "Caution: Contents Very Hot" printed on the cup. In 1994 a jury awarded $2.9 million to an 81-year-old woman scalded by McDonald's coffee.[1] The risk was the decision to litigate rather than settle.
- Reputation risk is the risk to the image of the organization or company. This is known as consumer confidence in a brand or company and influences the perceived quality of the goods or services being offered. According to the

Associated Press report of April 12, 2005, LexisNexis, a large data broker, found a breach in security compromising the information of 310,000 people. Information accessed included names, addresses, Social Security numbers, and driver license numbers.

■ Personnel risk is the potential for loss of key personnel. Critical knowledge often resides undocumented with key personnel. Consideration of the risk drives succession planning, training, and mitigation plans.

■ Physical or environmental risk involves the ability to secure areas where critical information, software, or hardware reside. These risks may include natural disasters like planning for tornados, floods, earthquakes, hurricanes, etc. They also include physical proximity to terrorist activity, unstable governments/civil unrest, pandemics such as the avian flu, or the physical separation of employees working with secure data.

Performing a risk assessment is the first step to compiling the information necessary to evaluate the importance to the business and the likelihood of the risk occurring. An assessment entails a series of questions used to dimension the business operation and the information, software, hardware, and systems critical to the operation (see Table 14.1).

Individual departments must participate in the risk assessment process and own the risk management process. Most organizations assign some centralized ownership for aggregated risk reporting and oversight; however, those with the most effective risk management operate as though it is a shared responsibility (e.g., Toyota, Johnson & Johnson). The expertise necessary to identify and manage risk resides with the people performing the day-to-day work. Only they can effectively determine all critical assets necessary to performing the work. The prioritization of those assets to address backup and recovery standards requires the knowledge of those who use the systems or data and the managers who govern the process.

Risk assessments seek to identify the functions or contributions of the department to the company.

What is the importance of the functions performed?
What assets, information, hardware, software, applications, or data are critical to the performance of the key functions?
What people or functions are critical to the performance?
What vulnerabilities exist?
What threats could expose or exploit these vulnerabilities?

A process or system weakness is called a "vulnerability." The definition of "vulnerable" according to *Webster's Dictionary* is

1. Susceptible to physical injury
2. Susceptible to attack

Table 14.1   Sample Risk Assessment

Company
Risk Assessment
Date

Department

1. State the mission of the department	
2. What are the primary functions performed to implement the mission?	
3. What assets, information, software, or hardware are critical to the performance of those key functions?	

1. For each risk category, identify potential dangers to information and system (threats).
2. Identify the process or system weakness (vulnerability) that could be exploited (this generates the threat/vulnerability pair).
3. Identify existing controls to prevent the risk.
4. Determine the likelihood of occurrence for a threat exploiting a related vulnerability given the existing controls.
5. Determine the severity of impact on the business by an exploited vulnerability.
6. Determine the risk level for a threat/vulnerability pair given the existing controls.

Category: Financial
(continue with each category for evaluation, legal, reputation, personnel, physical, or environmental)

#	Threat Name	Weakness or Vulnerability	Risk Description	Existing Controls	Potential Impact	Likelihood of Occurrence

Table 14.2   Vulnerability/Threat Pairs

Vulnerability	Threat Source and Action
Identified flaws in the security design of the system	Unauthorized users obtain access to sensitive data
Terminated employees' system access is not revoked in a timely manner	Terminated employees access proprietary data from the company's network or launch an attack
Data center does not enforce a policy of covered beverages	Careless employee spills coffee on a server
Internet application does not process customers' opt-out of solicitation requests	Unhappy customers receive unwanted solicitations, causing a public backlash and non-compliance with the Gramm–Leach–Bliley Act

According to the National Institute of Standards and Technology, in the system environment, vulnerability is a flaw or weakness in the system security procedures, design, implementation, or internal controls that could be exercised accidentally or intentionally and result in a security breach or a violation of the systems security policy.

The danger identified during the assessment is known as the "threat." Together with the vulnerability, these create vulnerability/threat pairs. The goal of the exercise is to identify the threats that could expose or exploit the system, process, or security vulnerabilities.

Examples of common vulnerability/threat pairs are shown in Table 14.2. Once a risk assessment has been completed, the prioritization of the risks can be addressed. The information from the assessment forms the initial requirements for security and disaster recovery planning.

Referring to Table 14.1, risks are considered for their likelihood of occurrence and potential impact. Data is used to graph the risks as shown in Figure 14.1. Risks that have a high impact and high probability of occurring appear in the upper right-hand side of the graph. These should be addressed with individual risk plans to mitigate or plan for the risk if it is likely to occur.

A risk mitigation plan can be as basic as assigning an owner and a few sentences of steps to be taken if the risk occurs. The risk mitigation plan can also take the form of an entire detailed plan with a dedicated team to create extensive alternate plans if the event occurs. An example of this is a disaster recovery plan.

The disaster recovery plan is a risk mitigation plan. It plans for the series of detailed tactical steps that will be executed if a pandemic or catastrophic event occurs. By compiling risk assessments for the departments in the organization, the mission-critical processes have been identified. This forms the basis for disaster recovery planning. Once created, disaster recovery plans must be considered living documents that are reviewed, updated, and possibly tested once a year.

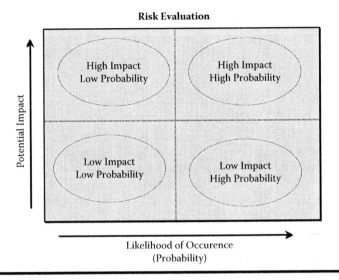

Figure 14.1   Risk evaluation.

How Does Security Relate to Risk Planning?

The risk assessment identifies the functions that require specific security measures. Security is comprised of two areas: physical security and information security.

Physical security is intended to secure a location and counter external threats. These are measures that prevent or deter access. Physical security includes locked doors, barriers, fencing, electronic access control, intrusion detection, and guards.

The National Institute of Standards and Technology (NIST), the Health Insurance Portability and Accountability Act of 1996 (HIPAA), the Internet Security Forum (ISF), and the International Organization for Standardization (ISO) standards 27001/17799 each provide robust guidance on physical security. However, it falls to the organization to assess its unique physical security needs and determine which parts of these and other standards are most applicable.

Information security is the process of protecting information from unintended access or use. The efforts focus on protecting the confidentiality, integrity, and availability of information. Protecting confidential information is a business requirement, and in many cases also an ethical and legal requirement.

There are many sophisticated approaches, such as cryptography and neural networks, designed to detect or prevent a breach. Often overlooked are account and password management (the simplest ways to guard against unauthorized access, but they are often neglected). The account and password combinations create the single greatest barrier to unauthorized users. Yet in the development of many applications the account or user name is repopulated or displayed upon login. This carelessness negates half the value of the security measure. Even more risky is the use of common accounts where the account names and passwords are shared or even printed in common work areas. The risk is not just the event but the climate created in the workplace: "It's okay to share passwords; here, use mine."

Information security requirements vary widely depending on the operation. Centralized standards exist; for more detail consult

- ISO/IEC TR 15443:2005 Information technology — Security techniques — A framework for IT security assurance
- ISO/IEC 17799:2005: Information technology — Security techniques — Code of practice for information security management
- ISO/IEC 20000:2005 Information technology — Service management
- ISO 27001:2005: Information technology — Security techniques — Information security management systems
- ISO/IEC 27006:2007 Information Technology — Security techniques — Requirements for bodies providing audit and certification of information security management systems
- The NIST's Computer Security Division develops standards, metrics, tests, and validation programs as well as publishes standards and guidelines to increase secure IT planning, implementation, management, and operation

What Legislation Has Affected Risk Planning, and Why?

Recently, legislation has become an unfortunate but necessary force driving new standards in business behavior. The three pieces of legislation the authors selected for this book are the most influential in driving operational change through their impact on IT Providers. Each has a different catalyst and meaning for different types of organizations.

To translate these pieces of legislation into operations and technology requirements, the business must work with their IT counterparts. Each of these has unique implications for different business interactions.

Sarbanes–Oxley Act of 2002

Sarbanes–Oxley (SOX) is one of the most controversial and challenging pieces of legislation for businesses today. It was conceived in the wake of corporate and accounting scandals, namely Enron, Tyco International, and MCI WorldCom and others. Critics of SOX believe it is too onerous and is a penalty to companies operating in the United States. Supporters believe the legislation is overdue and introduces executive accountability, corporate transparency, and separation of responsibilities that were previously lacking.

SOX is a U.S. federal law requiring the Securities and Exchange Commission (SEC) to implement rulings on requirements to comply with the new law. The SEC governs all publicly traded companies, enforcing the federal securities laws regulating the securities industry/stock market.

The following summary of the intent of the Sarbanes–Oxley Act of 2002 comes from the Sarbanes–Oxley Accounting Oversight Information Center:

- To improve quality and transparency in financial reporting and independent audits and accounting services for public companies
- To create a Public Company Accounting Oversight Board
- To enhance the standard-setting process for accounting practices
- To strengthen the independence of firms that audit public companies
- To increase corporate responsibility and the usefulness of corporate financial disclosure
- To protect the objectivity and independence of securities analysts
- To improve Securities and Exchange Commission resources and oversight
- And for other purposes

The SEC is adopting rules that require conformance with specific sections of the Act. These rules require company officers to certify that they are responsible for establishing, maintaining, and regularly evaluating the effectiveness of the company's internal controls; that they have made certain disclosures to the company's auditors and the audit committee of the board of directors about the company's internal controls; and that they have included information in the company's quarterly and annual reports about their evaluation and whether there have been significant changes in the company's internal controls or in other factors that could significantly affect internal controls subsequent to the evaluation. In practice, this has meant that executives in control of IT Providers are required to sign each quarter that their IT operations are "under control." What does this mean?

The Sarbanes–Oxley disclosure/internal control primer includes chapters on internal control framework, audit considerations, methodology, risk/control matrices, self-assessment questionnaires, and audit programs regarding Certification of Disclosure and Managements' Internal Controls and Procedures. The risk/control matrices, self-assessment questionnaires, and audit programs are based on the framework established by COSO/SAS-78.

Health Insurance Portability and Accountability Act of 1996 (HIPAA)

HIPAA established a set of national standards for the protection of certain health information. It applies to all in the health care industry and those who handle individuals' health information.

The challenge faced by companies is interpreting HIPAA into operational and technology requirements specifically for information (data) storage requirements.

Operationalizing limitations on the aggregation of this data is equally as challenging. The HIPAA.org Website offers help through checklists and implementation guides.

The Privacy Rule standards address the use and disclosure of individuals' health information — called "protected health information" by organizations subject to the Privacy Rule — called "covered entities" — as well as standards for individuals' privacy rights to understand and control how their health information is used. Within the U.S. Department of Health & Human Services (HHS), the Office for Civil Rights (OCR) has responsibility for implementing and enforcing the Privacy Rule.

A major goal of the Privacy Rule is to assure that individuals' health information is properly protected while allowing the flow of health information needed to provide and promote high-quality health care and to protect the public's health and well being. The rule strikes a balance that permits important uses of information, while protecting the privacy of people who seek care and healing. Given that the health care marketplace is diverse, the rule is designed to be flexible and comprehensive to cover the variety of uses and disclosures that need to be addressed.

Gramm–Leach–Bliley Act of 1999 (GLB Act)

The GLB Act, also known as the Financial Modernization Act of 1999, created standards on the disclosure of non-public personal information. It includes provisions to protect consumers' personal financial information held by financial institutions. There are three principal parts to the privacy requirements: the Financial Privacy Rule, the Safeguards Rule, and pretexting provisions.

According to the Federal Trade Commission (FTC), the GLB Act gives authority to eight federal agencies and the states to administer and enforce the Financial Privacy Rule and the Safeguards Rule. These two regulations apply to "financial institutions," which include not only banks, securities firms, and insurance companies but also companies providing many other types of financial products and services to consumers. Among these services are lending, brokering, or servicing any type of consumer loan, transferring or safeguarding money, preparing individual tax returns, providing financial advice or credit counseling, providing residential real estate settlement services, collecting consumer debts, and an array of other activities. Such non-traditional "financial institutions" are regulated by the FTC.

The Financial Privacy Rule governs the collection and disclosure of customers' personal financial information by financial institutions. It also applies to companies, whether or not they are financial institutions, who receive such information.

The Safeguards Rule requires all financial institutions to design, implement, and maintain safeguards to protect customer information. The Safeguards Rule applies not only to financial institutions that collect information from their own customers but also to financial institutions such as credit reporting agencies that receive customer information from other financial institutions.

The pretexting provisions of the GLB Act protect consumers from individuals and companies that obtain their personal financial information under false pretenses, a practice known as "pretexting."

Summary

Planning for risk, identifying vulnerabilities, and creating risk plans are responsibilities shared by everyone in the organization. Risk management or execution of risk plans is the responsibility of both IT and the business departments the IT functions support.

Risk is not limited to the initial loss through theft. Often the loss of confidence by consumers can have a much greater impact as the erosion of trust is more difficult to regain. Failing to invest in risk planning or in adequately planning for the unknown could lead to an event causing suppliers and consumers to move on to find a more secure source for doing business.

Legislation has given rise to new requirements for the management and usage of data and corporate reporting. Being cognizant of the legislation arising from irresponsible corporate behavior requires risk planning to avoid being in violation. Risk reviews can no longer exist only in the bowels of the organization; more and more boards of directors require at least annual review and adherence to risk plans. According to the CIO Executive Board in 2006, 51 percent of company boards required annual review of risk plans. This percentage is expected to continue to climb.

Reference

1. "McDonald's callousness was real issue," *Wall Street Journal*, September 1, 1994.

Chapter 15

How Should IT Manage Its People?

In the ITIL® version 3 Service Transition Appendix, there is an excellent summary of the value of people as assets:

> The value of people assets is the capacity for creativity, analysis, perception, learning, judgment, leadership, coordination, empathy, and trust. Such capacity is in teams and individuals within the organization, due to knowledge, experience, and skills.

Of course, it is always dangerous to generalize about people. A memorable quote from the movie *Men in Black* (1997) highlights the problem of attributing individual characteristics to "people" in general:

> Agent J: "Why the big secret? People are smart, they can handle it."
> Agent K: "A person is smart. People are dumb, panicky, dangerous animals, and you know it."

The management of IT people is a huge topic. For the purposes of this chapter, it is necessary to narrow the focus. Hence, we will concentrate on what the business should care about, which is specific to its IT Providers, visible outside the IT Provider organization, and different from, or needing more sensitivity than the management of all the other people in the organization.

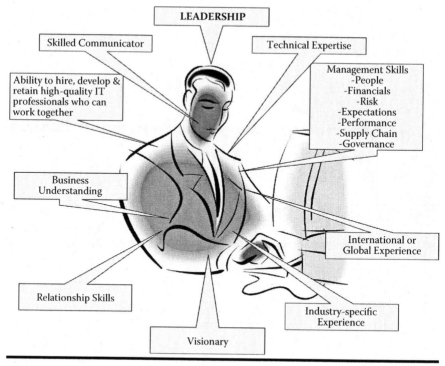

Figure 15.1   The ideal CIO.

What Should You Expect From Your CIO?

To borrow from the real estate world, the three most important things you should expect from your CIO are leadership, leadership, and leadership. Of course, the real needs are slightly more complex. A set of expectations for an ideal CIO are illustrated in Figure 15.1.

The individual who excels in all of the areas shown in Figure 15.1 is very rare indeed. In practice, the importance of these attributes will vary from organization to organization and from situation to situation over time. Is it better to have a CIO who scores evenly across all the attributes but does not excel at any or a CIO who is a star at a few of these things but weak on the others? Of course, "it depends." The best advice is, if you are not sure, go back to basics and look at their leadership capabilities. If you are still not sure, then don't hire!

Leadership

What is leadership? There are innumerable sources of information and opinion on this subject going back to the beginning of history. We have referred to the Broadbent and Kitsis book, *The New CIO Leader,*[1] a number of times in this book and we certainly recommend reading it for a deeper insight into what might reasonably be expected from modern CIOs. A simple definition that has served the authors well is that a leader is someone who can get people to follow him or her. Ask for, and look for, evidence that when your candidate is "out front" on a project or initiative, his or her team is following, supporting, and enabling.

A leader who is a strong motivator can help to build a strong team. Too often, this is over-simplified by would-be leaders as simply expecting as much from their team as themselves. This sometimes leads to teams built in the CIO's image. CIOs must recognize that a team with mixed backgrounds and perspectives is much more likely to identify a wider range of potential opportunities and problems than a team with a narrow background. This is especially important in IT where the ability of teams to solve problems is the stuff of life. In recognizing the importance of a diverse team, the CIO must also recognize the existence of diverse motivations.

The authors believe that, generally, leaders are born, not made, but there are important qualifiers to this belief. Many people who are very capable of being leaders are not aware of their capabilities, or do not demonstrate their capabilities until they are given an opportunity to exercise them. Many people can be trained to be extremely effective managers without ever being leaders. This is valuable to the organization but the difference must be recognized. Finally, in a few instances, good leaders sometimes cannot be trained to be good managers and, in these cases, being a good leader is not enough unless appropriate managerial support is provided.

Management Skills

Proficiency in directing and supervising people, projects, resources, budgets, vendors, and other business partners is essential. Great managers are also expected to be accomplished team builders, motivators, coaches, and mentors. Setting priorities, assigning the appropriate resources against those priorities, and delivering projects on time and on budget are always seen as key requirements for a top CIO.

Increasingly, whether dealing with purchased equipment or software or outsourced services, CIOs must be experienced and competent in making arrangements for managing the supply chain that feeds their own output. Supply chain management means working with people outside your organization, particularly service and product vendors, who must prioritize their own organizations' needs as highly as they prioritize yours (if you choose your vendors well!). It is imperative to be able to manage service providers effectively. This can be very tricky but, as we have described elsewhere in this book, there are best practices that can help. The business must expect these best practices to be implemented and challenge the CIO accordingly. It will always be tempting for the business to limit investment in IT, delay upgrades, and hope equipment and software on hand will last just a little longer. This adds to the difficulties of vendors who must maintain versions of hardware and software that may no longer be current. Together, the business and its IT providers must decide on the most cost-effective way to sustain existing infrastructure at an acceptable level of risk.

This brings in the next two key management skills for a CIO: a solid understanding of financial management and risk management. There is no doubt that the spirit of the old saying, "a stitch in time saves nine," applies to IT. The challenge for IT Providers is to take a particular highly technical risk issue and boil it down to a set of risks with probabilities and financial consequences associated with them that are comprehensible to the business. Further, the CIO must understand the organization's financial climate to understand just how much risk that organization can tolerate at any given time. In other words, how hard should they push? Businesses must be very careful not to react to either the CIO who pushes unjustifiably hard or the CIO who does not push hard enough.

This judgment on how hard to push the case for IT also applies more generally to the effective management of expectations. A good CIO with an understanding of the business will be internally marketing IT Providers' abilities to help the business reach its goals and objectives. What the great CIO does is sell IT without overselling it. Software projects, and large software projects in particular, are renowned for failing too often on cost, quality, delivery date, or all three. The CIO must be able to demonstrate that the IT Providers' projects have a high probability of success.

This requires management of performance. Many people have been attributed with first coining the phrase, "if you can't measure, you can't manage." The phrase is a core message of this book. Regrettably, it is still possible that there are CIOs out there who either do not regard the measurement of IT and software development as important or who believe that some or most of these processes cannot be measured. Clearly, such a position must be unacceptable to the business.

To monitor whether all of the CIO's management skills are being effectively applied, it is important for the business and the CIO to agree on a clear policy on IT governance. As described previously, the simplest definition of governance boils down to answers to the following questions: What decisions need to be made? Who makes them? How do they get made? The answers to these questions must be clearly documented to provide accountability.

Communication Skills

In the authors' experience as managers, "communications" is always on the list of things that the IT staff thinks could and should be improved. This is true regardless of how much effort is put into communicating. Of course, that does not mean that you should stop trying. On the contrary, the ability to articulate strategies and feelings intelligently in a clear and appropriate manner is essential for IT managers and particularly so for the senior leaders. This ability is required for written and verbal communication to individuals, groups, or audiences. Great listening skills as well as strong abilities in negotiation, persuasion, and conflict resolution are equally important. It is important to create regular opportunities for both speaking and listening to staff. Remember that your IT staff's collective knowledge of your situation is always greater than the CIO's and that one of them is likely to be the first to know most of the good or bad things that are going to happen to your IT Providers. Finally, in any communication to more than one person, always remember Agent K's advice: "A person is smart. People are dumb, panicky, dangerous animals, and you know it."

One of the signs of a CIO with excellent communication skills is the ability to talk technology fluently among peers and yet be an equally skilled translator among the less technically savvy. This person can communicate with others in the organization about what IT can do to move the company forward. In other words, good communication is key to developing good business relationships and sustainable success.

Technical Expertise

For the purposes of this book, it is important to distinguish between a CIO and a chief technology officer (CTO). There are no hard and fast rules, and every organization has a different interpretation. In fact, some companies have a CIO but no CTO, or vice versa. In this book, our use of the term "CIO" is meant to represent the leader of the group responsible for delivering IT services to the rest of the organization. As Figure 15.1 suggests, this implies a much wider span of skills, knowledge, and experience than just technology.

However, although it's possible for a department of IT professionals to be managed by a leader who doesn't have a technical background, the lack of a technical background significantly impedes the leader's ability to make critical judgments at the technology/business interface and to earn the respect of their senior staff. Hence, being technically knowledgeable usually helps a CIO to succeed in aligning and leveraging technology for the advantage of the enterprise. That said, it is not usually necessary, unless industry-specific needs prevail, for the CIO to have deep expertise in any particular aspects of technology such as specific application software packages, operating software platforms, or hardware.

Business Expertise

In the eyes of senior management as well as peers, the most visible and frustrating shortcoming of senior IT managers is a lack of business understanding. Usually and understandably, this is not a generic observation but a specific one as in, "our

CIO doesn't know anything about the commercial loan business," not, "our CIO doesn't know anything about financial services." Frankly, if this level of specific business knowledge is vital, then the pool of potential CIO candidates will be very small and the organization that chooses this path will most likely be burdened with mediocre CIOs.

However, it is reasonable and necessary to expect that a CIO has a solid foundation in the principles of accounting, finance, supply chain management, marketing, sales, and distribution channels, both traditional and online. Any gaps can, and should, be filled with formal training. From this foundation, a good CIO will have the capacity to develop a deeper understanding of the organization's specific business models and customers. If not, they are doomed to fail because they are inherently limited in the value that they can add to the organization's progress and well-being.

A CIO with this ability to think strategically to support the business' goals and objectives can position IT to be an important player in moving the organization forward. It establishes credibility which generates attention when IT Providers propose proactive solutions or participate in problem solving at the organizational level rather than just the IT level.

Vision — Ability to Create and Manage Change

The capabilities of IT solutions in the market change quickly. It is very difficult, expensive, and inefficient to have the organization's infrastructure change as fast as the external environment. Businesses must look to their CIOs and IT Providers to keep them in contention without expending too many resources. A great analogy for this is the Tour de France cycle race (if we ignore some of its less savory challenges in recent years). It is very hard to win the race by staying at the front all the time. Most successful stage and race winners stay in the peloton (the group behind the leaders) and share the load of leading to save energy. The trick, of course, is never to be so far back that you cannot make a breakaway to win or respond to a sudden breakaway by your competitors.

The rapid changes in IT make vision and the ability to manage change very important because change can take many forms and not all changes are sustained in the longer term. Hence, it is important for CIOs to have a vision that they can articulate and use as a guide for whether the latest technology is one that will help, hinder, or be irrelevant to their vision or, more accurately, the shared vision that they have developed with the business. The ability to evaluate the potential impact of new technology on the corporation's operating and business processes, for both efficiency and competitiveness, is a necessary first step to introduce the right change and then manage the implementation of that change. Business process re-engineering and continuous process improvement are on the minds of many CEOs, especially in tougher economic conditions.

Ability to Hire, Develop, and Retain High-Quality IT Professionals Who Can Work Together

In their book *What Really Works*,[2] Joyce, Nohria, and Roberson describe a "4+2" formula for sustained business success based on their research which showed that successful business did not just follow but excelled on all four of what they identified as the primary management practices and any two secondary management practices:

- Primary management practices
  - Strategy: Devise and maintain a clearly stated, focused strategy
  - Execution: Develop and maintain flawless operational execution
  - Culture: Develop and maintain a performance-oriented culture
  - Structure: Build and maintain a fast, flexible, flat organization
- Secondary management practices
  - Talent: Hold on to talented employees and find more
  - Leadership: Keep leaders and directors committed to the business
  - Innovation: Make innovations that are industry transforming
  - Mergers and partnerships: Make growth happen with mergers and partnerships

It is worthwhile to make explicit note that these were not management practices for IT but more generic practices for any successful business. Nonetheless, these are great expectations for a business to have for its CIO and IT Providers. Note the importance of how people are managed in all four of the primary management practices.

So, for which two of the four secondary management practices should business expect excellence from their IT Providers? Based on the introductory comments in this chapter, the first is clear — secondary management principle #1, businesses should expect their IT providers to hold on to talented employees and find more. Assuming the fourth choice is not really relevant to IT, the choice between the remaining two secondary principles is not so obvious. It is tempting to jump at the obvious connection between innovation and technology. That may be appropriate for some businesses whose success is truly based upon IT innovation. However, in most cases, the authors would choose leadership over innovation especially with the qualifying statement of "… committed to the business."

In *Good to Great*,[3] another book based upon research into what makes some organizations more successful than their peers, Collins identifies three characteristics that great organizations share: disciplined people, disciplined thought, and disciplined action. He stresses that disciplined people must be in place first before a transformation from good to great can occur.

Surprisingly, the ability to hire, develop, and retain high-quality IT professionals who can work together is often not high on the list of required attributes of a great

CIO. Selecting a good team is particularly important in IT because very often both the information and the ability to understand it to deconstruct complex problems or synthesize complex solutions are split between different people and disciplines. Building a good team also helps a CIO position IT to help a company achieve its goals and objectives. As discussed earlier, an important step in that direction is listening. Organizations should expect their CIOs to delegate authority "carefully," understanding that empowered teams will tend to achieve more but solving some challenges will require inputs from all perspectives of a bigger picture. Businesses should expect IT Providers to make mistakes when they are seeking to innovate. There can be no innovation without experimentation and occasional failures.

The delegation of authority by the CIO is also a key component of one of the CIO's most important jobs: succession planning. Usually, succession planning is focused on the top few layers of the organization. Businesses should require a succession plan from their CIO at least annually. The succession plan should not just be a set of names but should include the strengths and weaknesses of the individuals with mitigation plans for the weaknesses, and contingency plans if the succession plan is disrupted for some reason.

Succession planning is particularly important in IT because it is a field in which detailed knowledge of the current working environment is invaluable for continued success. Hence, it should go deeper than most succession plans to look for individuals who have developed a unique set of knowledge and skills that do not exist elsewhere in the organization. Succession or knowledge capture/transfer plans for these individuals are imperative because of the two main forces currently at play in the IT world: offshoring and the availability of good jobs for good people (especially those with scarce knowledge/skills). The ITIL Service Transition Appendix quoted at the beginning of this chapter goes on to give us an important reminder about people assets: "They also are assets that can be hired or rented but cannot be owned." Assume that anyone important in your IT Providers could leave at any time (from the only database analyst who knows how to make a certain database work, on up to the CIO).

The impact of offshoring is more complex. The availability of good jobs for good people in IT is just as important a factor in China, India, and elsewhere. If anything, perhaps more so as the offshore turnover rates show. Furthermore, the offshoring of IT jobs seems to be leading to the observed phenomenon of reducing the attractiveness of IT as a career to young people in the United States and Western Europe. Taken with the loss of "veteran" skills as the baby boomer generation retires, this compounds the scarcity of good IT resources.

The serious shortage of software professionals grew dramatically during the 1990s. Initially, the availability of offshore software talent to support outsourcing of software development, or to apply themselves as visiting workers, disguised the building talent crisis. However, by the late 1990s, turnover rates among software companies in countries such as India had risen to levels between 15 percent and 30 percent annually as these companies began competing for increasingly scarce talent within their borders. The shortage of talent in these countries is undoubtedly only a timing problem as the education systems of those countries struggle to catch up with the unprecedented growth of the industry but the shortage of software talent has created a constellation of problems including:

- High turnover
- Loss of critical system knowledge
- Escalating salaries and benefits
- Staffing shortfalls
- Increased workloads, overtime, and stress
- Increasing product and service costs
- Unfinished work

At the Massachusetts Institute of Technology, as in other schools across the United States, computer science enrollments have been dropping, raising questions about the country's future technology leadership. In three recent successive years, new undergraduate majors in MIT's electrical engineering and computer science department fell from roughly 385 to about 240 to just under 200, a fall of about 48 percent. The Rutgers University computer science department has canceled some course sections and expects total enrollment in classes in the major to be thousands less than its peak of 6500 several years ago. Saul Levy, chair of the undergraduate computer science program, said the ongoing decline stems from the way students perceive career prospects. "They don't believe in the job market in computers anymore," Levy said. At Carnegie Mellon University, 2000 students applied to the school of computer science recently, down from 3200 in 2001.

Data from the Higher Education Research Institute at the University of California at Los Angeles shows the percentage of incoming students interested in majoring in computer science plummeted between the fall of 2000 and the fall of 2004. The percentage dropped by 60 percent and now is 70 percent lower than its peak in the early 1980s.

For women, the drop is even more dramatic. The number of women interested in computer science as a major has plummeted 80 percent between 1998 and 2004 and 93 percent since its peak in 1982. The proportion of women to men interested in the field is the lowest since the 1970s. The trend is in sharp distinction to other fields, including biology, physical sciences, and engineering, where the representation of women has continued to rise.

Even the best CIOs have a battle on their hands in the current and future IT talent market.

International or Global Experience

In today's global economy, a CIO needs to possess an appreciation of foreign cultures and an understanding of doing business in foreign markets for both the demand and supply sides of the equation. Knowledge of a specific market, country, or language is sometimes required. More generally sought is an openness and awareness, based on experience, that there are different ways of interacting and diverse modes of conducting business in other parts of the world.

Industry-Specific Experience

As mentioned earlier, it is possible that requiring a CIO to have industry-specific experience might result in too small a pool from which to expect a great CIO to emerge. It is certainly true that the "ideal" CIO would have industry-specific knowledge. The value of industry-specific knowledge is that the CIO will be able to get to know the business faster, and will know what questions to ask and what surprises to expect. For example, in financial services, the CIO will know to expect a raft of regulatory changes that will need to be implemented at different times of the year.

Relationship Skills

Dysfunctional connections and low rapport between the CIO and other C-level officers and business unit leaders is a highly observable and an all-too-common reason for failure in organizations. Visibility of that issue readily extends to customers, suppliers, and partners. Relationship building takes interpersonal communication to the next level by establishing and maintaining a strong understanding, rapport, bond, and trust between peers. It is one thing to discuss, conceptually, where a company is headed and how IT can be used to get there. It's quite another to recognize the office politics that will be involved along the way. Corporate politics can be an obstacle or an asset. A great CIO will strike a delicate balance between building alliances and — either because of them or in spite of them — making good business decisions. There does come a time when you have to help make decisions that are good for the company, not just a matter of self-preservation. Self-preservation is doomed to backfire; doing the right thing will tend to establish credibility and integrity, and sometimes even lead to rewards!

IT Staff as Assets

We started this chapter with the quote from ITIL about the value of people as assets:

> The value of people assets is the capacity for creativity, analysis, perception, learning, judgment, leadership, coordination, empathy, and trust. Such capacity is in teams and individuals within the organization, due to knowledge, experience, and skills.

Given the amount of detailed knowledge embodied in the staff of its IT Providers, an organization must expect those IT Providers to manage their people assets to grow their value in a sustainable way. Investment in the following approaches will help to achieve sustainable growth in the value of people assets:

- Training — The development of subject matter knowledge
- Coaching — The development of emotional intelligence (or situational intelligence or social intelligence)
- Mentoring — Subject matter intelligence (which often manifests itself as "do as I do and you will be successful in this company/career")

We are artificially differentiating here between the passive "knowledge" and the interactive "intelligence" to separate the difference between the accumulation of received information and the application of that information in, more or less, real-time. Coaching and mentoring must become more important in IT Providers if they are to bridge successfully the middle management gap created by the retirement of the baby boomers, and the mix of fewer young onshore staff and frequently moving young offshore staff.

In Chapter 1, we introduced a number of formal frameworks for IT Providers. These all emphasize the importance of training, coaching, and mentoring. Taking the example of CMMI®, it requires that people should be trained in two dimensions: to fulfill their role and to fulfill the specific needs of the project. Business should expect IT Providers to establish formal training and competency databases.

ITIL takes this a step further by requiring IT Providers to:

- Formalize how the competencies of individuals responsible for the IT assets and related services can be regarded as an asset within the organization and are managed as such
- Specify how the IT asset life cycle applies to people assets, particularly in terms of measurable competencies such as skill, knowledge, understanding, qualifications, experience, attitude, and behavior
- Ensure the documentation of the competencies is currently in place and specify how these can be reused or enhanced
- Ensure organization standards are compatible with existing standard competency frameworks for the IT sector, such as SFIA (Skills for the Information Age)[4] and skills and competencies are incorporated into roles and responsibilities

Concerns about preserving and developing the capabilities of developmental engineering staff led the SEI to create the People Capability Maturity Model® (People CMM® or P-CMM)[5] in 1995. This model, now revised as version 2, can also be used by any kind of organization as a guide for improving its people-related and work force practices.

The People CMM adapts the maturity framework of the CMM for Software, now CMMI (see Chapter 6), to managing and developing an organization's work force. The motivation for the People CMM is to improve radically the ability of IT Providers to attract, develop, motivate, organize, and retain the talent needed to improve software development capability continuously. The People CMM is designed to allow IT Providers to integrate work force improvement with software process improvement programs guided by CMMI.

Version 2 of the People CMM adds enhancements learned from five years of implementation experience with version 1 and better integrates the model with CMMI. In addition, other improvements have been made in version 2 to bring the People CMM closer to its maturity framework roots in process-driven organizational improvement. An institutionalization goal has been added to each process area to align the goal structure better with that used in the CMMI.

After lengthy review of the literature and experience gathered from implementers on programs to improve work force practices, it was determined that these programs often fail when work force practices are not introduced as a system of practices or in reinforcing bundles, but rather are deployed in isolation. For instance, efforts to install empowered teams are likely to fail if compensation practices continue to reward individual performance without recognizing contribution to team performance and team success.

Based on the current best practices in fields such as human resources and organizational development, the People CMM provides organizations with guidance on how to gain control of their processes for managing and developing their work force. The People CMM helps organizations to characterize the maturity of their work force practices, guide a program of continuous work force development, set priorities for immediate actions, integrate work force development with process improvement, and establish a culture of software engineering excellence. It describes an evolutionary improvement path from ad hoc, inconsistently performed practices, to a mature, disciplined development of the knowledge, skills, and motivation of the work force, just as the CMM describes an evolutionary improvement path for the software processes within an organization.

The philosophy of the People CMM can be summarized in the following ten principles:

1. In mature organizations, work force capability is directly related to business performance.
2. Work force capability is a competitive issue and a source of strategic advantage.
3. Work force capability must be defined in relation to the organization's strategic business objectives.
4. Knowledge-intense work shifts the focus from job elements to work force competencies.

5. Capability can be measured and improved at multiple levels, including individuals, work groups, work force competencies, and the organization.
6. An organization should invest in improving the capability of those work force competencies that are critical to its core competency as a business.
7. Operational management is responsible for the capability of the work force.
8. The improvement of work force capability can be pursued as a process composed from proven practices and procedures.
9. The organization is responsible for providing improvement opportunities, and individuals are responsible for taking advantage of them.
10. Because technologies and organizational forms evolve rapidly, organizations must continually evolve their work force practices and develop new work force competencies.

The People CMM consists of five maturity levels (see Table 15.1) that lay successive foundations for continuously improving talent, developing effective teams, and successfully managing the people assets of the organization. Each maturity level is a well-defined evolutionary plateau that institutionalizes a level of capability for developing the talent within the organization. Except for Level 1, each maturity level is decomposed into several key process areas that indicate the areas an organization should focus on to improve its work force capability. Each key process area is described in terms of the key practices that contribute to satisfying its goals. The key practices describe the infrastructure and activities that contribute most to the effective implementation and institutionalization of each key process area.

IT Staff and Change

A career in IT is a career dealing with constant change. Successful IT managers are, almost by definition, successful change managers. Hence, an IT Provider can be a great agent of change and leader of change in an organization. Certainly, IT Providers should have all of the necessary tools and skills to provide project management on a variety of change projects that might benefit the business. Business should expect high standards of change management and regular reporting of progress at appropriate levels of detail.

However, three cautionary notes are appropriate. First, as mentioned elsewhere in the book, software projects often fail to meet their objectives in terms of functionality, cost, quality, or schedule, sometimes notoriously so, due to the immaturity of the IT teams implementing them or the unreasonable expectations of the business. Second, IT Providers can be masters of manipulating change to suit their own goals. This can manifest itself as inactivity in the direction in which the business wants to go or a pedantic change control process that requires more time and money for every small change, or the introduction of the latest, greatest technology

Table 15.1 People CMM Version 2 Process Areas

Maturity Levels	Developing Individual Capability	Building Work Groups and Cultures	Motivating and Managing Performance	Shaping the Work Force
1 Initial		Work force practices applied inconsistently		
2 Managed	Training and development	Communication and coordination	Compensation Performance management Work environment	Staffing
3 Defined	Competency development Competency analysis	Work group development Participatory culture	Competency-based practices Career development	Work force planning
4 Predictable	Competency-based assets Mentoring	Competency integration Empowered work groups	Quantitative performance management	Organizational capability management
5 Optimizing	Continuous capability improvement		Organizational performance alignment	Continuous work force innovation

Source: Curtis, B., Hefley, W.E., and Miller, S.A., 2001, People Capability Maturity Model® (P.CMM®), Version 2.0, Software Engineering Institute, Carnegie Mellon University, http://www.sei.cmu.edu/publications/documents/01.reports/01mm001.html (accessed Sept. 21, 2007). With permission.

out of technical curiosity. Finally, IT Providers can get into a mode of "change for change's sake," where too many changes, too often, destroy the stability of the underlying systems and services.

Think back to the Tour de France analogy earlier in this chapter and adopt the appropriate strategy depending on whether the business needs to win the race, the current stage, or both.

IT Staff as Stakeholders

Different levels of IT staff and, indeed, different individuals at the same level, have varying perspectives of the organization. These perspectives are valuable in any part of the organization, but particularly so in IT because of the extraordinary amount of attention to detail required in the first two or three levels above entry level and the high degree of "detail drop-off" that is unavoidable at each step up the hierarchy. IT staff at different levels also have different needs from the organization, and from the business, in terms of information. As generally creative types, IT staff often share a need to be seen doing an effective job efficiently. They are likely to have a real stake (as in shares, options, or bonuses) or perceived investment (as in pride or career success) in the success of the organization.

These two things, perspectives and needs, can be grouped together as staff awareness. IT staff need to be aware of the different levels and what the business and the IT Provider are trying to achieve, and how they are trying to achieve it. Specifically, IT staff need regular updates for the following questions:

- What am I supposed to be doing?
- Where is the information I need?
- What are the priorities in the short term so that I know how to deal with the unexpected?

The rapid changes in technology make IT providers very dependent on the rapid entry of the next generation of staff conversant in or ready to absorb the next generation of technology. If CIOs are able to tackle the challenges of finding staff described earlier in this chapter, they will then need to address the challenges of dealing with the different perspectives of a new generation. By way of example, some interesting research has been carried out on the traits of the new generation of IT staff, the so-called "Generation Y." There are several different definitions for "Generation Y" but it is reasonable to think of it as those people born in the United States between 1978 and 2000. The different traits are shown in Table 15.2. The key point here is that if communication with, and motivation of, Generation Y is going to require some different approaches, how does the CIO plan to understand the perspectives of the next generation of IT staff working in completely different countries and cultures?

Table 15.2   Common Generation Y (Gen Y) Traits

Trait	Characteristics	Tips for the Business To Help IT Manage
Bluntly expressive	Gen Ys have their own thoughts, ideas, and opinions — and you are going to hear them, like it or not!	■ Give them a structured forum to be heard. ■ Let them know you do care about what they think. ■ When they say something inappropriate, do not take it personally. ■ Distinguish between real grievances and just letting off steam. ■ Establish firm boundaries for their interaction with customers.
Committed	Gen Y is fiercely loyal to the institutions they believe in.	■ Try to get them to buy into the company mission (and listen if they don't). ■ Demonstrate you care about them as individuals. ■ Believe in the Gen Y employees and they will believe in the company. ■ When something good happens in the workplace, make sure your Gen Ys hear about it.
Disrespectful	Gen Ys crave respect and will go to great lengths to get it, but they don't give respect easily.	■ Fight the urge to demand their respect. ■ Instead, treat them with the same degree of respect you would have them give you, and your actions will be mirrored.
Efficient	Gen Ys are masters of multi-tasking and time management.	■ Reward efficient work with employee incentives.

Impatient	■ Use Gen Ys' talent for multi-tasking and digesting information quickly.	■ Give them freedom to explore new methods for doing repetitive tasks. ■ Keep meetings short and to the point; vary methods for delivering the necessary content. ■ When change happens, let the Gen Ys ride the wave and help you adjust.
Innovative	■ Gen Ys are full of revolutionary ideas and have no fear of technology.	■ Unleash their unconventional approach to solving problems. ■ Invite them to express their ideas for keeping your business in step with or even ahead of the changes. ■ Listen to and look at their ideas carefully to find the mine of innovation that may first appear as rubble.
Skeptical	■ Gen Ys are capable of sniffing out "spin" and "bullshit" very quickly.	■ Aim for 100 percent truth, 100 percent of the time. ■ Nothing wins their respect and admiration like honesty. ■ Truth works like a magnet to attract Gen Ys and helps you earn their unshakable confidence and trust.
Tolerant	■ Gen Ys have a refreshing spirit of openness clearly demonstrated in their willingness to embrace each other regardless of outward differences.	■ Use Gen Ys as the building blocks for a truly effective team. ■ Do not segregate them from your established work force; integrate them immediately. ■ Disregard your notion of traditional roles and relationships for men and women.

Source: Martin, C.H. and Tulgan, B., 2001, *Managing Generation Y*, HRD Press Inc. With permission.

Summary

By and large, the people working for your IT Providers will be different in some important ways from the rest of your staff. It is important for businesses to understand these differences and ensure that the leaders of the IT Providers have the right characteristics to understand and appreciate the diversity and lead the IT Providers to success.

References

1. Broadbent, M. and Kitsis, E.S., 2005, *The New CIO Leader,* Harvard Business School Press.
2. Joyce, W.F., Nohria, N., and Roberson, B., 2003, *What Really Works,* HarperCollins Publishers.
3. Collins, J.C., 2001, *Good to Great,* HarperCollins Publishers.
4. www.sfia.org.uk (accessed Sept. 21, 2007).
5. People Capability Maturity Model — Version 2, Software Engineering Institute, Carnegie Mellon University, www.sei.cmu.edu/cmm-p/version2/ (accessed Sept. 21, 2007).

Chapter 16

What Should IT Expect From the Business?

In this chapter, we'll cover what IT Providers should expect from the business by conveying the importance of developing a shared understanding of the working relationship and expectations. We'll review communications and operating norms.

It's the Relationship That Matters

To properly define expectations, one must first understand the relationship. Your expectations of values, commitment, and quality cause you to think of certain characteristics if considering a new family doctor, yet very different characteristics if considering a marriage! How one defines the relationship forms the foundation for all other expectations.

Thinking about marriage there are many different types of marriage and much written about them. Sticking only to the positive ones, there are marriages of convenience, partnership, love, romance, status, etc. The most lasting types of marriage are ones where both people are in the same type. This example may seem a little tongue-in-cheek but setting the expectations of the relationship between the business and IT Providers is the first step to having a more successful and lasting pairing.

The business must convey the type of relationship it expects to have with IT and ensure the environment supports it. Flowery speeches of collaboration are meaningless unless there is follow-through by the rest of the business staff. Defining the expectations of the relationship is important, and communicating this to staff is equally important.

IT Providers can perform based on the expectations set by the business and evolve over time. There are many different ways IT Providers can perform from "order-taker" to "trusted advisor," or even to performing in roles of strategic business partner.

When acting as an "order-taker," the IT Provider might be fully outsourced where projects are defined in-house and then placed out for bid to multiple vendors. The advantage of this type of relationship is that it is the most controlled. It is work for hire. The disadvantage is that communications are often challenging because there is no real understanding of the business intent behind the requirements and communications are stunted. Projects are performed by the best bidder and business knowledge is not invested in, retained, or developed.

When acting as a "trusted advisor," the IT Providers are knowledgeable about the business and the systems landscape. They attend planning meetings to produce order-of-magnitude input for new projects. The advantages are that IT staff can often contribute to tactical sessions and are proficient at evolving business requirements to achieve the desired goals. The disadvantages are that there are only a few subject matter experts, and long-term planning is a challenge due to the limited view of the strategic direction.

When acting as a "strategic business partner," the leaders of the IT Providers are invited and regularly attend senior planning sessions of other business leaders. Leaders of IT Providers are aware of the multi-year strategic plans, including growth for all other departments. The business proactively plans for the needs of IT by including IT Providers, providing transparency into the business processes, and considering how IT will be affected. The business provides insight, answering "why," not just "what," will be needed in the future. IT Providers are able to contribute to the recommended approach. The advantage is a shared ownership of business goals. Also, if there are holes in the business strategy, they become more visible. The disadvantage is a front-loaded investment in the time and energy of IT leadership.

The business needs to consider the type of work it requires from IT Providers. The complexity, the business understanding required, and the contribution to a longer-term strategy all drive the framework for the relationship required. Once determined, it's important for the business leadership to involve IT leadership in regular discussions and reviews to develop or evolve and improve the engagement or operating model.

Develop an Operating Model

The goal of an operating model (see Figure 16.1) is to provide an essential guide for business decision making and provide everyone with a strong focus in setting collective and individual work priorities. According to the Berkeley Partnership, the process considers the nature of the business process, size of transaction throughput,

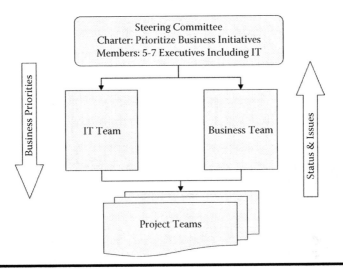

Figure 16.1 Operating model.

people skills, and information technology capability. It describes how your operating units and functions will work together toward shared goals.

An operating model describes what is important for an organization. The Center for Information Systems Research (CISR), a research group at the MIT Sloan School of Management, has defined and recommended a model that describes how the business cooperates across its business units and defines the business needs for business process standardization and integration (data sharing). CISR recommends this type of operating model to build reusable core capabilities and follow this base to guide IT investment decisions. The operating model will drive the architecture and infrastructure development, ensuring that business needs are met with the right IT foundation. The result is a foundation that enables the company to grow its business with the right level of IT, without having to do deep surgery on the IT systems each time the business grows either organically or through acquisitions. The implementation of business processes and IT systems is the realization of the operating model.[1]

In their book *IT Governance,*[2] Weill and Ross state,

> IT decision making becomes joint decision making. When senior managers abdicate to IT executives responsibility for IT success, disaster often ensues. Successful firms not only make better IT decisions, they also have better IT decision-making processes. Specifically successful firms involve the right people in the process. Having the right people involved in the IT decision making yields both more strategic applications and greater buy-in. These more involved people then produce better implementations.

Businesses should begin to develop the model by answering the following questions:

- What is the goal or mission of the department?
- Who is defined as the leadership team?
- Who are their counterparts in the IT Providers?
- What is the frequency of interaction between the groups?
- Are there formal channels for these groups to connect (meetings, reporting, project reviews, monthly review sessions, etc.)?
- What mechanism is used to communicate the needs of the business to the IT Providers?
- What review mechanisms exist to ensure projects or programs are progressing as needed?
- To whom are issues escalated?
- How are decisions ultimately made?

Answers to these questions assist in completing the operating model shown in Figure 16.1.

Table 16.1 assists the organization by providing common terminology to the teams on the roles and responsibilities within the operating model.

A charter for the steering committee (Table 16.2) is established in the first session and updated as needed. It is used as a communication vehicle for new members of the committee and the organization to clarify roles and the appropriate channels for decision making.

Table 16.1 Operating Model Roles

Business	Mission
Steering committee	Communicate business goals and objectives Translate business goals into a prioritized list for IT Set expectations related to resource assignments and associated behavior Communicate policies Generate support for IT
Business managers IT managers Project managers	Create awareness of, and support for business priorities Perform in accordance with goals and objectives Communicate resource assignments Communicate policies Communicate project status, provide awareness of risks, escalate issues when necessary and share success Manage issues and risks

Table 16.2 Steering Committee Charter: Meetings

Frequency	Twice monthly
Attendees	Steering committee members
Facilitator	
Purpose	Review and prioritize the business needs of IT
Recommended topics	Business prioritization of new and existing programs; administrative items relating to prioritization including resources, expected timing, assumptions, and dependencies
Minutes	Updated prioritization lists will be distributed to staff
Input	Project report, new project requests, work order report, new work order requests

Statement of Commitment

A statement of commitment serves as a published artifact of the organization's commitment to perform. This sets the norms of behavior for the business when working with IT. The exercise of coming together with other business and IT leaders to establish the commitment is often the greatest challenge. Once completed, much like a defined set of values, it serves to guide the expectations for both IT and the business.

By way of example, consider an executive with a track record for success (who shall remain nameless here). He is a 20-year veteran of his niche in financial services and leads one of the largest and highly regarded brands in the industry. He promotes an environment where there is "creative tension" between the marketing department and IT department. The belief is that you can never get everything done and IT could never be funded to achieve everything requested. If it were, the business wouldn't be profitable. By encouraging the large demand from marketing, he is guaranteed to have a large choice of the most and best ideas available. Also, by constraining supply from IT there is a real filter only allowing the most salient and prepared projects to proceed. This is one way to achieve the desired results.

Taking another look at this approach, what seems stellar in results can leave a lot to be desired in execution. Communications between the departments are naturally strained as capacity in IT is capped, leaving marketing to feel they cannot meet their goals for the year. Competition for the scarce resources translates into a lack of key information sharing within the ranks of the other departments. This leaves the organization with more internal competition than collaboration.

The challenge lies in the skewed expectations that exist among the departments. Both are striving for unattainable states of interaction and delivery. This results in frustration and competition among business groups.

In this circumstance, a statement of commitment from the business would represent the intent of the business units. It is not the needs of the businesses for IT. It is the stated contributions and operating norms of the business spelled out for the understanding of the IT Providers. These could include collaboration from the businesses to prioritize the needs for the IT Providers, participation in planning sessions, discussions of capacity and timing, etc. It is important to remember that a statement of commitment is not another iteration of any service level agreements that may already exist. SLAs are standards of delivery and availability for operations or IT.

IT is a key element of all businesses; defining the interaction for these critical resources serves to bring clarity and define and formalize any unstated intent further. IT can drive business innovation; a true partnership with open communication and an ongoing dialogue creates the environment for a flow of ideas and information.

Summary

Reflecting back on the example of the marriage, the most important element for success is both parties sharing a common understanding of intent. Communication, setting the expectations of the relationship between the two parties, and fostering an open dialogue is the path to success for the business with IT. IT is part of the business. Developing a collaborative open relationship provides the path to engaging in a successful business relationship.

References

1. Wikipedia, 2007.
2. Weill, Peter and Ross, Jeanne, 2004, *IT Governance: How Top Performers Manage IT Decision Rights for Superior Results,* Harvard Business School Press.

Index

255

Q

R